SELECTED PLAYS
OF
LENNOX ROBINSON

Irish Drama Selections

General Editors

Joseph Ronsley
Ann Saddlemyer

SELECTED PLAYS
OF
LENNOX ROBINSON

chosen and with an introduction by
Christopher Murray

Irish Drama Selections 1

COLIN SMYTHE
Gerrards Cross, Bucks.

THE CATHOLIC UNIVERSITY
OF AMERICA PRESS
Washington, D.C.

Copyright 1912, 1921, 1924, 1928, 1929, 1933, 1935
by Lennox Robinson
This selection copyright © 1982 by The Abbey Theatre, Dublin
Introduction copyright © 1982 by Christopher Murray

This selection first published in 1982 by
Colin Smythe Limited, Gerrards Cross, Buckinghamshire

British Library Cataloguing in Publication Data
Robinson, Lennox
  Selected plays of Lennox Robinson. — (Irish drama
  selections, ISSN 0260–7962; 1)
  I. Title   II. Series
  822′.912   PR6035.O55
  ISBN 0–86140–087–9
  ISBN 0–86140–088–7 Pbk

First published in North America in 1982 by
The Catholic University of America Press, Washington, D.C.

Library of Congress Cataloging in Publication Data
Robinson, Lennox, 1886–1958.
  Selected plays of Lennox Robinson.
  (Irish drama selections; 1)
  Bibliography: p.
  Contents: Patriots — The whiteheaded boy —
  Crabbed youth and age — [etc.]
  I. Title   II. Series.
  PR6035.O56A6   1982   822′.912   82–71455
  ISBN 0–8132–0574–3   AACR2
  ISBN 0–8132–0575–1 (pbk.)

Set by An Grianán, Galway, Ireland
Produced in Great Britain
Printed and bound by Billing & Sons Ltd., Worcester

CONTENTS

INTRODUCTION

I

Lennox Robinson was born on 4 October 1886 in Douglas, County Cork. His father, a stockbroker by profession, suddenly went for the ministry in 1892, thus providing the future playwright with the unlikely background of a strongly Protestant, and, indeed, politically Unionist home. Lennox, born Esmé Stuart Lennox, was a frail child, destined to be tall and thin in appearance. He received little formal education, because of ill health, but he read extensively and received private tuition at the rectory in Ballymoney, County Cork. In *Curtain Up: An Autobiography* (1942), Robinson says he was "a disagreeable, unhappy child", as the youngest of the five Robinson children who survived infancy. Yet his home life was by no means repressive, and the imaginative boy was free to develop his literary bent by editing a family magazine with his brothers and sisters. Out of this activity came his first play, *The Clancy Name*, based on a story written by his sister. The play, however, did not transpire until Robinson had first seen the Abbey players on tour in Cork. The effect on him of the realistic style was explosive. "It came on me in a flash, as a revelation," he says in his autobiography, "that play-material could be found outside one's own door, at one's own fireside." At the same time, August 1907, he was also fired by nationalist feeling, especially upon seeing the Abbey players in Yeats's *Cathleen Ni Houlihan* at the Cork Opera House. His family, antipathetic though they were to the idea of Home Rule for Ireland, did not stand in Lennox's way now, when he submitted *The Clancy Name* to the Abbey Theatre, where it was staged with such success on 8 October 1908 that Robinson's career was settled upon forthwith.

The Clancy Name, in one act, has for theme the passion for respectability which can stifle small-town life. Mrs Clancy, a hardworking widow, will do anything rather than have it known that her son is guilty of a local murder; when he is brought into the house after a serious accident all of her efforts, ironically, are directed at covering up his incoherent confession before the neighbours. She barely conceals her relief when her son dies with the "Clancy name" left unsmeared. One of the reviewers, that for the *Freeman's Journal*, took exception to Robinson's Ibsenist study of Irish hypocrisy, and blustered: "the whole thing is a shame and a disgrace . . . there ought to be some sort of censorship applied to those things." But Robinson was already busy on his second play, *Cross Roads*, "peasant tragedy of the most ruthless kind", as he himself described it. In two acts, with a prologue, it was staged at the Abbey on 1 April 1909, having been postponed for one week following the death of Synge. With Sara Allgood and Arthur Sinclair in the leading roles, it "had a success beyond its deserts", according to Robinson. It was followed by *Harvest*, his first full-length play, of which one commentator said that "it out-Synges Synge. It gives us all the suggestiveness of the malodorous problem play without any intelligible problem." To have his name coupled with that of Synge was no mean achievement, and Robinson's talents must have struck Yeats and Lady Gregory as of considerable potential since they offered him the joint position of manager and director of plays at the Abbey. The salary was one hundred and fifty pounds a year. The year was 1910, a turning point in the Abbey's history.

It was at this time that the Abbey lost the subsidy which it had enjoyed since its opening in 1904. Miss Annie Horniman, the English woman whose money subsidized the theatre, flew into a rage when the Abbey failed to close its doors on the day following King Edward the Seventh's death, 7 May 1910, and immediately demanded the resignation of the manager, Lennox Robinson. Robinson had been too inexperienced to take the decision Miss Horniman expected, but Yeats now came to his defence and, as a result, Miss Horniman, dissatisfied for some time with policy at the Abbey, withdrew her subsidy. It was a hard blow. It was acutely embarrassing for Robinson, who felt obliged to take on extra work, as secretary at the Abbey, in order to save costs. In addition, when the tours of the Abbey company began to the United States, in 1911, as a means of raising funds for the theatre, Robinson had the burden of tour organizer. He travelled with the company on that first, riot-torn tour and also during the third tour in 1913-14, while in between he dashed back to direct his own new play, *Patriots*, at the Abbey.

He must surely have felt he had been thrown in at the deep end. After all, he had had no training in the theatre, nor had he even had much experience as a theatregoer, when he was appointed director of productions at the Abbey. The story at the time was that Yeats chose Robinson because he liked the back of his head, on seeing him in the Abbey audience. Yeats had, no doubt, strange powers of clairvoyance. He did not leave all to the spirit world, however, for he sent Robinson to London on what might be called a crash course in practical stage-management. He arranged for Robinson to work with Shaw and Granville-Barker in their rehearsals, and in a matter of six weeks, early in 1910, Robinson no doubt picked up a few valuable hints from these experts in the new stagecraft of realism. Back at the Abbey, Robinson's first directing job was with an established comedy, *The Eloquent Dempsey*, but far more of a trial was Pádraic Colum's new play, *Thomas Muskerry*, which opened on 5 May 1910. This sombre tragedy in four acts, Colum's best play, demands careful control if the atmosphere is to be right, and it seems likely that Robinson learned more from the cast here than they were likely to learn from him. The cast included Sara Allgood, Maire O'Neill, Arthur Sinclair and Sydney Morgan, well experienced in the production style introduced a decade earlier by the Fay brothers. *Thomas Muskerry* was an artistic success, and as time went on Robinson became a skilled director, although it has been said that he was never good on the visual side of production.

When the Abbey tours to America came to an end in 1914, Robinson resigned from the theatre. He was given the impression that he was to blame because the tours did not make money, and, in addition, he was concerned about his own work as playwright. He took five years off, but when he returned in 1919 as manager and director of productions he was never to leave again. In 1923 he was created member of the Board of Directors, finally filling the vacancy left by the death of Synge in 1909.

During his respite from managerial work at the Abbey Robinson became involved with Sir Horace Plunkett in a scheme to set up a public library system in Ireland under the Carnegie Trust. He was organizing librarian in the district of Limerick-Kerry from 1915 until 1924, staying for four of those years at the house of the O'Briens of Cahirmoyle, a noted Irish family, and getting to know Irish rural life from the point of view of a detached observer. He was later to write a biography of his landlord, the painter Dermod O'Brien (*Palette and Plough*, 1948), but the main effect of his stay was the turning of his genius into the fresh channel of comedy. *The Whiteheaded Boy* (1916) was written at Cahirmoyle, and used Mrs Mabel O'Brien as model for Aunt Ellen in the play. Its success at the Abbey later led to a London production, and secured Robinson's reputation as a rising new playwright. He was also writing short stories at this time, and it was a short story that ended his career with the Carnegie Trust. The committee took exception to a story of his, "The Madonna of Slieve Dun", published in *To-Morrow*, edited by Francis Stuart. It was regarded as blasphemous, which it certainly is not, and Robinson as author was asked to resign from the Carnegie Trust position. Supported by Yeats (whose poem *Leda and the Swan* appeared in the same controversial publication), Robinson refused. He was then dismissed, in December 1924. This case of blatant censorship aroused much interest at the time.

Towards the end of 1918, Robinson was instrumental in founding the Dublin Drama League, dedicated to staging international drama. Mainly on nationalist grounds, Yeats was opposed at this time to the inclusion of foreign plays in the Abbey repertory, but had no objection to the League's filling this gap as a complementary company. Thus the Dublin Drama League was granted use of the Abbey stage, and some of its players, on Sunday and Monday evenings. During its most active years, from 1919 to 1928, the Drama League staged modern European and American plays, usually of an experimental nature. Robinson was at various times secretary, Vice-President and President, directed some of the productions and occasionally acted in them (under the name 'Paul Ruttledge', taken from the hero of Yeats's *Where There is Nothing*). After 1928, when MacLiammóir and Edwards founded the Dublin Gate Theatre, the *raison d'être* of the League was largely removed, although it continued to function until 1941. So far as Robinson's own plays are concerned, there is discernible after the arrival of the Drama League a greater sophistication and willingness to experiment. In addition, Robinson must be credited for encouraging an international repertory in Dublin during the 1920s, something that not only influenced the work of O'Casey and Denis Johnston but helped create an audience which, in turn, patronized the new *avant-garde* theatre at the Gate.

By 1930, the year he first travelled to the United States as visiting professor and director (at Amherst, Carnegie Institute, University of Michigan, and University of Montana), Robinson was something of a celebrity. His plays, ever-increasing in number, were securely established in the Abbey repertory and occasionally to be seen in London and New York; publication by prestigious houses usually followed. He was called upon to edit several anthologies of Irish poetry, and became a founder-member of the Irish Academy of Letters in 1932. In 1931 he married Dorothy Travers-Smith, the scene designer, and they lived in Dalkey, County Dublin.

In August 1938 Robinson organized a special Abbey Theatre

Festival, the lectures for which he edited in *The Irish Theatre* (1939). He himself contributed an essay on Lady Gregory, who had died in 1932, and whose *Journals* he was later to edit. Although she was at times critical of Robinson, considering him vague or morose (he was, indeed, given to depression), he was never less than generous in his praise of her and of her work for the Abbey. Yeats he admired this side idolatry, and in 1940 contributed a long essay to a volume in commemoration, *Scattering Branches*, in which he both paid tribute to the man and offered lengthy analyses of Yeats's plays. Robinson held a high opinion of Yeats as playwright, and since he had directed several of the plays he now wrote with an unusually informed view on this subject. Much of that essay he reprinted in *Curtain Up* (pp. 44-72), and it retains to the present day the imprint of a keen analyst of what constitutes effective theatre. In 1949 Robinson was commissioned to write the official history of the Abbey Theatre, which was published two years later. In 1949, also, Robinson was made honorary Doctor of Literature by Trinity College, Dublin. Towards the end of his life he took an interest in the amateur drama movement, and was appointed patron of the newly-founded All-Ireland Drama Council in 1953, acting as adjudicator at the first all-Ireland drama festival at Athlone. From first to last, Robinson dedicated himself to serving the interests of Irish theatre. He died in Dublin on 14 October 1958 and was buried in Saint Patrick's Cathedral there.

II

Lennox Robinson was one of the most prolific Irish playwrights of modern times. Twenty-two plays and one adaptation (of Sheridan's *The Critic*) were staged at the Abbey, while three more were done by Edwards-MacLiammóir Productions, and one, *Give a Dog—*, was staged by the Dublin Drama League after rejection by the Abbey. Most of these plays were published, but all are now out of print. The time is well past for a re-issue of some of the plays as a reminder of how good a writer for the theatre Robinson could be. He has tended to be neglected in recent years, which is a great pity since Robinson's work has permanent value both as entertainment and as material for the study of craftsmanship in the theatre.

The plays included in this volume are selected so as to represent the various phases in Robinson's career, and also the varied forms in which he wrote. What unifies all six plays collected here is on the one hand Robinson's technical skill—especially his fine use of dialogue and his almost classical sense of dramatic form—and on the other hand his love of Ireland and its people. This love was neither idolatrous nor uncritical, but it was nonetheless profound and enduring. Indeed, Robinson concludes his autobiography, *Curtain Up*, with the remark: "this strange Irish thing has been the commanding force in my life." His work, lacking the passion of Synge or O'Casey, nevertheless takes its inspiration from the source that gives those writers their places among the greatest of Irish writers: national feeling. It takes its significance, however, from its value as theatrical art, unremittingly pursued. This inspiration and this significance can be seen again and again in the six plays in this volume.

All but one of these plays, *The Whiteheaded Boy*, were from the first directed in the Abbey Theatre by Robinson himself, which gives to the texts a quality unique in the history of the Irish dramatic movement. He knew the acting company intimately, and knew the (quite restricting) stage on which the actors worked; his plays were thus tailor-made, and should be read with a small proscenium stage clearly in mind. The last thing they claim to be is literature; they are scripts for performance, pre-eminently.

Patriots (Abbey, 11 April 1912) stands as an example of Robinson's early work in the realistic, Ibsenist vein. It is also indicative of Robinson's nationalist feelings. He was, in his own way, a strongly political writer, as can be seen by the two plays which followed *Patriots*, namely *The Dreamers* (1915), a play about Robert Emmet, and *The Lost Leader* (1918), a play about Parnell. Political fervour is also seen in Robinson's only novel, *A Young Man from the South* (1917), which is partly autobiographical, and in four short stories written 1915-16 at the time of, and stories saturated with, powerful national feeling. These stories were published under the title *Dark Days* (1918).

At the time when *Patriots* is set, prior to 1912, Ireland was in a political limbo. The movement to obtain Home Rule, with political independence implied for all Ireland, was about to come to nothing. Indeed, *Patriots* opened on the same day as the third Home Rule Bill was introduced in the British House of Commons. At this time, the revolutionary spirit which was to lead to the rising of 1916 had not yet manifested itself in the founding either of the Volunteers or of the Irish Citizen Army. Robinson is writing about a period of apathy among Irish people, and his play hinges on the contrast between such people and the passionate commitment of the released Fenian prisoner, James Nugent. Nugent is like a prophet, out of phase with his own time, a Jeremiah come to rural Ireland. Although it is clear that to Robinson Nugent is the real hero, violent though his republicanism is, it is equally clear from the ending of *Patriots* that the majority reject Nugent's dream. The play is thus a study of a social leader passed by and isolated by a change in public mood. The irony of the ending provides a sharp critique of this public mood, and adds, as it were, a bold question mark to the play's title.

Because of the swing towards violence which entered Irish political life after 1915, *Patriots* was soon out of date. The James Nugents of a former time came into their own again. Yet this fact does not minimize the force of Robinson's play. In his autobiography, he himself praised its "precise construction, the tightness of its dialogue... the humour springing out of character." The reviewers of the first production praised *Patriots* in just those terms, and the noted critic Andrew Malone said in *The Irish Drama* (1929): "In thought, in dialogue and in construction *Patriots* is one of Lennox Robinson's best plays."

The Whiteheaded Boy (Abbey, 13 December 1916) marks a complete change in mood and style. "Lady Gregory said of me years later that I 'waded through blood to write, at last, *The Whiteheaded Boy*'," remarked Robinson in his autobiography. This play proved a turning point in his career as playwright, for here he struck for the first time that vein of comedy which probably best expressed his talents as a writer. It settled into the Abbey repertory as a lasting success, and by 1962, according to Ernest Blythe, it had accumulated a greater number of performances than Synge's *Playboy of the Western World*.

A good deal of the charm of *The Whiteheaded Boy* derives from the atmosphere of good-natured mockery which pervades the play. This atmosphere is immediately established by the narrator who speaks through the stage directions. (In a revival of the play at the Abbey in 1974, these directions were voiced through a loudspeaker.) It is important to bear in mind that a persona is being used here; unlike, for example, Shaw's plays, *The Whiteheaded Boy* does not employ the author's own voice in the stage directions.

A curious, informed, yet ill-educated person (who uses quaint turns of phrase and even dialect at times) takes the spectator into his confidence and comments on the setting, the characters, and the action in such a way as to provide a filter for the comedy. The best comedies seem always to allow an audience a certain superiority of attitude, a vantage point from which, like Shakespeare's Puck, the audience can enjoy the thought, "Lord, what fools these mortals be!" Robinson achieves this comic distance by interposing an invisible commentator who controls the mood in which the story is received.

In other respects, *The Whiteheaded Boy* is a well-crafted play. Robinson set great store by what is called, sometimes disparagingly, the "well-made play", whereby each scene contributes directly to the growth of an organically-conceived plot. From the expected return of Denis Geoghegan (pronounced "Gaygan") in the first scene, the plot advances through the crisis in the middle of act two (when Aunt Ellen tries to buy off Duffy and meets a proposal instead), to the marriage of Denis and Delia at the end, with full victory for Denis over his family's attempts to exile him. All of this development is handled with great ease and naturalness, because the characters are shrewdly adjusted to milieu and act in a probable manner. The characterization centres on Denis himself, the "whiteheaded boy" or family pet, a scapegrace who never alienates sympathy because he has both spirit and a sense of decency. Here, it might be said, Robinson closed his Ibsen and opened his Goldsmith and Sheridan. For Denis is a new version of the "good-natured man" of earlier comedy, whose integrity eventually shows up against the background of double-dealing engaged in by the society around him. While the others think primarily about the Geoghegan "name" (like Mrs Clancy in Robinson's first play), Denis refuses to do anything which might injure Delia. He is, in his way, a rebel, whose relationship with his family is analogous with that of Ireland to Great Britain, though it is not necessary to see the play altogether as "political from beginning to end", which was how Robinson himself described it later. If the political implications are given too much weight, the genial satire of small-town life is endangered, and a character such as Aunt Ellen, that lovable busybody, is likely to be turned into an abstraction. As it stands, the play is beautifully balanced, its theme of individual independence happily reconciled to a social structure amusingly exposed but tolerantly accepted.

The Whiteheaded Boy stands out as not only the first but the greatest of Robinson's comedies. Over a decade later he achieved a comparable success with *The Far-Off Hills* (1928), which, as it marks no advance on *The Whiteheaded Boy*, is not included in this volume. The latter was not only one of the best of all Abbey comedies, but, in the opinion of Michael J. O'Neill in his fine book on Robinson, "there are not many comedies to rival it on the contemporary stage." Small wonder that it was recommended to Sean O'Casey as model, when he was starting out to write for the Abbey. After he had seen a production in December 1923 O'Casey wrote to Robinson: "It is a glorious work... I envy you every word of the White-headed Boy. This is no hasty opinion, for I read the Play before I went to see it, and though honestly, I thought at first, I was going to be disappointed, I soon found myself laughing, and it takes a good man to make me laugh, now."

Crabbed Youth and Age (Abbey, 14 November 1922) shows Robinson's skill with a one-act play. From its beginnings, the Irish dramatic movement had cultivated the one-act form, seen in the work of Yeats, Lady Gregory and the early Synge. But these one-acts usually had a rural setting (or in Yeats's case a mythological setting), so that Robinson, while working within the tradition, here left the famed "peasant quality" behind and wrote instead a miniature comedy of manners.

He found it harder work than *The Whiteheaded Boy*. Indeed, he spent almost six months in writing *Crabbed Youth*, "foreshortening and further foreshortening, making it in the end the seemingly careless, easy thing I hope it is," he says in his autobiography. The result is a model of good craftsmanship. The "point of attack", as Robinson called that moment in a story at which the playwright enters, is when the three unmarried daughters are at breaking point in their frustration over their widowed mother's superior attractiveness. The mother, Mrs Swan, is not on stage when the play opens, a favourite trick of Robinson's; and we encounter instead an atmosphere of incipient revolt by her daughters, who fail to hold the attention of one young man while the sounds of Mrs Swan's success with two other young men filter from the next room. Robinson's first title for the play was the punning "Revolt of the Swans", and this provides the theme: the girls decide they will confront their mother and force her to retreat. Comically, this revolt misfires, and we see why as soon as Mrs Swan enters. (The character was based on an actual person, the artist Sarah Purser.) She is not at all a vamp or a *femme fatale*. Her vivacity and bubbling good

15

spirits, devoid of all egotism, make her naturally magnetic, and the young men simply cannot accept that she should leave them. The excuse that she is ill only activates their zeal to find medicine and make her comfortable; in short, it makes more pronounced their preference of mother over daughters. There is a neat reversal when Mrs Swan joins the company again, and takes over, with everybody rushing to do what she wants. This comic reversal, implied in the title *Crabbed Youth and Age*, makes her place in the family similar to that of the "whiteheaded boy" in the earlier play.

Because of its well-observed characterization, its economic use of dialogue, and its tolerant yet lively appraisal of the youth *versus* age motif, this little play has long been regarded as among the best work Robinson ever did. It repays study for its techniques; and it warrants production for its entertainment value.

The text here printed is the later version of *Crabbed Youth and Age*, published by James Duffy in Dublin in 1956, collated with the earlier version included in *Plays*, published by Macmillan in 1928. Robinson updated Mrs Swan's references to her honeymoon, originally put at 1897 and now at 1924, with a nice inclusion of Shaw's *Saint Joan*, which actually opened in that year.

The Big House (Abbey, 6 September 1926) has Robinson tackling a major theme in Irish literature. Because of its colonial status under English rule, Ireland for much of its history knew the importance of the "Big House" in rather a different way from England or Russia, for example. Jane Austen's *Mansfield Park* would be only half the story of the status of a Big House in an Irish landscape. The political question was always present, whether consciously or not, in the relations between Protestant, Anglo-Irish aristocracy and Catholic, native, perhaps Gaelic-speaking, peasantry. When the old order began to change, and Irish independence became a reality in 1921, the place of the Big House in Irish life and Irish culture was taken away. This change cannot be seen simply as a victory for democracy or as a symbol of the achievement of national independence, for there was loss as well as gain in the event. Yeats was to lament the loss of Lady Gregory's family home in his moving poem *Coole Park, 1929*, and later in his play *Purgatory* (1938), where the Old Man voices an elegy for the Big House as symbol of culture in the community.

But this elegiac note blends with a sharper, more insistent sound in Robinson's *The Big House*. By setting his play between the years 1918 and 1923, Robinson uses the 'Big House' theme to focus on that political question which was inherent in it. Ballydonal House, owned by the Alcocks, is besieged by history; a tide seems to turn violently against it, and we see the expulsion of a family innocent of wrongdoing in the community. Catholic servants turn against their Protestant employers; the house is betrayed from within, invaded by Republican soldiers and burned to the ground. Just as truly as O'Casey was writing of the destruction of the tenement community through the 1916 rebellion, the Black-and-Tan campaign of 1920 and the civil war of 1922-3, in his three great Dublin plays, so Robinson was truthfully recording the assault on a Protestant segment of Irish society which took place about the same time. In *Three Homes* (1938), Robinson's sister Nora testifies that life in County Cork in the years 1920-22 was very much as Lennox had depicted it in *The Big House*.

The permanent value of Robinson's play lies, it may be said, in the sensitivity with which he charts both the inevitability of the destruction of the house and the sense of outrage he articulates, through Kate Alcock, at the action which seeks to drive out a people as if they had no right to be there. The play thus has a continuing relevance to Irish history, for it still comments on the "Brits Out" policy of the latter-day extremist republicans, the Provisional IRA. Robinson may also be said to have established a genre of Irish drama, that of the besieged Protestant class, seen again in Jack White's *The Last Eleven* (Abbey, 1968) and William Trevor's *Scenes from an Album* (Abbey, 1981), while a different version of the Big House theme is seen in Brian Friel's *Aristocrats* (Abbey, 1979).

Some years after *The Big House*, Robinson wrote what is in some respects a sequel, *Killycregs in Twilight* (1937), concerning the decay of an Anglo-Irish family, the De Lurys. Here the dying fall is sounded in a Chekovian style, and in a key speech Judith de Lury says: "I wish we'd been burned out in the Troubles.... I wouldn't have behaved like that fool-girl in the play, *The Big House*. I would never have rebuilt Killycregs, I'd have thanked God to be quit of it." Perhaps Robinson had adopted a more pessimistic view of Ireland by 1937, but twelve years earlier he was writing out of a felt need to affirm his own identity, in pride and in freedom.

Drama at Inish (Abbey, 6 February 1933), which was entitled *Is Life Worth Living?* when it played in London and New York, is an extended joke on two levels. On one level it pokes fun at the lack of sophistication of small-town audiences, unable to distinguish between drama and reality. This humour is as old as

A Midsummer Night's Dream, but there Shakespeare makes the provincials into would-be actors; here, Robinson makes them into would-be cultured citizens. The failure, in each case, exposes the absurdity of the provincial mind. Taking too seriously the plays of Ibsen, Strindberg and other naturalistic writers, the "hempen homespuns" of Inish apply to their own lives a philosophy ludicrously out of keeping with their circumstances. "Is life worth living?" becomes the pessimistic attitude of the naive playgoers, with the result that attempted suicides and other extreme solutions, borrowed from drama, become commonplace in the village. It is through the exaggeration of this point beyond what is credible or plausible that Robinson derives one whole area of amusement.

On the second level, *Drama at Inish* is a play about actors and theatrical styles. Hector de la Mare and Constance Constantia are exaggerated types, travelling players of Dickensian proportions, whose lofty demeanour is at once awesome and absurd. With their theatrical talk, of "vibrations" and so forth, they contrast sharply with the homely normality of John Twohig's hotel; but it is their direct importation of theatricalism into the hotel itself that starts off that confusion of illusion and reality (as in the maid Helena's reaction to the rehearsal in Act I) which provides the play's main source of comedy. The gap narrows between the theatricalism of the De La Mare Repertory Company and the realism of the residents of Inish, to the point where the residents become "actors" themselves, striking attitudes and declaiming romanticized versions of their past lives. Robinson's mockery of this development is seen at the end of Act II, where Lizzie and Eddie are shown as self-dramatizing, *"entirely engrossed in making pretty, untrue pictures for themselves."* It is also seen in the voting decision of the local member of Parliament, Peter Hurley —inappropriately influenced by the hero of Ibsen's *An Enemy of the People*—which brings down the Government. Theatricalism of this kind (and other examples are available in Act III) is finally suspended by John Twohig, who banishes the De la Mare Repertory Company and restores the *status quo*.

Drama at Inish, then, is very much a play for and about actors. The fun resides largely in role-playing for its own sake, but Robinson also satirizes a certain kind of playwriting. Hector de la Mare tells of his youthful conversion to Ibsenism (Act I), after which he felt a sense of "mission" to the public. In an essay entitled "Ibsen", in *I Sometimes Think* (1956), Robinson says of Hector's speech here, "if you will substitute the Gaiety Theatre [Dublin] for the Cork Opera House you may take [it] ... for a fragment of autobiography." The older Robinson is therefore laughing at the dedicated young playwright who Ibsen-like exposed the hypocrisies of Irish provincial life in his earliest plays.

Drama at Inish proved among Robinson's most popular plays at the Abbey, and in September 1975 it received a musical adaptation at the new Abbey, by Fergus Linehan and Jim Doherty. Robinson himself set two more plays in his invented seaside town of Inish, *Bird's Nest* (1938) and *The Lucky Finger* (1948), but neither of them was as successful as the whimsical *Drama at Inish*.

Church Street (Abbey, 21 May 1934) shows Robinson in more experimental vein. He was too intelligent a man of the theatre not to want to break away from realism now and again. He did this in a couple of plays in the 1920s, *The Round Table* (1922) and *Ever the Twain* (1929), in which he introduced touches of symbolism and expressionism. These and other such ambitious plays as *Give a Dog—* (1929) and *All's Over, Then?* (1932) had nothing specifically Irish about them, and it seems plain that Robinson strained to extend his range in line with the achievements of European and American drama. The failure of *All's Over, Then?* in its London production in 1933 made him think again about subject-matter and to consider whether the provincial Irish life he knew best might not, after all, best suit his talents as playwright. Consequently, *Church Street* is autobiographical, presenting in the playwright Hugh Riordan (returned from London after failure there) a man compelled to recognize that the stuff of tragedy underlies the mundanity of life in his home town. But *Church Street* is also experimental in form, thus bringing together the two impulses in Robinson's mature work.

Where *Drama at Inish* had taken a light-hearted approach to the metaphysical question of what illusion is, *Church Street* explores this theme in a more profound and thought-provoking manner. In a speech in Act III of *Drama at Inish*, Annie Twohig admits that the town scandals existed before the players came, but that nobody knew of them "except the parties concerned". The problem plays "began to put ideas into our heads", i.e. they turned private affairs into public (and extreme) expression. Robinson now takes this duality and uses it to illuminate the nature of dramatic art. That is to say, he takes as theme, to borrow Thoreau's famous remark, that most men "lead lives of quiet desperation", but he is simultaneously saying, with Judge

Brack after Hedda Gabler's suicide, "people don't do such things" as might show up the desperation. Robinson does show up the desperation, the hidden poverty, the "pangs of despised love" and so on, that underlie the outwardly calm social order such as his community in *Church Street* typifies; but he does so only by letting the characters conduct scenes which they would not "in reality" experience. Inverted commas around the latter phrase are appropriate, because one of the effects of Robinson's method is to force on his audience a fresh consideration of what reality is. What kind of reality do we expect in the theatre? How does the playwright arrive at the version of reality (or truth) which he proposes for our acceptance? Luigi Pirandello had already probed such questions in *Six Characters in Search of an Author* (which was staged at the Abbey 3 December 1934) or in *Henry IV* (in which Robinson himself played the lead when it was staged by the Drama League in 1924). Robinson rather teases with such philosophical questions than provides sufficient exploration in *Church Street*, which is ultimately more of a scenario than a play.

The form of *Church Street* was highly innovative, so far as Abbey plays of the day were concerned. Robinson calls for a contrast in style between the disorderly way in which the houseguests first make their entrance and the "directed" way they move and speak when Hugh evokes imagined scenes in their private lives. Special lighting effects are also called for in these scenes, and swift rearrangement of furniture by Hugh himself, making clear theatrically how dramatic art presupposes the intervention of the designing hand. A second actor was needed for the Evoked Hugh, so that the audience had the experience of seeing the "real" Hugh (played by Arthur Shields) watching the imaginary Hugh (played by Denis O'Dea) on stage. With Hugh as director, these scenes-within-the-scene can defy the conventional, realistic usage of time and place, to very powerful effects at times, as in the sequence involving Sallie's abortion:

DOCTOR SMITH: Nothing bad can possibly happen, Miss Smith. As I said, in a short time, a very short time —
(*The scene suddenly goes black. The platform at the back on which the bench was is illuminated as a surpliced clergyman appears.*)
CLERGYMAN: I am the resurrection and the life, saith the Lord, ...

When the Clergyman's voice fades, the scene darkens again and a light comes up on Sallie's lover, Jim, writing to his mother in a vein totally out of keeping with the tragedy of Sallie's death. Although Robinson abolishes this sequence by Hugh's insistence that "it's all in my mind", it remains a moving story, skilfully told by means of stage techniques. Robinson tries to weld such theatricalism on to a realistic framework, and the result is experimental writing of a high order. The brevity of the play, however, remains a problem. None of the imagined scenes is long enough to sustain the tragic feeling evoked. Robinson was aware of the awkward length of the play, and remarked in *Towards an Appreciation of the Theatre* (1945): "it lasts about an hour and twenty minutes without a break; no English-speaking management outside the Abbey Theatre will consider it for a minute, but translated into Italian it plays contentedly in Rome."

It is a measure of his own estimation of this piece that it was, of all his plays, *Church Street* that represented Robinson the playwright during the Abbey Theatre Festival of August 1938, which he helped to organize. It was also the play of his included by Curtis Canfield in his anthology *Plays of Changing Ireland* (1936), alongside such experimental plays as Johnston's *The Old Lady Says 'No!'*. Canfield considered that Robinson was only at this time "reaching his full powers as a dramatist", thus implying great things to come. They did not, in fact, come. The course of Robinson's career after *Church Street*, or at least after *Killycreggs in Twilight* (1937), was a slow decline. Yet Canfield's judgement of Robinson remains just, and may stand for conclusion here: "his technique is more polished and his structure more certain than that of any of his contemporaries."

Christopher Murray
University College
Dublin

October 1981

A NOTE ON THE TEXTS

Patriots, never reprinted in Robinson's lifetime, is the text published by Maunsel (Dublin and London, 1912). *The Whiteheaded Boy* is the text reprinted by James Duffy (Dublin, 1973). *Crabbed Youth and Age* is the text reprinted by James Duffy (Dublin, 1964) in *Two One-Act Comedies: Never the Time and the Place, and Crabbed Youth and Age*. This is a revision of the text published in *Plays* (London: Macmillan, 1928). The text of *The Big House* is that published in *Plays of the Irish Renaissance 1880-1930*, edited by Curtis Canfield (New York: Ives Washburn, 1929), but the spellings have been restored to the English forms. *Drama at Inish* is substantially that reprinted by James Duffy (Dublin, 1972), but collated with the text in *Killycreggs in Twilight & Other Plays* (London: Macmillan, 1939), where the title is *Is Life Worth Living?*, a form never used at the Abbey Theatre. It is possible that the Duffy text represents some changes made by Robinson after 1939, but as it omits a few lines from the Macmillan text these have been included here. The text of *Church Street* is from *More Plays* (London: Macmillan, 1935).

PATRIOTS

A play in three acts

To
the James Nugents
of history

COSTELLO. It's a statue of Liberty Brian Hosty was talking about
in the commencement.
MANNION. Ah, who the hell cares about liberty? . . . .

The Image
Lady Gregory

CHARACTERS

JAMES NUGENT
ANN, his wife
ROSE, their child
BOB ⎫
HARRY ⎭ ANN'S brothers
DAN SULLIVAN
MRS SULLIVAN
WILLIE, their son
FATHER KEARNEY
PETER O'MAHONY
JIM POWELL
TWO YOUNG MEN

"Patriots" was first produced in the Abbey Theatre on April 11th, 1912, with the following cast:

Peter O' Mahony	SYDNEY J. MORGAN
Ann Nugent	SARA ALLGOOD
Rose Nugent	KATHLEEN DRAGO
Mrs Sullivan	EILEEN O'DOHERTY
Bob	ARTHUR SINCLAIR
Harry	J.A. O'ROURKE
Willie Sullivan	C. POWER
James Nugent	FRED O'DONOVAN
Father Kearney	J.M. KERRIGAN
Dan Sullivan	PHILIP QUINEY
Jim Powell	J.M. KERRIGAN
First Young Man	U. WRIGHT
Second Young Man	PHILIP QUINEY

The Play was produced by the Author

ACT I

Scene — ANN's *sitting-room over the shop in a country town in Ireland. The room is well furnished, and in fairly good taste.* ANN *is forty-four years old* — *but her hair is already grey. She is capable and methodical, a splendid business woman, and she has lived with two fools for eighteen years, so she speaks as little as possible.* O'MAHONY *is older than her in years, but appears younger. They are seated at a table with books and papers before them. They are making up the half-yearly accounts of the shop. It is evening.*

O'MAHONY: Six hundred and forty pounds seven and eight pence?

ANN: No. Six hundred and thirty-seven pounds seventeen and eight pence.

O'MAHONY: Dear me, I can't find the mistake. This is the third time I have gone over it.

ANN: (*taking some papers from him and pushing a book towards him*) Read the items out to me.

O'MAHONY: Wolff, twenty-five pounds ten; Brady, sixteen pounds two and six pence; Farmer, fifty-seven pounds; Burke, fourteen pounds ten and sixpence; Caughlan, twenty-one pounds sixteen and sixpence; Maybury —

ANN: You have Caughlan twenty-three pounds six and sixpence. That's where you're wrong.

O'MAHONY: Have I really? How stupid!

(ANN *finishes the accounts with a few decisive pen-strokes.*)

ANN: Now it's finished.

O'MAHONY: I congratulate you, Ann; it's by far the best half-year you've ever had.

ANN: Yes, it's been very good.

O'MAHONY: Three eighty — yes — nearly four hundred better than this time last year.

ANN: And there are really not so many outstanding debts — ones that I'm anxious about I mean — except the Clarkes.

O'MAHONY: And of course the Sullivans.

ANN: Oh, I've made up my mind about the Sullivans. They've got to go.

O'MAHONY: Go?

ANN: (*calmly*) If they won't pay their rent they've got to be put out.

O'MAHONY: It's not that they won't, it's that they can't.

ANN: Well, it doesn't make any difference to me. Ten pounds is all I've got out of that house in Main Street during the last three years. That's not good enough, Peter. It's a fine house in one of the best positions in the town. If I put them out and do it up thoroughly, I can get double the rent the Sullivans are supposed to be giving me.

O'MAHONY: Do you really mean this, Ann?

ANN: Of course I do.

O'MAHONY: Sullivan has had a long struggle.

ANN: It's quite easy to make a good living out of the grocery business; I've proved that.

O'MAHONY: Well, you know they say that it's because you're doing so well, that he's doing badly.

ANN: Yes, I *have* got the best part of the custom of the town .... It's Sullivan's own fault. He had it and he lost it by laziness and drink. I won it by downright hard work.

O'MAHONY: If they managed to pay up their arrears....

ANN: No, they must go altogether. I want to put up the rent, and it's not good for my property to have it occupied by shiftless, failing people.

O'MAHONY: But Mrs Sullivan's your friend... how can you ever face them if you do a thing like this... without... why ... they'll never expect you to do such a thing... Willie Sullivan is Rose's greatest friend.

ANN: It won't hurt Willie, he's got his place with Hughes.

O'MAHONY: Oh, you're a rich woman, Ann; you can afford to be a little generous.

ANN: I'm not rich. I can't afford it.

O'MAHONY: (*in a lower voice*) Sullivan was one of *James*'s greatest friends, Ann. Have you forgotten that?

ANN: (*stonily*) I don't see that that makes any difference.
(O'MAHONY *sighs. There is a pause during which they put away the papers.*)
Oh, I made my will today, Peter.

O'MAHONY: A fresh one?

ANN: Hm... nothing very different from the old one except that when I die the business is to be sold at once and the purchase-money shared up. I've made you sole executor of Rose's share.

O'MAHONY: Why, Ann?

ANN: Well, I can't run any risk about Rose's future. Of course

Bob and Harry might get a good manager for the shop—but then they mightn't, they might try to run it themselves—they'd be bankrupt in five years. It's better to sell it out at once. You won't find it hard to get a good price for it.

O'MAHONY: Yes, I see. And Rose's money is to be invested?

ANN: Yes... (*her voice gets softer, more anxious*). You... you'll be very careful, won't you, Peter? Get something very safe... never mind if the interest's small... it's got to be safe. We can't take any risks about Rose.

O'MAHONY: Don't you worry about Rose, Ann, she'll be all right.

ANN: I'm sure she will. You've been very good to me, Peter, I don't know what I'd have done without you all these years.

O'MAHONY: Oh, nonsense. You've had your brothers...

ANN: Ph, they're no good.

O'MAHONY: Where is Rose tonight? In bed?

ANN: No. She took a fancy to go to that Irish concert at the last minute, and I hadn't the heart to stop her. Mrs Sullivan took her.

O'MAHONY: Had she a good day?

ANN: Yes, very.

O'MAHONY: I really think she's getting stronger and stronger.

ANN: Oh, there's no doubt of it. Doctor French is very pleased with her. But she'll always need great care and attention of course.

O'MAHONY: Yes... (*taking a small bust off the chimney-piece.*) Where did this come from?

ANN: Oh, that's Rose's. Willie Sullivan gave it to her the other day.

O'MAHONY: It's Emmet, isn't it?

ANN: Yes.

O'MAHONY: Willie's at the concert with them, I suppose?

ANN: Oh, no. This is the Committee night of the League.

O'MAHONY: You don't say that Willie's on the Committee? Sure, he's only a boy.

ANN: Yes, but he's very enthusiastic, I believe.

O'MAHONY: Oh, nonsense. I wish he'd keep clear of that political set. He's got the makings in him of a good business man, but that silly League would ruin him.

ANN: I quite agree with you.

O'MAHONY: That's what ruined his father. We must save Willie from it.

ANN: I hear people passing in the street. I expect the concert is over.

O'MAHONY: (*going to the window*) Yes, it must be. I see a lot of people passing, and there's Rose and Mrs Sullivan.

(ANN *pulls out a comfortable chair to the fire, and pours some milk into a saucepan and makes other preparations.* MRS SULLIVAN *and* ROSE *come in.* MRS SULLIVAN *is middle-aged, with the anxious, helpless expression of a woman whose business is on the edge of bankruptcy, and whose husband is a drunkard. It is not in her character to do more than pray "God help me."* ROSE *is eighteen, petulant, enthusiastic, a torch longing for the match, a sick child — all in one because a cripple.*)

ROSE: Why, Peter, are you here? (*She kisses him affectionately.*)

O'MAHONY: Well, Rose. Good evening, Mrs Sullivan.

MRS SULLIVAN: Good evening, Mr O'Mahony.

ANN: Come and sit by the fire, Rose; you must be cold.

ROSE: No I'm not. (*She sits by the fire and* ANN *takes off her coat and shoes.*)

MRS SULLIVAN: I won't wait, I only wanted to see Rose safely in. Good night.

ANN: Thank you for looking after her, Susan; good night.

MRS SULLIVAN: Good night, Rose.

ROSE: Good night, Mrs Sullivan, and tell Willie that I managed to get that book about the Fenians from a second-hand shop in Dublin — he'll know the book I mean — and I'll give it to him if he comes round tomorrow night.

MRS SULLIVAN: I'll tell him. Good night. (*Goes out.*)

ROSE: Where's everybody?

ANN: Your uncles haven't come in yet.

ROSE: Oh, I remember uncle Bob said they had all the winter lectures to settle, and that always means a lot of work. I do hope they'll have some one new this session.

O'MAHONY: You know they won't. They always have the same old lot set.

ROSE: Well, I like the League all the same. I'm going to make you come this winter, Peter.

O'MAHONY: No, you won't get me to go. That sort of talk, talk, talk, doesn't interest me. I've got to look after my baking.

ROSE: Perhaps it won't always be a place for talk. Willie would do something if he got the chance.

O'MAHONY: Yes, but he won't get the chance, and a good thing for him that he won't. That sort of thing is all very well as a sort of — well as a sort of amusement... but to go in for it seriously....

ROSE: Why not?

O'MAHONY: You don't understand.

ANN: Now, Rose, your milk is ready.

O'MAHONY: That's it. Drink up your milk and don't bother your head about politics and Leagues. Good night, dear. Good night, Mrs Nugent. (*Goes out.*)

ANN: (*holding a cup of milk*) Here, dear.

ROSE: (*petulantly*) I don't want it, take it away.

ANN: Oh, come, you must drink it — just to please me —

ROSE: No, mother.

ANN: A tiny sip . . . that's it. (*She feeds her like a little child.*)

ROSE: I wish Peter wouldn't talk like that about the League.

ANN: Never mind Peter, he was only joking you. Tell me about the concert.

ROSE: There's nothing to tell.

ANN: You're tired, aren't you?

ROSE: Yes. No.

ANN: Is your back bad?

ROSE: No, only a little.

ANN: I'll put this cushion behind you . . . . There, is that better?

ROSE: Yes.

ANN: And I'll move the lamp so that the light won't catch your eyes . . . . Now, finish this and then I'll put you to bed.

ROSE: I don't want to go to bed yet. I want to wait until Uncle Bob comes in.

ANN: He may not be in for a long time.

ROSE: Oh, yes he will; it's half-past ten.

ANN: What do you want to see him for?

ROSE: I want to hear all about the meeting.

ANN: You could hear it in the morning.

ROSE: No, mother, no. I want to hear it now. I'm not tired. I'm not really.

ANN: You're looking so white, darling.

ROSE: I'm all right, I am really, do, do let me stay up.

ANN: Very well, dear, just for ten minutes, but if they're not in by that time, off you go. We don't want to have Doctor French shouting at us, do we?

ROSE: I hate Doctor French.

ANN: I'm just going down to the shop to look for a receipted bill of Bolton's. I know it must be somewhere. Would you drink a little more milk if I heated it?

ROSE: No, mother, I couldn't, I couldn't.

ANN: Very well, dear. (*At the door.*) I hear your uncle's latchkey. Put on the saucepan of hot water.

(*She goes out. A moment later* BOB *comes in. He is a small stout man, always very busy about nothing.*)

29

BOB: Well, Rose.

ROSE: There you are at last!

BOB: Where's your mother?

ROSE: Downstairs looking for something. Where's Uncle Harry?

BOB: Oh, coming. Macnamara called after him in the street and I came on. Knew you'd wonder what was keeping us, and I couldn't risk catching cold.

ROSE: Isn't it a beautiful night out?

BOB: Hm.... I'd say there was a touch of frost. I must start using my winter muffler. I'm sure I caught a chill coming out of the hot room.

ROSE: Sit here near the fire. How did the committee go?

BOB: Oh, very well, very well. Starkie wasn't there, I'm glad to say.

ROSE: So I suppose you got through a lot of business.

BOB: Well, we settled the winter lectures at any rate — up to Christmas that is — and that's no joke I can tell you.

ROSE: No indeed. Who are you getting? Do show me the list.

BOB: It will be published in the "Watchword". Where's my cocoa? Don't wait for Harry of course.

ROSE: Your cocoa isn't ready yet. Do read me the list now.

BOB: (*importantly*) Well, you know, Rose, it's not quite regular.

ROSE: Oh, rubbish. What's the good of you being secretary to the League if I don't hear everything before everyone else?

BOB: Well, here it is. Shall I read it to you?

ROSE: Yes, please.

BOB: October 4th, Hugh Tanner, "Through the Appenines with a Camera". October 18th, J.H. Lockley, "The Folk Songs of Ireland" (that's the new doctor at the Asylum — clever young chap — nice tenor voice). October 31st, Rev. Patrick Coakley, C.C., "Ireland under Elizabeth".

ROSE: You had something about Elizabeth and Ireland last session, hadn't you?

BOB: Yes, yes. But it's an interesting period, very interesting. November 14th, your uncle Harry on "Old Dublin Newspapers". November 28th, William Sullivan, "Two Irish Patriots".

ROSE: Yes, Willie told me about that.

BOB: December 12th, Edgar Stockton, "The Nationalisation of Irish Railways". That's the list up to Christmas. What do you think of it?

ROSE: I think it's very good. It's so varied.

BOB: Yes, yes.... Er — you've read Willie's essay, have you, Rose?

ROSE: He read me a rough draft of it some time ago.

BOB: Yes .... Now, would you mind telling me is it very extreme?

ROSE: Extreme? Well, Willie couldn't write about Stephens and Emmet without enthusiasm.

BOB: Of course no one admires Stephens and Emmet more than I do, but — but times have changed, and I sometimes think Willie doesn't realise it. We've some very respectable young men in the League now — new members — and I don't want to hurt their feelings. There's the two Casey boys, their father is Clerk of the Petty Sessions, and Smith, the Postmaster's son — you know — you know their fathers mightn't like it — to say nothing of Doctor Lockley, a most superior young man.

ROSE: Well, I know Willie feels that father started the League to revive the national spirit in Ireland, and he thinks it can be done better by thinking of Stephens than a trip to the Appenines.

BOB: But sure, Tanner never saw Stephens and he did go through the Appenines last summer.

ROSE: Willie's terribly in earnest about things.

BOB: He goes too far, Rose, he does indeed. It's very bad for him professionally. Hughes won't keep him if he goes on like this; I expect Hughes will give him a rise soon, I know he thinks well of him, he told me so. But the other day I heard some one speak of Willie as "that wild young revolutionary clerk of Mr Hughes". Now, you know, Hughes won't like it if he hears that.

ROSE: How proud Willie would be if he heard himself called that. Anyway, I don't see that one's political views need affect one's business.

BOB: They needn't — if you're sensible. Look at us. We're — we're a desperate family. Everyone knows that Ann's husband is in prison for life for murder — political murder. Everyone knows what Ann's own views were... everyone knows what I was twenty years ago before my wretched health broke down — why we're a desperate family, but we keep our views to ourselves, and the consequence is we draw our custom from every class in the community. The shop's thriving. Willie will have to learn to hold his tongue if he wants to get on.

ROSE: Willie would rather earn a pound a week till the Day of Judgment than hold his tongue about his views.

BOB: Ah, well, he'll grow out of it, he'll grow out of it. I thought the same when I was his age.... I was a desperate fellow. I remember one night I swore six soldiers into the League — six — Rose.

ROSE: (*wide-eyed*) Did you really? How splendid of you, Uncle Bob.

BOB: Ah, yes, I'd have had the country in a flame only for my wretched health. But I done what I could, I done what I could. It's no joke being Secretary to the League, I can tell you. Why, getting up these winter lectures is a big job in itself, and then there are always resolutions to be framed and addresses and — and people like Starkie to pacify — oh, it's very wearing. I sometimes think that if I had withdrawn from it altogether I might have got back my health. But I'll never withdraw. I've given my life willingly — for Ireland.... Isn't that cocoa ready?

ROSE: Just. Aren't you going to lecture at all this session?

BOB: No, not at present. I might after Christmas if I could find an interesting subject.

ROSE: Why not have a lecture on father?

BOB: Your father? Why we've often had lectures about him, his life, his trial, his sentence — they all know the story.

ROSE: I was looking at the old lists yesterday. There's been nothing about him for three years.

BOB: As long as that? Are you sure?

ROSE: Yes. And I think it's a shame that the founder of the League who's in prison today for his patriotism should be forgotten like that.

BOB: Oh, come, come, Rose, he's not forgotten.

ROSE: He will be very soon.... He's been in for eighteen years, he'll be released soon perhaps — have you forgotten that? You don't want him to find himself forgotten when he comes out.

BOB: No, of course. But how can I lecture on him? I can't find anything fresh to say.

ROSE: Why don't you go and see him?

BOB: In prison? No, Rose, I couldn't do that. Nothing would make James suffer more than for me to see him in the day of his humiliation. I've never seen him since he was taken from the dock. You may think that heartless of me, but it would make him and me suffer too much.

ROSE: I hoped you'd go, because I meant to have gone with you.

BOB: You, Rose?

ROSE: Yes.

BOB: But your mother wouldn't let you. She'd never let you go to the prison. She's always gone alone.

ROSE: I know, I know. It's cruel, that's what it is; it's unfair to father and me.

BOB: Hush, Rose, you mustn't say that about your mother.

ROSE: (*stormily*) It is unfair. She never speaks of him to me. If I speak of him she — she —

BOB: Hush, hush, Rose. You don't understand these things, you're only a child. You must make allowances for your mother, she's never been the same since that long illness she had when you were born — just the time James was condemned to death. I've never quite understood her since.

ROSE: She — she loved father, didn't she?

BOB: Loved him? I should just think so.

ROSE: And she never speaks of him.... I suppose to have the person you love most in the world shut up like that is perfectly unspeakable.

BOB: Yes, yes, and I think your mother was right. There's no use fretting over what can't be helped.... I'll have another biscuit ... your mother's a wonderful woman, Rose, a great manager....

(HARRY *enters. He is very like his brother, as busy and as useless.*)

HARRY: Bob, Bob!

BOB: What is it, man, what is it?

HARRY: Is Ann there? Where's Ann? I've great news.

ROSE: What is it, Uncle Harry?

HARRY: James is released, at least he's going to be.

BOB: My God!

ROSE: What!

HARRY: It was Macnamara — that's what Macnamara wanted me for — it was on a Dublin evening paper.

BOB: But is it true, Harry?

HARRY: Don't I tell you it's on the paper. Listen. (*Opens paper.*) I'm so excited I can't find the place. Here it is. "We learn on the best authority that James Nugent, the famous revolutionary, is about to be released from prison. He was condemned to death in 1893 for the murder of Henry Foley, one of his confederates, but his sentence was commuted to penal servitude for life. He is a native of Coolmore, where his wife and child are still living." There now.

ROSE: It must be true.

BOB: It must then....

HARRY: But, Bob, I thought he wouldn't be out for another couple of years.

BOB: It's maybe the new Chief Secretary that's done it.

HARRY: Oh, maybe you're right.

ROSE: Will he come here, Uncle Harry?

HARRY: I suppose he will.

BOB: Where else would he go to?

ROSE: Oh, isn't this splendid! We must call mother.

BOB: Who's to tell Ann?

HARRY: You'd better do it, Bob.

BOB: No, no, let Rose, let Rose.

ROSE: I wonder how she'll take it.

BOB: You'll have to break it to her gently, you know. Sort of hint at it at first and then — oh, my God, here she is.
(ANN *comes in.*)

ANN: I've got it, Rose.

ROSE: What, mother?

ANN: The bill. Bolton's receipted bill. I knew I had paid it. That's the second time Boltons have done a thing like that. Have you had your supper yet, Bob? Don't forget that tomorrow's fair day, and we must have the shutters down by half-past seven, so you'd better go to bed as soon as you can. What's the matter with you?

HARRY: Ann — (*stops*)

ANN: Well?

HARRY: It's — something's happened, Ann.

ANN: Happened? What's happened?... What is it, Harry? There's nothing wrong in the shop I know — unless — is Clarke bankrupt?

HARRY: No, it's not that, Ann.

BOB: Now, Ann, calm yourself.

ANN: Oh, tell me what it is, I'm not a child; I can bear things.

HARRY: Well — (*stops*)

ROSE: Father is coming, mother.

ANN: What?

ROSE: He's going to be released at once.

ANN: James... coming... back.... Harry, is this true?

HARRY: Yes, Ann; at least I think so.
(ANN *sits down.*)

BOB: Quick, Harry, get her a glass of water.

ANN: No, no, I'm not going to faint. Who told you?

HARRY: It's on the evening paper.

ANN: Show me. (*He hands her the paper, she reads it and hands it back.*) Thank you. (*Her voice is quite expressionless.*)

BOB: It's extraordinary to think after eighteen years... well, well....

HARRY: He'll be greatly changed.

BOB: Bound to be after all those years; his health ruined, I suppose, with jail fever and the like....

HARRY: And his spirit broken too. Man, but he had the great spirit long ago. Do you remember, Bob, that day in Kilkenny? I came on the account of it the other day in an old "Freeman" — no, but an "Independent" it was — Where are you going, Ann?

ANN: (*at the door*) I'm going to write to the Governor to find out if it's true.

BOB: Did — did they say nothing about this, Ann, when you were there last?

ANN: No.

BOB: You haven't been since April, have you?

ANN: No. (*Goes out.*)

ROSE: (*almost crying*) Uncle Bob, what does she mean? Why doesn't she say something? Is she disappointed he's coming back, or what?

BOB: Oh, no, Rose.

HARRY: Never think that, Rose; never think that about your mother. She worshipped your father — she gave him all her money, she went with him everywhere, she left me and Bob to manage the shop as best we could. Why, I've newspapers upstairs full of accounts of the speeches James made and the speeches she made and the way they went about together — oh, it's very interesting reading.

BOB: I think it's most satisfactory — most satisfactory — your mother has taken it splendidly. You know it might have given her a great shock — I felt quite faint myself for a minute — Hello, there's a ring.

HARRY: You'd better open the door, Bob.

BOB: Oh, damn. Who on earth can it be at this hour? (*Goes out.*)

ROSE: It's — it's all so wonderful. Somehow I never expected he'd come back — I don't know why. It's wonderful to think I'll see him.

HARRY: Ah, you'll never have seen the real James Nugent, Rose. You'll only see an old broken man creeping home to die.

ROSE: Poor, poor father.... Why that sounds like Willie's voice — it is Willie.

(BOB *and* WILLIE SULLIVAN *come in.* WILLIE *is nineteen and very young.*)

WILLIE: I had to come in and see you all. Isn't this tremendous. Think of James Nugent coming back. He's just what we want — a real fearless honest man. My God, he'll save Ireland.

HARRY: I'm afraid — as I was just saying to Rose — poor James won't have much spirit left after all those years in prison.

BOB: His health, you know, will be quite broken down.

WILLIE: (*blankly*) But — do you mean — you think he'll be too broken to do anything in public?

HARRY: Well, eighteen years in prison, you know —

WILLIE: I never thought of that.... But after he's had a bit of a

35

rest — he's not more than forty-five, is he?

BOB: Well, well, I dunno. Anyway I'm glad the League is still going at Coolmore. It's the only one of the twelve branches he started that is still in existence. We've kept the flag flying in great style. I'm wondering what sort of a demonstration we ought to have for James.

HARRY: Oh, I hadn't thought of that.

BOB: It's so awkward now about our fight with the Town Band — we won't be able to get it now — of course we might try illuminations.

WILLIE: I think the best thing would be a monster meeting at which he could make a speech.

BOB: Well, I was thinking of that, but then he may not want to make a speech.

HARRY: No, no. I think we'd better not do anything rash. Let's wait and see what his views are, and anyhow we ought to wait till the Canon comes back from Palestine.

BOB: Stockton will probably —

HARRY: Oh, I forget, Stockton told me to tell you he can't lecture after all.

BOB: Can't lecture? But he promised.

HARRY: Yes, but he didn't know then that Tanner was going to lecture. He says he won't let his name appear in the same series as Tanner — you know they've never patched up that row over the building contract.

BOB: Well, that's just like Stockton — he promises you a thing and then when your back is turned he — and my list all made out and ready for the "Watchword" — who am I to get now?

WILLIE: Oh, Stockton's no loss, he's an old woman.

BOB: He is a loss. The Nationalisation of the Railways is a most important question, and one which the League has not yet passed an opinion on. I know there are many important men waiting to hear what we'll say on the subject, and Stockton has got relations on two of the railways in Ireland, so he's in a position to speak with intimate knowledge. Who am I to get now?

WILLIE: Maybe if you ask Father Kearney he might speak?

BOB: No, he wouldn't. I know he wouldn't. He's another. It's most disheartening really. There he was in the thick of things with James and he won't open his mouth. He sends in his subscription all right — I wish others were as regular — but as to doing anything practical — helping in a commemoration or — or — decorating a grave, he's useless. I'll resign the Secretaryship, I declare I will; this sort of thing is killing me.

ROSE: Perhaps father would give a lecture.

WILLIE: Yes.

BOB: Your father? The very thing. Why, he'll have any amount to tell us, all about prison and how he was treated – most interesting – most interesting – it'll be the best lecture of the lot. By the way, Rose, this knocks out the idea for my lecture – it's a pity, but no matter – of course James will speak. (ANN *comes in.*) Oh, Ann, we're going to get James to give us a lecture. Stockton has played me false.

WILLIE: That'll be splendid.

HARRY: It should be very interesting.

BOB: I'll have to put off advertising the list until next week's "Watchword". I must wait and get the title from him. "Behind Lock and Key" would sound good now, or "Prison Bars", or – oh, Ann, what sort of demonstration should we have for him?

ANN: Demonstration?

BOB: Yes, when he comes back.

HARRY: We can't get a band – unless we get one from Dublin.

BOB: Too expensive, too expensive.

WILLIE: (*a little doubtfully*) I hope Mr Nugent will like the list of lectures. I'm sure he'll think we should have had more national subjects.

BOB: Oh, he can't find any fault with them, they're so varied. I know Tanner's on the Appenines will be most interesting – and your one, Harry, on Dublin Newspapers.

HARRY: Yes, *it* will be good. If I can only get that "Freeman" for May 30th, 1886.

(ANN *laughs.*)

ROSE: What is it, mother?

(ANN *still laughs.*)

BOB: What are you laughing at, Ann?

ANN: It will be very funny – when James comes back – and asks you what you've been doing – for eighteen years – and you tell him about the League, and show him the list of lectures –

BOB: What's wrong with the list?

HARRY: Well, we've done a lot.

BOB: The membership is larger than it's been for years.

HARRY: We're the only branch that's still in existence.

WILLIE: I don't suppose he'd approve of our supporting the United Irish League candidates.

HARRY: He'll have to realise that things have changed.

BOB: We done what we could.

HARRY: We stood out for compulsory Irish.

BOB: You attended classes yourself for two winters.

HARRY: Yes, indeed, I know a lot of Irish — not — not to speak it of course.

WILLIE: Still I can realise James Nugent wanting something more than that.

HARRY: We passed a resolution against the Irish Council's Bill.

BOB: We done what we could.

HARRY: And things have changed.

BOB: Yes, things *have* changed.

WILLIE: I suppose they have.

(*But they look at each other uncomfortably and in silence.*
ANN *laughs again.*)

CURTAIN

ACT II

Scene. — The same. A week later. ROSE *is alone.* WILLIE *comes in.*

WILLIE: Mr Hughes sent me across with this letter for your mother.

ROSE: What's happened to Johnny?

WILLIE: Oh, Johnny's all right, but I offered to run over with it. The fact is I wanted to know if he's come. Has he, Rose?

ROSE: No, not yet. The train must be late. Uncle Bob and Uncle Harry have gone to the station to meet him. They're so frightened, they've never had a minute's happiness since the night they heard he was going to be released, and mother laughed at them.

WILLIE: I know. I feel miserable too. I don't know what he'll expect.

ROSE: Poor father. I don't suppose he'll expect very much, except care and quiet and attention. It's his heart you know, Willie; it's on account of his weak heart he's been released. The doctor wrote to mother about him.

WILLIE: It's like Christ coming to earth again twenty years after His ascension. I wonder will he realise how hard it is to do things nowadays.

ROSE: But the League has done a lot, Willie.

WILLIE: It's done nothing. Nothing that he'd call anything. That's what makes his coming back so frightful.

ROSE: At any rate he won't blame you. He can't. You're one of the youngest members.

WILLIE: Do you know what, Rose, I've made up my mind. I'll chuck my place if necessary. I mean if he wants people to go with him and help him, I won't hesitate. I'll leave Hughes.

ROSE: What would your people say? Oh, Willie!

WILLIE: Oh, they'll be all right. They've got the shop.

ROSE: And then there's your own career. Oh, Willie, I don't like your doing such a desperate thing.

WILLIE: Do you think my career matters a hang compared with — with —

ROSE: Of course we've always said that it doesn't. But when it

39

comes to the point.... However, I'm sure father won't want you to do anything of the kind.

WILLIE: No, he may not. Has your mother gone to the station?

ROSE: No, I think she's in her room changing her dress.

WILLIE: You're all dressed up.

ROSE: Of course.

WILLIE: How does she — I mean what does she think of it?

ROSE: I don't know. I never know what mother thinks. She's hardly spoken about him, she got his room ready and everything, but — oh I don't know. She handed us the doctor's letter, but I don't know whether she doesn't care or whether she cares very much. Yesterday I was looking over a bundle of old papers of Uncle Harry's and I came on a long article all about her, her personality and her influence. It was dated about a year before father's trial. They spoke of her "magnetic personality", her "queenly bearing" and now she's — she's not a bit like that, Willie.

WILLIE: Yes, she must have changed a lot. But she's a splendid woman all the same. I wish we had her brains down at our place and maybe the shop would begin to look up.

ROSE: Are things very bad?

WILLIE: Ay .... He's drinking again.

ROSE: Oh, Willie!

WILLIE: You see at any rate I've got to get away from this town. I can't live here with a thing like that going on.

ROSE: What would your mother do without you, you're all she has?

(ANN *comes in.*)

ANN: Oh, Willie, that you?

WILLIE: Yes, I just came over with this note from Mr Hughes. I'll be off.

ANN: (*taking note*) Thank you.

(WILLIE *goes out.*)

ROSE: (*hurrying to the window*) I see people coming from the station. They'll be here in a minute, and — oh, mother, you haven't changed.

ANN: Me? No.

ROSE: I thought you were going to.

ANN: Oh, no, why should I?

ROSE: You — you don't seem to care a bit.

ANN: Your blouse is open behind, Rose. Let me fasten it for you.

ROSE: (*looking out of window*) He'll be here in a minute.

ANN: (*with sudden passion*) You'll always love me, Rose?

ROSE: (*with surprise*) Mother?

40

ANN: (*kissing her passionately*) My darling, my darling, remember he's nothing — nothing — you've been mine — mine —

ROSE: Mother, what is it? Don't cry.

(ANN *moves away abruptly.* ROSE *turns to the window again.*) They're coming, I see them. Mother, he doesn't look old, come and look. I'm going to open the window and wave to him.

ANN: Don't, Rose. (ROSE *tries to lift the sash but stops with a little cry of pain. Going to her swiftly.*) What is it, Rose, have you hurt yourself?

ROSE: No, I just — it's only my back.

ANN: You shouldn't try to lift that sash, it's too heavy. Are you sure you haven't hurt yourself?

ROSE: Yes, quite sure. Where are they now?

ANN: (*looking out*) They've just turned in at the shop door. Come away from the window, dear.

ROSE: I wonder what he'll think of me.... Has he ever seen a photograph of me, mother?

ANN: No.

ROSE: Wouldn't the prison people let you give him one?

BOB: (*very fussy and nervous outside the door*) I think Ann is here — I'm sure she is — come in, James, come in. (*Looks in.*) Oh, Ann, there you are. He's come. Come in, James, Ann is here.

(JAMES *comes in, followed by* HARRY. JAMES NUGENT's *hair is nearly white, but he holds himself erect and walks and speaks with vigour.*)

JAMES: Ah, Ann, how are you? (*He kisses her.*)

BOB: And this is Rose, James.

JAMES: Is this Rose? Will you kiss me, my dear, I am your father.

ROSE: (*crying*) I'm very glad to see you.

JAMES: We should have met long ago. Ann, why would you never bring her to see me? ... Ah, well, perhaps you were right.

ANN: Won't you sit down?

JAMES: (*not sitting*) Thanks. (*Goes to the window.*) Everything looks just the same — I might have been here only yesterday — how wonderful it is to be back again — the room seems bigger, I think — How wonderful —

ANN: Had you a nice journey?

JAMES: Yes, a delightful journey, Ann, the train passed through such beautiful country, and everything looking so prosperous and well-to-do.

BOB: Yes, the country's thriving. Business is very good just now.

JAMES: How is the shop doing?

ANN: We've done very well the last half year.

BOB: My dear James, there's been a revolution since Ann came and looked after things. You remember what it was in the old days, waste, neglect — yes, Harry, there was neglect — but that's all altered now. We're thriving, thriving, it's the best grocery shop in the town.

JAMES: I'm very glad to hear it. It used to make me unhappy to think that perhaps you were badly off.

ANN: (*drily*) Did it?

JAMES: Yes... Rose is a Nugent, Ann. Don't you think she's very like my father?

ANN: No, I don't see any likeness to the Nugents.

JAMES: Well, well, what matter. (*He kisses* ROSE *very affectionately.*)

ANN: (*stung to jealousy*) See if tea is ready, Rose.

ROSE: Kate is getting it.

ANN: Please go and see about it.

ROSE: Oh, very well. (*She limps out.*)

JAMES: (*watching her*) She's hurt herself, hasn't she?

ANN: She's a cripple.

JAMES: Oh... I never knew, you never told me, Ann. It was the result of an accident, I suppose?

ANN: Yes.

JAMES: Recently.

ANN: No, a good many years ago.

JAMES: (*after a pause — briskly*) Well, now, I want to hear all about everything. I tried to make Ann understand a code for giving me information at our interviews in prison, but you never understood what I was aiming at, did you, Ann?

ANN: No, I didn't.

JAMES: Well, now, tell me everything.

HARRY: Well, we got several of the workhouse contracts this winter.

JAMES: Oh, I don't mean the shop; I mean the Cause.

HARRY and BOB: The Cause?

JAMES: I've seen some papers of course, but they had very little information — I may say none — in them. I gathered, however, that you have been working very quietly and discreetly for some years. That is quite right. Discretion was what we wanted in the old days. The organisation is better now, I am sure.

BOB: Oh, yes, yes.

JAMES: I see they are still playing that old Parliamentary game. I thought they'd have learnt its futility by this time. I'm sorry to see O'Brien in it. Really he was made for better things.

HARRY: I tell you, James, Parliament has done a great deal of late years; there's been the Land Act and —

JAMES: Oh yes, sops, sops. Parliament may have passed some good bills in its time, but it passed a devilish lot of bad ones too. And it's not the fellows at Westminster we have to thank for the good ones; it was some man in Ireland who maimed a bullock or shot a landlord that did the work. I'd like to repeal every bill for the last thirty years.

HARRY: What?

JAMES: They're only chains, Harry. The better the bill the stronger the chain. The better you house your slave, the better you feed him, the less just appears his demand for freedom, the less he wants freedom. Isn't that true?

HARRY: I dunno.

JAMES: How is the League doing?

BOB: The membership of the Coolmore Branch is larger than it's been for years.

JAMES: Splendid!

BOB: By the way, there's a small deputation from the League coming in a little while to welcome you. Only two or three, Father Kearney and a couple more.

JAMES: I'll be glad to see John Kearney again. How are we off for arms?

BOB: (*quickly*) I want to show you, James, the list of lectures for the coming winter. I thought perhaps you might like to give us a lecture yourself about your experiences in prison, and how the Government treated you.

JAMES: No, I won't lecture on that. What does it matter how they treated me — I'm out, I'm free, that's what matters. But, of course, I'll speak for you. (*Reads list.*) Ah, the police are watching you at present, I see.

HARRY: The police? No.

BOB: Why do you think that?

JAMES: Well, this list — it's so very harmless — unless — is there a double meaning in it? (*His voice drops significantly.*)

HARRY: What?

JAMES: The lecture on the Nationalisation of Irish Railways, for instance; does that by any chance point out the best way to set about getting possession of them when there's a rising?

HARRY: Oh, no, no. But we all think that if the Government was to take over the railways and —

JAMES: Well, well. The police are not active at present then?

BOB: No. Very quiet, decent men.

43

JAMES: I see. Effete. Good. "Old Dublin Newspapers" — what on earth is that about?

HARRY: (*with pride*) That's *my* lecture.

JAMES: But what is there interesting in old newspapers?

HARRY: My dear James, you find everything interesting in old newspapers. I've been collecting them for over twenty years, but lately I'm making a speciality in accounts of the funerals of patriots, you've no idea what interesting comparisons can be drawn between — say — the funeral of O'Connell and Parnell, or the —

BOB: Oh, talking of funerals, James, I want to know is it a kind of a twitch in the heart you feel, or a dull pain, or do you feel anything at all?

JAMES: In my heart?

BOB: Yes. You know I've a wretchedly weak heart myself, and I want to compare my symptoms with yours.

JAMES: Oh, I won't talk about my health.

BOB: Well, I think that's selfish of you, James. Maybe I could do something for you. I have a bottle recommended to me by —

JAMES: What about arms?

HARRY: Of course the language movement has come along since you were imprisoned.

JAMES: Oh, I don't attach much importance to that. Let's get a country first and then we'll see about the language. The idea's all right in moderation, but it's apt to draw people's attention away from the main thing. Are we well armed?

BOB: (*miserably*) Ann, don't you think tea is ready?

ANN: (*cruelly*) Rose will call you when it is. James is asking you something, Bob.

BOB: Oh, is he?

JAMES: I only wanted to know how we were off for arms. How many rifles have we?

BOB: Well — er — well —

HARRY: You see, James, you mayn't realise it yet, but things have changed —

BOB: Yes, James, very much changed.

HARRY: We work in a different way nowadays.

BOB: We've changed.

JAMES: In what way?

BOB: Well, one organises differently — we believe in educating the people — there's the Gaelic League, you know.

HARRY: And then I had to think of the shop and your wife and child, and Father Brady advised me and — and —

BOB: That's it.

JAMES: (*quite bewildered*) What do you mean? I don't understand what you're talking about.

ANN: They mean, James, that they've no arms, and don't intend to get any.

JAMES: What... But — the League?

BOB: The League is flourishing.

JAMES: But — but —

BOB: Now, James, you mustn't blame me. It's been my wretched health. Two months after your conviction I got a dreadful chill, I've never been the better of it since. I've been to every doctor in the country — that's why I never went to see you in prison — the doctor said it would be too much for me, not that there's any doctor here who can do anything for me, the only thing that does me any good is the advice I get from the "Sunday Globe's" medical column, and they always say that my symptoms are very serious and that I should see a specialist. That will make you understand my wretched health. Only for that I'd be in the forefront of the battle today.

JAMES: Has nothing been done?

BOB: We done what we could, James, we done what we could. Of course your conviction was a great blow to us, and it crippled us for years, but we recovered it and went on as if nothing had happened. We've always stood for the best nationalism in the country, we supported compulsory Irish (though I don't suppose you believe in that) and — and the United Irish League and — and all the best interests of Ireland.

HARRY: And then there was the shop; I felt it, and your wife and child were left to me as a sacred charge, and my first duty was to them. I consulted Father Brady about them, and he advised me to take no active part in politics for some years, but I've never stopped being a member of the League — never — and I've given them a lecture or a reading from the old papers every session for the last fifteen or sixteen years — you can look up the records.

JAMES: (*realising at last*) I see. I've got to begin from the beginning, all over again.

BOB: Well, you mayn't believe it, but I've proved that I've only half a lung and my heart is — well — wretched.

JAMES: What a fool I was to let myself be taken, but I didn't know I was so necessary, I thought others would take my place. I thought I was only one of a hundred — a thousand —

HARRY: No, there was no one like you, James.

JAMES: It can't be helped now. We won't waste time looking back, we'll look forward. D'ye know, personally, I feel glad. Of course from the national point of view it's terrible to think that all those years have been wasted, but one of the thoughts that tortured me in prison was that when I came out I wouldn't be wanted; that in the new organisation no place would be found for me. I see now I am wanted as badly — worse perhaps than I was wanted twenty years ago.

BOB: (*sneezes*) I knew I had caught cold. That's from waiting at the station.

HARRY: But, James, you'll find your views considered a little out of date.

JAMES: Out of date? They were supposed to be out of date then. Mitchel was out of date, Emmet was out of date, but I tell you that until Ireland gets out of date from north to south she'll never win anything.

BOB: I'm going to take some quinine. (*He goes out.*)

JAMES: We've got to start again. It's not too late. There was a Nugent out in '98, my two uncles followed Smith O'Brien, I had a cousin mixed up in the Invincibles, and now, Bob, I have got to... why, where's Bob?

HARRY: I think he went out. I'll go and look for him. (*He goes out.*)

JAMES: Your brothers have changed, Ann. They were not like that long ago. Well, well, it's you and me again, Ann, you and me against the world again.

ANN: No, not me, this time.

JAMES: Ann?

ANN: I have duties. There's the shop.

JAMES: Yes, the shop, I forgot the shop.... Do you know the shop may be one of our most useful assets. It makes a splendid headquarters for an organisation. You remember the part Flanigan's public house played long ago?

ANN: Yes. And the police heard all our plans next morning.

JAMES: That's where a shop like yours will have the advantage. There'll be no temptation to drink ourselves communicative. There will only be ourselves serving in the shop.

ANN: (*proudly*) I have three assistants.

JAMES: Oh... well they must be members of the League, of course.

ANN: Are you in earnest, James?

JAMES: About what?

ANN: Do you seriously want to begin the old thing again?

JAMES: Why, of course.

ANN: Then we must understand each other... You asked me a little while ago why I never gave you any information about the League or the political situation when I went to see you in prison. You said that I didn't understand you were trying to establish a code. I'm not stupid... I saw what you wanted, but I wouldn't help you... I was sick of it all.

JAMES: What do you mean?

ANN: When you were arrested, James, when you were dragged from my room on that awful night, I fainted. I went from one fainting fit to another. It was four months before I was able to stir from my bed.

JAMES: I didn't know you had been as ill as that, Ann.

ANN: And when I got up and saw myself in the glass my hair was grey — as grey as it is now. I was an old woman, James. I was just twenty-six years old. (*She can no longer keep the passion out of her voice.*)

JAMES: Ann!

ANN: But it wasn't my face and hair only that were changed... while I lay there helpless for four months I wasn't able to do anything but think, and lying there I saw everything clearly at last. I saw my life here with mother before you met me — calm, sheltered, playing at patriotism as we all played in those days. Then you came and I was fascinated by you. You were so passionate and impetuous, so in earnest, so desperate, so different to anyone I had ever met, so.... You wooed me passionately, you married me passionately, and for five years you dragged —

JAMES: Dragged!

ANN: Me after you round the country kindling my patriotism at the flame of yours, speaking through me with your passionate voice. I was never myself all those years, I was only you. You took my health, my strength, my beauty, my money, and you spent them prodigally, and at twenty-six I found myself old and ugly and grey and worn out.

JAMES: I loved you very much, Ann.

ANN: (*stormily*) Perhaps you did. But you never thought of me. You never had the least consideration for me.

JAMES: How can you say such a thing?

ANN: I know it because you did me a wrong—a terrible, unforgivable wrong.

JAMES: What was it?

ANN: I won't tell you, I'll spare you that.... I saw all this, James, as I lay in bed. Sickness makes some people feel that nothing really matters, but I was made to feel that all these things mattered tremendously. And then by a miracle I was freed from you. For a certain number of years I would be my own mistress again. Perhaps for the rest of my life. If you had been dead I would have gone abroad, far away from Ireland and its stupid politics, but while you lived I couldn't do that. You still claimed me, I had a duty to do, I had to visit you. Well, I came here and took the shop over from my brothers. I found it a miserable little place, badly managed, on the verge of bankruptcy. It's now the best grocery shop in the town. I've built up a splendid business; I draw my custom from the Prescotts and the Canon down to the poorest working man. Eighteen years ago I was a discredited woman; people spoke of me as if I was hardly respectable, a person decent people would shun. I'm the most respected woman in the town today, and now, just when I've reached this position you come and *you* think I'm going back into that old life, that I'll risk my position, ruin my business perhaps for — for something I care nothing about.

JAMES: You used to be patriotic, Ann.

ANN: No. I'd have gone to the stake for Ireland if you'd told me to, and I'd have betrayed Ireland if you'd told me to — you were my patriotism. I suppose I can't stop you going back to that nonsense if you want to, but you go alone without me or my money or my influence.

JAMES: You're shrinking from it, of course. I can understand that. Ann, I don't understand all you've been saying, I don't think it's true, but perhaps there's some truth in it. Forgive me if I treated you badly, I didn't mean to, and don't let a wrong I did you twenty years ago stand in your way now; don't let it stand in Ireland's way. Think of it, Ann. Think of all those long weary years, the injustices that have been heaped upon us, the way we've been plundered of money, starved with famine, drained of our best blood, the crucified of the nations. And think of it with the English driven out, a free country, a happy people, liberty at last. Think of it, Ann, Ann! (*It is the old enthusiasm, the old eloquence that swayed a countryside twenty years ago.*)

ANN: It's no use. You can't kindle me again. (*Bitterly.*) I suppose I'm too old.

JAMES: Oh, well, never mind. I can do without you if it comes to that.

ANN: You'll find it's no use, James. People will simply laugh at your kind of talk nowadays. They'll think you're mad. And I begin to think you are.

JAMES: I'm not mad. But this means everything to me. I've shot a man for the sake of it; I've given the best years of my life for it; won't you help me, Ann, if not for the sake of Ireland, for the sake of the love we had — we have for each other. (*He catches her arm.*)

ANN: Don't, James. Let me go. That love died eighteen years ago. I think... I think I hate you now.

JAMES: Ann!

(O'MAHONY, BOB, HARRY, SULLIVAN, FATHER KEARNEY *and* WILLIE *come in, and* ANN *goes out.*)

BOB: This, James, is the little deputation come from the League to welcome you.

FATHER KEARNEY: (*stout, middle-aged, and good tempered*) Not formally, James. We just came round to shake hands and bid you welcome home.

JAMES: I'm glad to see you again, John, glad to see you again. Peter, is that you?

O'MAHONY: Welcome back, James; you're looking well.

SULLIVAN: (*a little drunk*) You haven't forgotten me, have you?

JAMES: You are...

SULLIVAN: Dan Sullivan.

JAMES: Of course. But you've changed.

SULLIVAN: Well, I'm older to be sure, and this is my son Willie, one of the old stock.

BOB: And a most enthusiastic member of the League.

JAMES: How are you?

WILLIE: I'm proud to meet you, sir.

FATHER KEARNEY: Well, now, we want to mark your return by some sort of a little festival, James, and we're wondering what you'd like. Some thought of a public meeting, but I think we've all decided now on a nice quiet dinner at Fitzy's some day next week — just old friends there. How would that suit you?

SULLIVAN: Yes, yes, a nice little dinner at Fitzy's.

JAMES: I... I don't know, thank you very much.... Things are not exactly what I thought they were, and I've got to get to work at once.

O'MAHONY: Now, James, Bob has been telling me something of your notions and the things you've been saying since you came home, and you've got to understand from the beginning

49

that that sort of thing won't do. You're a bit behind the times — naturally — but you can take it from me that that sort of talk is no use nowadays; it never was much use, but it's absolutely ridiculous now.

JAMES: I understand that there is no physical force party in Ireland at present. That is not to be wondered at when there are men like you at the head of the League.

O'MAHONY: (coolly) Oh, I left the League fifteen years ago.

JAMES: Left it?

O'MAHONY: I hadn't time for that sort of nonsense.

JAMES: I'm going to start a new movement.

FATHER KEARNEY: (with a fat smile) Oh, come, come, James, absurd.

JAMES: (desperately) I'm going to save Ireland.

FATHER KEARNEY: Don't you bother about Ireland. She's getting along all right.

JAMES: She can't be right until she's free.

FATHER KEARNEY: What can you do anyway?

JAMES: I can do what I did twenty years ago — rouse the people, go through the country, build a new League on the ruins of the old.

BOB: (miserably) You'll only ruin the League, James, if you do that. That sort of advanced thing won't go down with a lot of the new members, I know it won't. Couldn't you keep quiet anyway until after Christmas, when the subscriptions are paid?

HARRY: I don't know what the Canon will say, and he's on his way home.

FATHER KEARNEY: Give it up, James. It was very good fun twenty years ago when we were all young and felt that life was a desperately serious thing, and that Ireland would sink under the sea if we didn't cut her free from England. But we're older now, and more sensible, and we feel that things are gradually working right.

SULLIVAN: Yes, you were pretty hot-headed, John. Do you remember the time you went about addressing meetings of the farmers and the Bishop's messenger following you all the time with a letter forbidding you to speak — and the way you dodged him?

FATHER KEARNEY: (hastily) Yes, yes, yes. But I stopped the minute I got the letter.

SULLIVAN: (To O'MAHONY) And the rifles you used to get, and they supposed to be crockery. Well, well, I love thinking of them old times. Come over to Fitzy's, James, and we'll have a drink.

JAMES: No, no. Oh, the waste of time, of opportunity. There was such a chance after Parnell's death for a physical force movement — it was the only thing that would have quickly put heart into the people. Then nine years of hard, quiet, effective work, and in 1900 the South African War, Ireland empty of troops, the best chance for a successful rising for a hundred and fifty years.

FATHER KEARNEY: I'm sorry, James....

JAMES: Oh, I don't blame you. I suppose there was no other leader, but if I had been out, Davitt, O'Brien and myself, we'd have done something; why did I let myself be taken....

BOB: Yes, 'twas a pity.

JAMES: But I had to kill Foley; he had all the names, all the secret papers — I found he was making terms to betray us. I couldn't risk another Carey... and I wouldn't order another man to do what I might be thought afraid to do myself.

FATHER KEARNEY: Well, you're going to spend the rest of your life quietly here, James. Mrs Nugent will make you very comfortable, and tonight you're coming up to have dinner with me, and over the fire and a glass of whiskey we'll talk of old times.

O'MAHONY: All your troubles are over now, James.

SULLIVAN: We'll have a nice happy evening, and James will tell us that story of his fight with Baker and the two policemen; won't you, James?

JAMES: Good God, you seem to think my life is an anecodote — a thing to be told stories about. John, I've been dead for eighteen years. I've come back from the grave, I'm free again, the doctor says I've only a few years to live. I've got to work desperately. I've dreamed of these years all the time I've been in prison. I was a passionate man when I went in, but I curbed my passion in there. I saw it was only by being very quiet and patient that I could ever hope to get out... and I was quiet and patient for eighteen years, and now that I am out and free you ask me to sit over the fire and exchange stories with you... John, you've forgotten me. (FATHER KEARNEY *shrugs his shoulders and turns away.*) I see you won't help me. Are you all against me?

WILLIE: I'm with you, sir.

JAMES: Good man. O'Mahony?

O'MAHONY: No.

JAMES: Dan?

SULLIVAN: Well, I'm... I'm not exactly against you, James....

JAMES: Will you help me?

SULLIVAN: What d'ye mean by helping you?

JAMES: Just what I meant long ago. The soft way isn't the way to save Ireland, it's got to be the hard way; it's got to be the fighting way — with rifle and sword.

SULLIVAN: (*hastily*) Oh, no, no, James. I couldn't do that.

JAMES: Ph, I thought not. Bob, you're the Secretary of the League still, aren't you? (BOB *nods.*) The meetings are on Tuesdays? Very well. Call a special important one for next Tuesday. I am going to speak.

BOB: But Tanner was going to speak next week.

JAMES: I don't care a damn about Tanner. Do what I tell you.

BOB: Well, it's upsetting all the list... oh, very well.

(ROSE *comes in.*)

ROSE: Come in to tea, father.

JAMES: Yes, Rose. Come, Willie, come in to tea with us. Good afternoon, gentlemen. I thought that at least in Coolmore — in my native town — I would be safe from traitors and cowards. I see I was mistaken.

(JAMES, ROSE *and* WILLIE *go out.*)

HARRY: Well, well.

SULLIVAN: (*snivelling*) He needn't have called us cowards. I'm as brave as any man, but when a fellow comes to my time of life he's not fit for... for... swords and rifles and... and... oh, I'm going over to Fitzy's.

BOB: And we all thought he'd be changed. Why he's just the same — only *worse.*

O'MAHONY: (*slowly*) He's mad of course. But he makes us all feel a bit ashamed, doesn't he? Ashamed of the things we didn't do.

FATHER KEARNEY: Poor James, poor James. God help him.

CURTAIN

ACT III

Scene. —A week later. The room where the League meetings are held. A platform and rows of empty benches. Evening. WILLIE SULLIVAN *and* JIM POWELL *(the caretaker of the hall) are alone in the room.*

WILLIE: I don't believe there's going to be a soul.

JIM: Ah, sure, there might yet, Master Willie. It's not much after half-past seven.

WILLIE: It's a quarter to eight — after it. Isn't it dreadful, Jim?

JIM: Well, it's a very wet night, you know, and then there's the Mission at the Chapel and them Moving Pictures at the Town Hall.

WILLIE: This will break his heart.

JIM: I'm going to see them tomorrow night; they say they're a wonder entirely. Dan Clancy was saying there's one there of a fight between a nigger and an Irishman — oh, the nicest thing you ever saw. I'd have gone tonight, but of course with this League meeting I couldn't. What'll Mr Nugent be doing? Will he be stopping at Coolmore, d'ye know?

WILLIE: I don't know. This meeting was to decide everything.

JIM: Well now, he'll be a foolish man if he leaves Coolmore, I tell you. The wife has a very tidy business up at the Square. Indeed I remember the Nugents before James came along, a queer cracked set they were, always having trouble about land, or poaching, or politics, or divilment of some sort; oh, believe me, they'll always be on for making trouble, them Nugents.

WILLIE: How do you feel about it, Jim?

JIM: Well, of course I don't want to say anything against Mr Bob, or any of his relations. He's been hiring this hall for meetings for the last twenty years, so I must have a respect for him, but I don't think it matters one way or the other. You see, Master Willie, this is the hall where nearly all the meetings of the town are held. When the Parochial Hall was burned even the Archdeacon had his prayer meetings here — yes, indeed! And a beautiful soft speaker he is — and so, you see, I hear every side speaking, and you can't expect me to be very much for anything — and the longer I live the harder I find it to make out what difference Home Rule is going to make. If James Nugent wants to go about having meetings and rousing the people, as he calls it, I don't see why he shouldn't — 'tis a free country — only, mind me, Mr Willie, to have been in prison isn't as respectable as it used to be — no indeed — and that's why there's a lot of people kept away tonight.... Here's this letter came a while ago for Mr Nugent. What'll I do with it?

WILLIE: Leave it here on the table, I'll give it to him .... Ah, here's someone at last. (*Goes down the hall.*) Why, Rose!

ROSE: There you are, Willie. Oh, isn't it wet... I thought the meeting was to be here. Where is it going to be?

WILLIE: It is here.

ROSE: But — but — there's nobody here... it's at eight, isn't it?

WILLIE: Yes.

ROSE: Don't you think anyone's coming? Oh, Willie!

JIM: You see, miss, there's them Moving Pictures and the Mission.

WILLIE: It doesn't look as if we'd have many, Rose.

ROSE: There'll be nobody at all. I know it. And it will kill father.

WILLIE: Oh, no, Rose.

ROSE: Yes, it'll kill him, it'll kill him. It will be just the last straw.

WILLIE: Perhaps I could go out and bring some people in. When was he to leave your house, do you know?

ROSE: He left it long ago. He went over to O'Mahony's, they are coming down together. I came on by myself because mother was so slow about getting ready.

WILLIE: Well, O'Mahony will be here and Father Kearney, I know, and your two uncles, and your mother. If I could only get ten or twelve more it wouldn't be so bad.

ROSE: No, it's no use, Willie. He expects a packed hall, great enthusiasm and crowds — oh, it's all too dreadful — (*She begins to cry.*)

WILLIE: Don't cry, Rose, it's not your fault. Ah, here are some people coming now. (*Two young men come in.*)

1ST MAN: (*to* 2ND MAN) I don't think this is the place.

2ND MAN: Searles said it was round the corner.

1ST MAN: (*to* WILLIE) I beg your pardon, but is this where the Moving Pictures are?

WILLIE: No.

1ST MAN: I thought not. Where are they, d'ye know?

WILLIE: Round the corner on the right.

1ST MAN: Thank you. (*Going.*)

JIM: They're at the Town Hall, and I hear they're grand.

1ST MAN: So I hear.

WILLIE: Wait a minute. Do you know a most interesting meeting will be held here tonight, when a speech will be made by James

Nugent, the famous revolutionary.

2ND MAN: The what?

WILLIE: The rebel. The man who was shut up for eighteen years by the English Government for attempting to free the country.

1ST MAN: What did you say his name was?

WILLIE: Nugent. James Nugent.

1ST MAN: Never heard of him.

JIM: Sure, don't you know Mrs Nugent's shop down the Square — opposite Fitzy's?

1ST MAN: Is it the grocery shop?

JIM: Yes, that's the one. Sure she's his wife.

WILLIE: It's going to be a splendid speech. You shouldn't miss it.

2ND MAN: (*in a low voice*) Come on away.

1ST MAN: Ah, well —

WILLIE: It's the only chance you'll have.

1ST MAN: Thank you, but we want to see the pictures tonight.

WILLIE: They'll be here till the end of the week — this man is a patriot — as great as Emmet or — or Stephens or Tone —

1ST MAN: Yes, yes. We'll be going, I think.

(*They go out.*)

WILLIE: It's pretty hopeless, isn't it?

ROSE: Yes . . . it'll break his heart.

WILLIE: I suppose it's no use trying to make a start down here, though yesterday — this morning even — several members told me they were coming tonight. I don't know what can have happened to them. Never mind, Rose; it only means that he'll have to go away up to Dublin and start there.

ROSE: You'll go with him.

WILLIE: Of course.

ROSE: I'm going too.

WILLIE: You, Rose?

ROSE: Yes, he's been deserted by everyone. I'm going to stand by him.

WILLIE: Will you ever be strong enough?

ROSE: Oh, I'm much better — oh, Willie, it's what we've always dreamt about to be doing something — something definite for Ireland.

WILLIE: Yes. And I sometimes was afraid it could never happen. I'm glad I'll have to give up Hughes. I want to feel I'm cutting myself right away from that money-making common, commercial life. Hughes gave me a rise this morning, Rose. He's sending me over to Bradyfield — he says I'll be manager there some day if I keep steady. Oh, in a few more years I'd have been so entangled in this business I'd never have broken free.

ROSE: You're giving up wealth and position.

WILLIE: And you're giving up a home.

ROSE: Yes.

JIM: (*appearing on the platform*) Here's Mr Nugent now, he's after coming in the side door.

ROSE: Oh, what can we do, what can we do? Willie, we mustn't let him come into the room — can't we tell him the meeting's put off — anything. (O'MAHONY *appears.*) Keep him back, Peter, don't let him come in.

JAMES: (*appearing*) Why, Rose, what is the matter?

ROSE: (*hysterically*) It's all right, father, it's all right — it's only the wrong night, they're all coming — all coming — tomorrow — we must go home now — we must — we must —

O'MAHONY: Hush, Rose, hush.... You see, James, there's no one here.

JAMES: No one here.

ROSE: It's not the night — tomorrow —

O'MAHONY: Hush, Rose.... They don't want to hear you speak, James. Do you understand, they don't want to hear you speak.

JAMES: They do, they do. They've been kept away against their will.

O'MAHONY: No, no, James, there's been no force used, but you've been going about all the week talking of arming and drilling until people are tired of it. They are tired even of laughing at you.

JAMES: You'll never get me to believe that the spirit that animated the men of '48 and '67 is dead.

O'MAHONY: Not dead, James, but grown wise. Ireland is going to be very prosperous, very well-to-do one of these days, but she's never going to fight again. She's got courage still, but it's a different sort of courage. She's got to fight her own self now. I drilled secretly twenty years ago for Ireland, now I make bread for Ireland — that's progress. Come, and join me in the bakery. (JAMES *moves away with an impatient gesture.*) I'm not laughing at you, I know what you're suffering. I didn't give up myself without a struggle.

JAMES: Do you think I'm going to go back now? Do you think because a few fools in a country town laugh at me and pay no attention to me, I'm going to give up what I've spent my life for?

O'MAHONY: What can you do?

JAMES: I'll go to Dublin. There I'll find some of the old friends, they'll help me.

WILLIE: I knew it.

O'MAHONY: Yes. You'll find Brennan — who spends all his time in public houses — gassing about his patriotism with every glass he takes; you'll find Regan sponging on his relations and never doing a stroke of work — those are all the old friends you'll find there. I tell you, you'll not find a man in Ireland to follow you.

WILLIE: There's where you're wrong, Mr O'Mahony. Mr Nugent, I'm with you heart and soul, and I'll follow you wherever you go.

O'MAHONY: I thought you had more sense, Willie.

WILLIE: Don't mind about this meeting, sir, it means nothing. Let's go away at once.

ROSE: And — father — I'm coming with you.

JAMES: You, Rose?

ROSE: Yes. I can be some use, can't I? I'm not very strong — but you said yourself the other day that women must play a large part in building up a nation. Can't I help?

JAMES: Of course you can, dear.

O'MAHONY: James, it's madness, taking away Rose with you. Why, she'll never stand it. She'll break down in a week.

JAMES: That's enough, O'Mahony.

O'MAHONY: (*under his breath*) Wait till Ann hears this.

WILLIE: Oh, this letter came for you.

JAMES: (*looking at signature*) Ah, from John Kearney.... Called away to ˙Tipperary on important business... sorry can't be here.... The coward, the coward!

O'MAHONY: James, you make us all feel cowards. When we see you we remember all the hopes and plans we had when we were young — long ago.

JAMES: I'll revive them for you. It's not too late, Peter.

O'MAHONY: It is too late. It was too late when we were young. You and I were born too late.

JAMES: Were we, I wonder?

O'MAHONY: Yes, forty years too late. What a chance you'd have had sixty years ago. You'll never get that sort of chance now.

JAMES: (*suddenly beginning to lose heart*) Won't I... Peter, are you right? Is it too late — am I the last patriot?
(MRS SULLIVAN *comes in quickly.*)

MRS SULLIVAN: Is Willie here. Where's Willie? Ah, there you are, Willie.

WILLIE: What's happened, mother?

MRS SULLIVAN: Your father —

WILLIE: Again?

MRS SULLIVAN: No, no, it's not that, it's worse; he's had a sort of a fit, but he's better now. The doctor's with him, and I ran across for you.

O'MAHONY: Oh, Mrs Sullivan, how did it happen?

WILLIE: Mother!

MRS SULLIVAN: It was when he read the letter. It made him so angry, and then —

O'MAHONY: What letter?

MRS SULLIVAN: The one from Ann giving us notice.

O'MAHONY: Oh!

WILLIE: Notice?

MRS SULLIVAN: We owe three years' rent. We'll be sold up.

WILLIE: Sold up?

JAMES: What?

WILLIE: I don't understand.

O'MAHONY: Mrs Nugent talked of doing this the other day, but I hoped she wouldn't at present.

MRS SULLIVAN: (*crying*) I never thought she'd do it on me — I never thought she'd do it on me. Of course I know we owe her money, but for the sake of old times I thought ... I thought ....

WILLIE: Mother, mother, don't.

MRS SULLIVAN: Oh, Willie, we'll be sold up. You're all I've got to hold on to now. Oh, thank God, you've got your good place with Hughes. He told me this afternoon about your rise, and that you were going to Bradyfield. It's like the hand of God. We'll all go away there and live together — I'll get lodgers and maybe we'll manage all right — come home, Willie.

WILLIE: You mean — there's nothing to live on but what I earn?

MRS SULLIVAN: Yes, but it will be enough, Willie, we'll make it do, when we've sold everything there may be something left — but never mind about that, come home now to your father. Oh, my poor Dan. (*Goes.*)

WILLIE: I see .... How — how beastly. I'm coming, mother. Mr. Nugent, I can't come with you at present; I've got to stay, you see, and look after them. I'm — I'm — Rose, I'll never get free now. (*Goes.*)

ROSE: Oh, poor Willie.

JAMES: It's shameful of Ann, shameful. How can she be such a grabber?

O'MAHONY: She's in her right.

JAMES: Oh, her right. Daniel Sullivan was one of my most trusted comrades. She mustn't do it, I won't let her.

O'MAHONY: You can't stop her.

JAMES: I can. I will. Oh, you've all so changed since I was in prison. I don't know any of you, you're all against me. (ANN *comes in.*) Ann, how could you do such a thing to poor Dan Sullivan?

ANN: What? Do what?

JAMES: Give him notice, sell him up. He's had a stroke — he's dying perhaps.

ANN: I'm sorry to hear that.

JAMES: You must write at once and tell them they can stay. Dan Sullivan mustn't be treated like that.

ANN: I'm sorry, but they've got to go.

JAMES: Why?

ANN: I've lost a lot of money on that house —

JAMES: Money. You think of nothing but money. I thought Mrs Sullivan was your friend, Ann?

ANN: If she wasn't she'd have been out of that house three years ago.

JAMES: You're rich, Ann. You've any amount of money put away in the Bank, more than you can spend, you usen't to be a miser.

ANN: I'm not a miser.

JAMES: What are you hoarding it up for?

ANN: Not for myself.

JAMES: Who for then?

ANN: Rose.

JAMES: Rose?

ANN: If I died tomorrow could she go out and earn her bread like another?

JAMES: Oh... I see what you mean. But you can be generous now. I'm taking her off your hands, she's going away with me.

ANN: Away. Where?

JAMES: To Dublin. I'm going to open my campaign in Dublin. Rose is coming to help me.

ANN: James, you don't know what you're talking about.

JAMES: Rose has said she'll come with me.

ANN: Nonsense, she can't. Think of her health, James.

JAMES: She is ready to come.

ANN: Oh, Peter, can't you explain to him — he doesn't seem to understand.

O'MAHONY: I don't think you know, James, how very delicate Rose is.

ANN: It would kill her, that sort of life would kill her — I know what it is — she needs every care and attention — she can't do anything for herself — she can't put on her clothes, she can't take them off.

ROSE: Father would help me.

ANN: No, no, no, I'm not going to let you be taken from me — it's madness.

JAMES: You've come between us before, you've kept her away from me for eighteen years — you're not to do it again, Ann, I won't let you.

ROSE: I want to go, mother.

ANN: You can't have Rose. I won't let her go. You have no consideration for her or you'd never suggest such a thing.

JAMES: I am thinking of my country. If patriotism demands —

ANN: Oh, don't talk to me of patriotism — I'm sick of it. It's made Sullivan a bankrupt; it's made Brennan a drunkard; you a murderer; it's destroyed my happiness; it's made Rose a cripple.

JAMES: Ann!

ANN: It's true, it's true. She's a cripple today because of your mad patriotic selfishness.

JAMES: Ann, how can you say such a terrible thing?

O'MAHONY: Mrs Nugent, please —

ANN: No, I won't be quiet — I wasn't going to tell him, I was going to spare him that — but now when he comes to snatch Rose away, I'll hide it no longer. Do you remember that summer of '93, you knew I was going to have a child, you knew how nervous I was about it — wouldn't any other man have been a little more considerate to his wife at such a time — but you — you told me that Foley might betray us, that he must be killed — when he was found shot I knew you had killed him — when you fled from the police I knew where you hid — when you came to our house was it to see me, to find out how I was? No, you came to burn some papers I had, and when the police surrounded the house did you go out and say, "My wife is ill, I give myself up to prevent you disturbing her." No, you fought to the end, and from my bedroom window — my bedroom window — as I lay in bed you fired your last shot. You were dragged from my room. And when in the morning I looked at the crippled, prematurely born child at my side I knew you were the cause of it.

JAMES: Ann!

ANN: She's lived in spite of you. I've had years and years of unceasing watching and care — I've fought and fought for her life, and I'm not going to let you come in now and rob me of her. You've crippled her but you shan't kill her, you shan't.

JAMES: Ann, Ann — how horrible —

ROSE: (*going to him*) Don't, father, don't.

JAMES: (*covering his face with his hands*) Go away, go away. I can never look at you again.

O'MAHONY: James. (*He stops, there is silence.* BOB *and* HARRY *come in.*)

BOB: Well, well, nobody here? I didn't think there would be. You know, James, I found there was hardly anyone coming to the meeting, and then this morning I heard the Canon had just come home — he's been in Palestine.

HARRY: No, Egypt.

BOB: Ah, well, it's all the same, and before he went he promised us a lecture when he came back, so I sent a message to know will he speak, and he will tomorrow night.

HARRY: And there'll be limelight views with it.

BOB: So I put off any few who were coming tonight, and they've all promised to come and hear the Canon tomorrow — it'll be welcoming him home again. We're to have a sort of conversazione, there'll be tea at seven — oh, Ann, you'll want to send down some cakes and things from the shop — and then a little address and a few Irish songs and a little step-dancing, and then the lecture on Egypt.

HARRY: And I've just been sent that "Freeman" I wanted! that's splendid, isn't it? Where's Jimmy? (*Goes up to platform.*)

BOB: I suppose you're a bit disappointed at things turning out like this, but what else could you expect — and indeed I've more good news for you. Who should I meet and I going about telling people of the meeting tomorrow but Major Moriarty, and he was asking me all about you, and he wants you to go out and be clerk in his co-operative store at Lusk.

JAMES: Me?

BOB: Of course I said you'd be delighted to go, isn't it a splendid thing! that's forty or fifty pounds a year — I think that's most satisfactory, most satisfactory. Jim, Jim, where are you?

JIM: (*appearing on platform*) Here, sir.

BOB: You can shut up, Jim; there won't be any meeting tonight; but there'll be one tomorrow and I'll be down here at six; there's going to be a tea to Canon Murphy, and a meeting after it — at six, mind, I'll be down.

JIM: Very good, sir.

BOB: And listen here. (*He talks apart.*)

O'MAHONY: Say something to him, Ann; look at him.

ANN: James, come home.

JAMES: Oh, Ann!

ANN: We're both old, James, we'd like to undo the past, but we can't. Come home.

ROSE: (*softly*) I'll always believe in you.

JAMES: My poor, poor child.

O'MAHONY: Go home with them, James.

JAMES: (*getting up — and he moves and looks like an old man — he catches* O'MAHONY'*s arm*) I've killed a man, I've crippled a child, I've got myself shut up for eighteen years — God knows what good came of it all — but — Peter — I meant — I tried.... I know I meant right — and in prison my cell used to be filled with the sad faces of men like me who had given everything for Ireland — they wouldn't have come to me, would they? if I hadn't been of their company. They are here now — I see them all around me — there is Wolfe Tone, and there is ... oh, quiet watching faces, I have tried — tried as you tried — and been broken....

(JAMES, ANN, ROSE, *and* O'MAHONY *go out.*)

BOB: That's all right, Jim; don't forget now, six o'clock — you can put out the lights — and of course we'll want a kettle boiled and the cups and saucers. Good night. Come on, Harry.

HARRY: I'm coming. Good night, Jim.

BOB: (*going out*) Most satisfactory, most satisfactory.

JIM: Good night to you. (*Looks at watch*) Only twenty past eight. I can go and see the pictures after all. (*He switches off the lights by degrees.*)

When the stage is quite dark the CURTAIN *falls.*

THE WHITEHEADED BOY

A play in three acts

To
"Aunt Ellen"

CHARACTERS

MRS GEOGHEGAN
GEORGE ⎤
PETER   ⎥
KATE   ⎥
JANE   ⎬ her children
BABY   ⎥
DENIS   ⎦
DONOUGH BROSNAN, engaged to JANE
JOHN DUFFY, Postmaster and Chairman R.D.C.
DELIA, his daughter, engaged to DENIS
HANNAH, a servant.
AUNT ELLEN

"The Whiteheaded Boy" was first produced at the Abbey Theatre, Dublin, on December 13th, 1916, with the following cast:

Mrs Geoghegan	EILEEN O'DOHERTY
George	BREFFNI O'ROURKE
Peter	ARTHUR SHIELDS
Kate	DOROTHY LYND
Baby	MAUREEN DELANY
Jane	MAY CRAIG
Denis	FRED O'DONOVAN
Donough Brosnan	PETER NOLAN
John Duffy	CHAS. C. O'REILLY
Delia	IRENE KELLY
Aunt Ellen	MAIRE O'NEILL
Hannah	SHEILA O'SULLIVAN

The Play was produced by J. Augustus Keogh.

ACT I

MRS GEOGHEGAN's *house is at the head of the street, facing the priest's house; the shop is at the other end of the village, between* MICHAEL BROSNAN's *public house and* DUFFY's *yard.* WILLIAM GEOGHEGAN (*God rest his soul*) *was a very genteel man, and when the wife brought him the house and the bit of land instead of getting a tenant for it like a sensible man (and the whole village knew* CLANCY, *the vet, was mad to take it), nothing would do him but live in it himself and walk down to his business every day like a millionaire. 'Tis too high notions poor* WILLIAM *always had — and his sister,* ELLEN, *worse again than himself, craning after anything new she'd be like a cow through a fence — but, indeed,* WILLIAM's *notions didn't stand too well with him, and when he died he left his family — six of them, no less — in a poor enough way. But the eldest boy —* GEORGE *— was always terrible industrious, and he made two of himself after the father died, and they managed to pull along. You can see from the appearance of the room we're looking at they're not wanting for comfort.* MRS GEOGHEGAN *— poor* WILLIAM's *widow (that's her behind the table setting out the cups) — is a hearty woman yet, and, after all, I suppose she's not more than sixty-five years of age. A great manager she is, and, indeed, she'd need to be with three unmarried daughters under her feet all day and two big men of sons. You'd not like to deny* MRS GEOGHEGAN *anything she's such a pleasant way with her, yet you know she's not what I'd call a clever woman, I mean to say she hasn't got the book knowledge, the "notions" her husband had or her sister* ELLEN. *But maybe she's better without them, sure what good is book knowledge to the mother of a family? She's a simple decent woman, and what more do you want? That plain girl behind, pulling out the drawer, is the eldest daughter* KATE. *She was disappointed a few years back on the head of a match was made up for her and broken afterwards with a farmer from the east of the county. Some dispute it was about the fortune, and he married a publican's daughter in the latter end. 'Tisn't likely* KATE *will ever marry, she's up to thirty-six by this time, with a grey streak in her hair and two pushing sisters behind her, but she's a quiet poor thing, no harm in her at* *all, very useful in the house, I'm told. I'm sure the mother'd be hard set to manage without her.*

You're admiring the furniture? 'Twas got five years ago at the Major's auction. A big price they had to pay for it too, GEORGE *didn't want to buy it but the mother's heart was set on it. They got new horse-hair put on the arm chair, the Major had it wore to the wood sitting all day over the fire, cursing the Government and drinking whiskey; the six plain chairs are as good as new.*

Aren't the pictures lovely? They're all enlarged photographs of WILLIAM's *family. That's* WILLIAM *himself over the chimney-piece, and that's his brother that died in Boston, hanging between the window and the door. The priest in the plush frame is* FATHER MAGUIRE, *no relation but a lovely man. There's one fancy picture, there on your right, "The Siesta" it's called — two young women asleep in some sort of a fancy dress.*

WILLIAM *bought the piano when he got married, I'm told it was old* DOCTOR PURCELL's. *Anyway it's a real old piano, the youngest girl,* BABY, *is a great one for music. The table's mahogany, the same as the chairs, only you can't see it by reason of the cloth. They're after setting the tea; they got that lamp new this afternoon, isn't it giving great light? Begob, there's a chicken and a shape and apples and a cake — it must be the way they're expecting company.*

Oh, the old one? That's HANNAH. *There's not a house in the village she hasn't been servant in. She was at a hotel in Cork once. Two days they kept her.*

HANNAH: Will I bring in the ham, ma'am?

MRS GEOG: Do. Reach me down the silver teapot, Kate.
(*'Tisn't real silver, of course, only one of them white metal ones, but catch* MRS GEOGHEGAN *calling it anything but the purest silver. She's smelling it.*) There's a sort of musty smell from it.

KATE: Sure we haven't used it since Denis was here in the summer.

MRS GEOG: I'll make Hannah scald it . . . . God help us, is that the kitchen clock striking six?

KATE: Ah, that clock is always apt to be a bit fast. Anyway the train isn't due till the quarter, and it being market-day, 'twill be a queer thing if it's not ten minutes late, or more.
(HANNAH's *in again with the ham.*)

MRS GEOG: Put it there. Now run across to Mrs O'Connell's, like a good girl, and ask her to oblige me with a couple of fresh eggs. Tell her it's for Denis they are, and she'll not refuse you.

HANNAH: There was a duck egg left over from the dinner.

MRS GEOG: A duck egg! Isn't it well you know Denis has no stomach at all for coarse food? Be off across the street this minute.

HANNAH: I will, ma'am.

MRS GEOG: Here, carry the teapot before you, and give it a good scalding; 'tis half musty.

HANNAH: I will, ma'am. (*And off with her.*)

MRS GEOG: Where's Baby?

KATE: She's above in the room writing.

MRS GEOG: Musha! writing and writing. Isn't it a wonder she wouldn't come down and be readying the place before her brother?

KATE: Ah, what harm? 'Twon't take us two minutes to finish this.

(*This tall girl coming in is* JANE. *She has a year or two less than* KATE. *A nice quiet girl. She and* DONOUGH BROSNAN *have been promised to each other these years past. Is it chrysanthemums she has in her hand?*)

JANE: These are all Peg Turpin had. She stripped two plants to get them.

MRS GEOG: They're not much indeed, but Denis always had a liking for flowers. Put them there in the middle of the table.

JANE: That's what Peg was saying. She remembered the way when he was a little child he'd come begging to her for a flower for his coat, and never could she refuse him.

MRS GEOG: Refuse him! And why would she refuse him? . . . Bring me the toasting-fork, Kate. I'll make the bit of toast here; 'twill be hotter.

(KATE's *off to the kitchen now. Amn't i after telling you she's a great help to her mother?*)

JANE: I met Aunt Ellen up the street.

MRS GEOG: For goodness' sake! Did she say she was coming here?

JANE: She did.

MRS GEOG: Oh, then bad luck to her, what a night she'd choose to come here! Where are we to put her to sleep?

JANE: If we put Denis to sleep in the room with George and Peter —

MRS GEOG: You'll do no such thing. I'll not have Denis turned out of his room. The three of you girls must sleep together in the big bed; that's the only way we can manage.... What crazy old scheme has Ellen in her head this time, I wonder?

JANE: She didn't tell me, but by her manner I know she's up to something.

MRS GEOG: God help us! And Denis will be making game of her,

and maybe she won't leave him the bit of money after all. . . .
There's a man's voice — 'tis Denis. (*What a hurry she's in to open the door.*) Ah, it's only Donough. (*He's not much to look at, is he? A simple poor fellow, it's a wonder he had the spunk to think of getting married at all.* JANE *could have done better for herself, but she thinks the world of the little man. God knows what she sees in him. Aren't women queer, the fancies they take?*)

DONOUGH: Good night, to you.

(*Here's* KATE *back with the toasting-fork.*)

JANE: Good night, Donough.

DONOUGH: Good night, Jane. Have you your tea taken?

JANE: I haven't.

DONOUGH: I wanted you to come across to the Temperance Hall to the concert. I didn't think I could get off in time, but I can. Swallow your tea and come on.

JANE: Oh, Donough, I'd like to, but, you see, Denis is coming on the six o'clock.

DONOUGH: Yerra, Denis will keep. Get your hat and come on.

MRS GEOG: What's that, Donough? Jane, where are you going?

JANE: Nowhere, mother. Donough wanted me to go to the concert with him.

MRS GEOG: She couldn't go out tonight, thank you, Donough. She must be here to look after Denis.

JANE: I'd better stay, Donough.

MRS GEOG: Tomorrow night, now, she'd be delighted. And maybe Denis would go with the two of you. That would be nice, now.

DONOUGH: Oh, faith, that would be grand — grand entirely! Only, you see, there's no concert tomorrow night.

MRS GEOG: Isn't that a pity, and Denis so fond of music. . . . I left a drop of cream on the kitchen table; fetch it for me, Kate.

JANE: Stay and have a cup of tea, Donough.

MRS GEOG: Sure, I suppose the man had his tea an hour ago.

DONOUGH: I had, indeed, Mrs Geoghegan. I'll say good night to you. Take care of Denis. (*He is going.*)

JANE: I'll see you as far as the door, Donough. (*They're gone.*)

MRS GEOG: What at all was Jane thinking of, asking a stranger to stop to tea tonight?

KATE: What stranger? Is it Donough? Sure he's like one of the family, and will be in real earnest the day he marries Jane.

MRS GEOG: I'm wondering sometimes what sort of a husband will he make her.

KATE: The best in the world.

MRS GEOG: I don't know. He's a queer selfish man. Wanting Jane to go out with him tonight. (*She's going to the door.*) Hannah! Hannah! ... God help us, she'll be all night gossiping at O'Connell's. (*She's listening at the door.*) Who's that going out?

A VOICE: It's me, mother.

MRS GEOG: Come in here to me, Baby.

(*Here she comes. Isn't she a great lump of a girl? She's thirty if she's a day, but she doesn't look it — 'tis the way she dresses, I suppose. She's a great idea of herself entirely, it's as much as her mother can do to hold her in. A long envelope she has in her hand.*)

BABY: Can I do anything for you?

MRS GEOG: We're through now, Baby, small thanks to you. Where are you off to?

BABY: Only to Duffy's to post this.

MRS GEOG: Is it love-letters you were writing all day?

BABY: You know well it wasn't. Only my shorthand for Skerry's.

MRS GEOG: Shorthand, moryah! I'd sooner they were love-letters. I've heard it said Thomas Naughton married Julia Roche for her lucky hand with butter, but I never heard yet of a man marrying a girl for shorthand.

BABY: I'm not wishing to get married, thank you. It's not my intention to spend my days in Ballycolman. Up to Dublin I'm going, and if I marry there, it's a gentleman I'll marry — a gentleman who works in an office. (*That's* BABY *for you!*)

MRS GEOG: Tell Jane to come in out of that. She's at the door saying good night to Donough for the last half hour. (*Off she goes.*) Kate, what did I ever do to have such a fool for a daughter?

KATE: Ah, she's young; little more than a child.

MRS GEOG: Faith, it's time she learned sense .... Now, if Hannah would bring the eggs we'd be ready. You brought in the drop of cream?

KATE: It was here all along, mother.

(*Here's* ELLEN GEOGHEGAN *herself along with* JANE. *You could tell from her appearance the sort she is, a bit cranky and a nasty twist to her tongue if she liked, full of notions and schemes, she's a terrible one for reading; 'tis that has her head turned, there's not a week she hasn't the "Free Press", the "Eagle", and the Supplement to the "Examiner" read to the bone. Still and all, she's a woman to be respected, she must have a couple of hundred acres back there at Kilmurray, and 'tis she*)

owns them three small houses at the other end of the village. . . .
Yes, indeed, a wonder she never married — too many notions,
maybe.)

JANE: Here's Aunt Ellen.

MRS GEOG: How are you, Ellen? I hope you're good?
(*How sweet they are, kissing!*)

AUNT ELLEN: I'm grand, thank you. How are all of you. Will it
bother you to put me up for the night?

MRS GEOG: Not the least bit in the world.

AUNT ELLEN: I've a lot to talk over with you all.

MRS GEOG: You have? And you'll see Denis. We're expecting him
from Dublin any minute.

AUNT ELLEN: Is that a fact? Did he pass his examination?

MRS GEOG: He did. At least, he told me he'd be sure to pass.

AUNT ELLEN: That's good news. Twice he's failed.

MRS GEOG: Small blame to him if he did. He got a sort of a
weakness the first time — too hard he was working, Ellen — and
the last time there was a cross old fellow examining. Denis told
me he couldn't come round him at all; nothing he said would
please him. Isn't it a wonder, Ellen, they'd have such a cross
man to examine them?

AUNT ELLEN: I'm told Dublin doctors are a fright for crossness.
Sure, there was a First Aid class over at my own place, and a
doctor from Dublin came down to examine them. Well, three
girls was all that he would pass out of the twenty, and one of
them had a brother a medical, and a mother who went mad and
drowned herself, so she was experienced like. But as to the lads,
divil a one would wait to be examined after they heard how the
girls had fared; they took to their heels and up to the mountains
with them. Oh, Dublin doctors!

MRS GEOG: I tell you then, they're clever men. No one knows
that better than myself after all I went through the time Denis
was born. And it's up in Dublin Denis will be when he's a
doctor. He'll never be one of your common dispensaries, hat in
hand to every guardian in the country.

AUNT ELLEN: You're right, Ann, you're right. He's a sight too
clever for that . . . . But tell me, are George and Peter inside?

MRS GEOG: George didn't come up from the shop yet, and
Peter went down to the station to meet Denis. George will
be up for his tea any minute.

AUNT ELLEN: I want to speak to them. I've a great plan in my
head. (*Look at them all looking at each other. She has them*
wore out with her plans.)

MRS GEOG: Don't tell me, Ellen, that 'tis goats again. I was thinking the other day it was only by the help of God you got shut of those queer outlandish goats you had.

AUNT ELLEN: I haven't had a goat these two years.

MRS GEOG: 'Tis well for you.

KATE: Another time you were for making a fortune out of tobacco.

JANE: Another time it was Muscovy ducks — cross, wild things; they had me in dread every time I went to see you.

AUNT ELLEN: Well, I have spirit in me and independence. I'm not like the common farmer people, plodding on in the same old rut from generation to generation.

MRS GEOG: Don't mind the children, Ellen. It's only joking they are. Tell us what's on your mind now.

AUNT ELLEN: Well, I've been reading a great deal lately about co-operation.

MRS GEOG: What?

AUNT ELLEN: Co-operation. They say it will be the salvation of Ireland.

MRS GEOG: Wisha, don't believe them. They're always blowing about this, that, and the other, and saying it's to be the salvation of the country. Sure, they must be talking, the creatures. In my young days it was the Land League; then it was Parnell; a couple of years ago 'twas them Sinn Feiners were to save us, or John Redmond — I don't rightly remember which, I wouldn't believe one of them. Pull away and do your work and put money in the Bank; that's the only thing to do. Anyway, George says co-operation will be the ruin of us. (*She's a rock of sense, that woman.*)

AUNT ELLEN: Well, I'm surprised at him, and he a shopkeeper and a farmer. By all accounts, it should be a great lift to him. Anyway, my co-operation is going to be a lift to the family. Listen here to me, Ann....

(*Here's* GEORGE *now. The eldest of the family, a steady man, a bit soured, maybe, but who wouldn't be and that string of sisters depending on him. He was forty last summer, but he looks more.*)

GEORGE: Is the tea ready, mother?

MRS GEOG: We'll have it the very minute Denis comes.

GEORGE: I didn't see you, Aunt Ellen. How are you?

AUNT ELLEN: I'm good, thanks. You're looking well.

GEORGE: I can't wait, mother. Let me have a cup of tea. I have to go back to the shop.

MRS GEOG: Don't sit there, like a good boy; you'll toss the table. (*But he sits all the same.*)

GEORGE: Ham, chicken, apples, a cake — is it a party?

MRS GEOG: Not at all — only Denis coming, and he'll want a bit after the journey.

AUNT ELLEN: You spoil Denis, Ann. He was always your white-headed boy.

MRS GEOG: Indeed he's nothing of the kind. I don't make a pin's point of difference between one child and another.... Hannah would give you a nice cup of tea in the kitchen, George. There's bread-and-butter there, and a lovely duck egg was left over from the dinner. Run and tell her, Kate.

GEORGE: I'll go myself.

AUNT ELLEN: Stay here a minute. I've been telling your mother about a great plan I have.
(*There's* KATE *off to give the message. Didn't I tell you that's the sort she was?*)

GEORGE: What ails you now?

AUNT ELLEN: Did you ever hear of a co-operative shop, George?

GEORGE: I did. I'd have nothing to do with one of them.

AUNT ELLEN: Why?

GEORGE They're bad. Ruining honest traders, that's what they're doing.

AUNT ELLEN: Is that a fact? Well, we're starting one over at Kilmurray.

GEORGE: You are?

AUNT ELLEN: Up there in the mountains you know how hard it is for us to get anything. Sylvester Brannigan is the only one who's by way of being a trader, and God knows I wouldn't have it on my conscience that I called him an honest one. So a lot of us have joined together and we're going to open a store there. It's going to be a great thing for the family.

GEORGE: How so?

AUNT ELLEN: The papers say that half the success of a co-operative shop depends on the manager. We're going to give a good salary to our manager — up to £150 a year — and there's a small house and an acre of land.

GEORGE: And who is he to be?

AUNT ELLEN: Your own brother, Peter.

GEORGE: Peter!

MRS GEOG: For goodness sake!

AUNT ELLEN: Isn't he just the man for the place? He knows all about a shop; he's clever and hard-working, and if he was out of this, Donough could marry Jane, and come in and work in his place.

JANE: Oh, Aunt Ellen, aren't you the great woman for plans!

AUNT ELLEN: A minute ago I was the greatest old fool in the world.

MRS GEOG: I hear steps in the street. Run out, Jane, and see if it's the train after coming in. (JANE's off.) Would it cost a deal of money, Ellen, to get that place? I suppose there'd be an amount of canvassing to be done?

AUNT ELLEN: Not at all. Isn't Jamesy Walshe, Donough's mother's cousin? Won't he want Peter to get it? Isn't Patrick Hogan married to John Duffy's sister, and is he likely to be unfriendly to Denis's brother, to the brother of the man his niece, Delia Duffy, is going to marry? Not at all. And then there's myself, who started the whole thing. I tell you, Peter wouldn't be called on to spend as much as half-a-crown in a public house.

GEORGE: It might suit Peter all right.

MRS GEOG: But, George, if them co-operative things are as bad as you say, maybe we oughtn't to let Peter be mixed up in them.

GEORGE: Sure, somebody's got to get that £150, and we might as well get it as another. God knows we want the money badly. I'm striving to put enough by for Jane's marriage — and now nothing will do Baby but to hyse up to Dublin learning book-keeping or shorthand or something.

AUNT ELLEN: Glory be to God! Is it notions she has?

GEORGE: Aye, notions. But they're notions that cost me money, and it costs a lot to make Denis a doctor.

AUNT ELLEN: Well, the Creegans made their son a doctor, and I'm sure they're in a very small way.

MRS GEOG: Is it that little snipeen of a fellow — Joe Creegan? Sure you wouldn't put him alongside my Denis. He's no smartness.

GEORGE: Denis is smart enough to run up debts in Dublin —

AUNT ELLEN: Debts!

GEORGE: Ay, and betting on horses.

MRS GEOG: From the time he was a little fellow he was always fond of horses, Ellen. I remember well one day, and he little more than a baby —

GEORGE: Well, he's a bit too damned fond of them for me. (Here's KATE back.)

KATE: I've a nice cup of tea ready for you in the kitchen.

GEORGE: Thank you, Kate. We'll speak again about this, Aunt. You're staying the night, I suppose?

AUNT ELLEN: I am.

(*And* BABY *and* JANE *in now.*)

BABY: How are you, Aunt Ellen. (*More kissing.*) Mr Duffy gave me this at the Post Office. I suppose it's for you, George. (*'Tis a telegram.*)

MRS GEOG: A telegram! Oh, has something happened to Denis? I knew he should be here before this — Oh, George, what is it at all at all?

JANE: Be easy, mother.

(*She's all in a flutter. Wisha, she's cracked about* DENIS. *'Tisn't so easy to stir* GEORGE .... *He's read it now.*)

GEORGE: It's not from Denis at all.... But I think it's for him.

MRS GEOG: What's in it?

GEORGE: "Hard luck. Geoghegan's Hope also ran. Sorry. Flanagan."

MRS GEOG: What does that mean?

GEORGE: I know no more than yourself.

AUNT ELLEN: Show me it. There doesn't seem sense or meaning in it.

JANE: You've some idea in your head about it, George?

GEORGE: I have. It's my belief it's about a horse-race. It's my belief Denis has been betting again. (*He'll be losing his temper in a minute.*)

KATE: He wouldn't. He gave you his word he wouldn't.

AUNT ELLEN: 'Tis a terrible curse. I read on "The Eagle" only last week of a young man who shot himself on the head of all the money he lost on horses.

MRS GEOG: You frighten me, Ellen.

GEORGE: You need have no fear of Denis. He'll not be the one to pay; 'tis us will have to do that.

BABY: That's a fact.

GEORGE: It'll be the last time. I'm damned if —

KATE: Hush, hush, George!

(JANE'S *looking at the telegram now.*)

JANE: Flanagan. That's the name of the young gentleman came to see Denis on a motor bicycle last summer.

MRS GEOG: I remember him myself. A lovely young gentleman. Seemingly he had a great liking for Denis — he talked to me about him for a long time, half laughing like. The "hope of the Geoghegans" he called him.

GEORGE: What's that? The "hope of the Geoghegans"? Did he call him that?

MRS GEOG: He did. Denis told me 'twas a sort of a pet name he put on him in college.

JANE: What is it, George?

GEORGE: "Geoghegan's Hope also ran." That's either a race horse, or it's Denis himself.

JANE: I don't understand you.

GEORGE: He's either broken his word to me and is betting on horses again, or else ... he's failed again.

JANE: His examination, you mean?

GEORGE: I do.

JANE: God help us!

MRS GEOG: Yerra, he hasn't failed. Don't think it, George. He told me himself last week in a letter he'd be certain to pass.

KATE: 'Twould be terrible for him if he failed.

BABY: 'Twould be terrible for us, you mean.

MRS GEOG: He'd never break his word to you about the betting.

GEORGE: For his own sake I'd almost hope he had. For if this isn't about a horse, if it's about Denis himself, if it means he's failed, I'll — I'll —

MRS GEOG: You're speaking very cross, George, about your brother.

GEORGE: I have reason to speak cross. If he's failed for the third time, divil another penny will he get from me — except his passage to Canada. (*They're staring at him; they don't believe him.*) I mean it. You're all looking at me as if I was out of my senses. It's out of our senses we've been all these years and years, spending lashings of money on an idle, good-for-nothing young fellow.

MRS GEOG: Yerra, George! ...

GEORGE: From the day he was born, hasn't everything been given to him? Look at the whips of money laid out for his education. He was too grand and too clever to be sent to the National School like the rest of us — poor Mr Lacy didn't know enough to teach him; oh, no! he had to go into the city every day by train — second-class — to be taught by the Christian Brothers. Look at Kate there, worn and grey before her time, an old maid. Wouldn't she have been married ten years ago to Jer Connor only we hadn't a penny to give with her, it all being kept for the laddo, to send him to college, Trinity College, nothing less would be fitting of course. And what's there to show for it all? Nothing at all. He doesn't even pass his examinations. What's keeping Jane from marrying Donough, only Denis? What's keeping Baby at home, and she mad to be learning up in Dublin, only Denis? What's keeping us straitened and pinching and saving, only Denis, Denis, Denis? But the old horse learns its lesson in the end, and I've learnt mine. Not another red half-penny will he get from me. You can tell him that when he comes in. (*And off with him, banging the door after him.*)

MRS GEOG: Ellen, what's come to him at all to speak like that?

BABY: It's true what he says. Every word of it's true.

MRS GEOG: Hold your tongue, girl! (*That's one for* BABY, *she's flouncing out of the room.*) Kate, run after your brother and pacify him. (*She's gone, but what can she do, the creature?*) What's come to him at all at all?

AUNT ELLEN: 'Tis true, you always made a pet of the boy — but sure we all did. I was reading in the "Girl's Friend" not long ago how foolish it was for a mother to be making differences between her children. They said that —

MRS GEOG: And why shouldn't I make differences? Is there anyone living who'd stand up on that floor and say that Denis isn't smarter and cleverer than his two brothers — or his sisters, either — or the whole menagerie of the Geoghegans lumped together? From the day he was born I knew he was different. Oh, Ellen, it will break my heart if George turns against him now! (*Is it crying she is?*)

AUNT ELLEN: Quiet yourself, Ann.... Go out, Jane, and speak to your brother. He always had respect for you.

JANE: I'll see what mood is he in. (*She's gone after him — she knows how to humour him.*)

MRS GEOG: From the day he was born I knew he was different. I was getting an old woman when he came... you remember, Ellen, it was nearly ten years after Baby was born. I thought I'd never have another child; it seemed like a miracle.... I thought I'd die with it.

AUNT ELLEN: You were nervous, I remember that.

MRS GEOG: Nervous? I was mad afraid. My sister — poor Bridgie — made me go up to Dublin to see a doctor there. Oh, Ellen, that doctor was a lovely man. He was a sort of a lord, Sir Denis Bellingham Burke, that was his name. He'd have nothing to do with common cases, 'twould be no use going to him with a broken leg or a sick stomach or the like — he wouldn't look at you. Women like me, those are all he'd see, and he told me.... (*She's whispering. We oughtn't to listen. 'Tis no place for us.*)

AUNT ELLEN: I remember you telling me that at the time. It was surprising.

MRS GEOG: Wasn't it now? Well, I did every mortal thing he told me to. I went into a sort of hospital — I'd be afraid to tell you what they made me pay — but I had the best of everything, and when Denis was born I called him after the dear doctor.

AUNT ELLEN: And made up your mind to make a doctor of him.

MRS GEOG: I did. 'Twas like a miracle, a boy to come after those three lumps of girls.... He was a lovely child... and now if George turns against him! Sure he has the money, and can do what he likes. Denis away in Canada! 'Twould break my heart. (KATE's back.)

KATE: He's ramping and raging in the kitchen. He says if the telegram is true, if he's missed his examination, he'll ship him off next week.

MRS GEOG: I'll go to George myself. I'll talk him over. He can't be in earnest. And what about Delia Duffy? Isn't he promised to her as soon as ever he's a doctor? Is she to be shipped to Canada along with him? Where's George? I'll go to him. (God help GEORGE when he meets her. Ah! here's DENIS in the other door. Isn't he lovely? You'd know he was from Dublin by his clothes and his smartness. He's just turned twenty-two.)

DENIS: Hullo, mother!

MRS GEOG: Denis! my darling boy! (She's flinging her arms round his neck; she'll have him choked.)

DENIS: Hold on, mother — or, rather, don't hold on! Don't kill me altogether!

MRS GEOG: How are you, my poor boy?

DENIS: Top hole. Hallo, Aunt Ellen; this is an unexpected pleasure. (I'd say he was codding her from the way he kissed her.) Well, Kate. (This young girl coming in is DELIA DUFFY. She's not as simple as she looks. She's her father's daughter. The fellow with her carrying all the luggage is PETER GEOGHEGAN, he's nothing much one way or the other.)

PETER: Where will I leave these?

DENIS: Oh, chuck them into my room, like a good chap. Here, I'll give you this coat. (Poor PETER.)

MRS GEOG: Oh, Delia, I didn't see you. Come in and sit down. You went to the station, I suppose?

DELIA: I did. I can't wait, Mrs Geoghegan, thanks.

MRS GEOG: Yerra, stay and have a cup of tea.

DELIA: I must be off home to give my father his supper. Denis will come down and see me later. There's questions I want to ask him. I have it in my mind he's been carrying on with a young lady in Dublin. (She is going.)

DENIS: Delia, I swear....

DELIA: Ssh! Don't tell lies on an empty stomach; wait till after tea. (*She's gone.*)

DENIS: But, Delia, I.... (*He's gone after her, she has him in good order.*)

AUNT ELLEN: He's looking gay enough now. Little he knows what's before him!

MRS GEOG: Oh, Ellen! (*Here's* GEORGE, JANE, *and* BABY.)

JANE: Has he come?

AUNT ELLEN: He has.

MRS GEOG: George, you won't be hard on him? He's dead tired and hungry.

GEORGE: Did he say anything about the examination?

MRS GEOG: He didn't; it's likely he doesn't know. It'll break his heart when he finds out he's failed — if failed he has. Couldn't we keep it from him for a day or two?

JANE: It's better he should know it, mother. George is right. It's time a change was made.

MRS GEOG: Jane!

JANE: You never think, maybe, I'd want my chance as well as Denis. You never think, maybe, Donough will get tired waiting. (*You wouldn't think* JANE *could be so bitter.*)

BABY: And I'm not going to stay in this hole of a place any longer.

MRS GEOG: You're an unnatural family, that's what you are! (DENIS *is back; he has a box of cigars in his hand.*)

DENIS: What's the confabulation about? Have you a match, George?

MRS GEOG: Tell Hannah to bring in the tea. (*Of course it's* KATE *that goes.*)

DENIS: Beastly cold, isn't it? (*Look at them moving aside so that he can have the centre of the fire.*) Well, Aunt Ellen, what's the latest? Is it true you've been making a fortune turning turf into paper?

AUNT ELLEN: It isn't.

DENIS: I'm surprised to hear that. A wide-awake woman like you, with a bog of your own. You should keep moving, Aunt Ellen, keep moving.

AUNT ELLEN: Thank you for your advice.

GEORGE: Aunt Ellen has some regard for the family. She's got a good position in her eye for Peter.

DENIS: What's that?

AUNT ELLEN: Manager of a shop, a co-operative shop.

DENIS: Co-operation? I see. That's the latest Sir What's-his-name, the hairy poet chap and all the rest of the gang — they'll

78

suit you down to the ground, Aunt Ellen. They're just your sort.

AUNT ELLEN: Do you know them?

DENIS: Me? No — thank God!

GEORGE: It's time some of us made a little money.

DENIS: Oh, if there's money in it. I'm sure there's no one knows better than I do how much we want money.

MRS GEOG: Poor boy!

GEORGE: No one knows better than you do how to spend it.

DENIS: Well, it's made to be spent, isn't it? What are you grousing about, anyway? Look what I brought you. (*He's giving him the box of cigars.*) They're good ones, too.

MRS GEOG: Oh, George, isn't it good of Denis? He never forgets you. (*She's glad of the chance to soften* GEORGE.)

DENIS: Wait till you see what I have upstairs in my bag for you, mother.

GEORGE: Thank you, but I'd rather you wouldn't spend your money — I mean my money — on me.

DENIS: Oh, I've been jolly economical lately. I don't believe I've had more than ten pounds from you since the summer.

GEORGE: Ten! You believe queer things.

DENIS: Well, not more than twenty — or twenty-five.

GEORGE: Tell me this; have you been betting lately?

MRS GEOG: George!

DENIS: No. Honour bright. Never once since you gave me that rowing. Though I don't mind telling you I missed a good thing last week; could have made twenty pounds as easily as lighting a cigarette.

JANE: You're sure you weren't betting?

DENIS: Absolutely .... Why you all look disappointed ... as if you wished I had been .... What's the matter?

GEORGE: What does this mean so? (*He's giving him the telegram.*)

DENIS: A wire? Is it for me?

GEORGE: Read it and see.

DENIS: Oh, I suppose it's from Flanagan. He said he'd wire the result of the exam.; it wasn't out when I left Dublin.

MRS GEOG: Don't mind it, Denis. Have your tea first — 'tis nothing at all.

BABY: Be quiet, mother. Can't you let him read it?

GEORGE: Well?

DENIS: Oh, I've lost my exam. Isn't that a beastly nuisance? I'm not surprised; I guessed I hadn't got it. (*Faith, it doesn't seem to trouble him.*)

MRS GEOG: Never mind, my poor boy. It doesn't matter the least bit in the world. (HANNAH, KATE, *and* PETER *are back.*) Here's Hannah with the tea.... Put this out of your head and have a bit of chicken and a sup of tea. (*She's coaxing him to the table.*) Sure what are those examinations after all? Only cross questions and botheration. I never could see the use of them. Run off and boil an egg, Hannah. (HANNAH*'s gone.*) There's a nice hot cup, now. Drink it and don't worry your head over this.

DENIS: Oh, I'm not worrying mother. I'll get it next time to a dead cert. (*He's eating his tea as if nothing had happened.*)

GEORGE: You won't.

DENIS: Oh, yes, I will. You'll see. I'll work like a nigger from now till June. Don't worry about it, old chap. Push me over the butter.

GEORGE: I've done worrying. I've gone through a deal of that in the last few years.

DENIS: That's right. Take life easy. That's what I do.

GEORGE: I've been thinking that. It's time you worried round a bit now.

DENIS: I'll worry till I get this exam. anyway.

GEORGE: I'm not going to ask you to.

DENIS: What do you mean? You're all looking dashed solemn. What is it? (*He's beginning to feel there's something up.*)

MRS GEOG: Don't mind George, Denis. He's a bit put out tonight, but —

GEORGE: Mother! We've been long thinking things over; we think you've been long enough at College; it's time you left.

DENIS: Left! Leave Trinity! But I'm only half through.

GEORGE: That's not my fault, is it?

DENIS: But I can't become a doctor. I'm not qualified.

GEORGE: I'm not asking you to be a doctor.

DENIS: But ... what ... I don't understand.

GEORGE: Well, here it is in two words. There's been enough and too much money spent on you; I'll spend no more. Yes, I will, though — twenty pounds more. That'll pay your passage to Canada and leave a bit in your pocket.

(*That's a slap in the face for him. There's not a word out of him.*)

DENIS: You're joking.

GEORGE: I am not.

DENIS: But ... but ... why?

GEORGE: Because there's a couple of others here to consider as well as yourself. It's fair they should get their chance. You've had yours.

DENIS: And what am I to do in Canada?

GEORGE: You can find out when you get there. You've a pair of hands, haven't you? When you've an empty belly and a pair of hands, I tell you you won't be long finding something to do.

DENIS: I see.... Are you all agreed on this — or is it only George?

MRS GEOG: Denis, darling, I'll never desert you.

DENIS: Are you all agreed on this?

JANE: I'd be sorry you'd go, but Donough is getting tired waiting for me.

BABY: You're not the only one wants education. I'm not going to stick in Ballycolman all my life.

KATE: George is right.

AUNT ELLEN: You've had your chance, Denis, and you've thrown it away. It's time you turned round and worked for yourself. Let this be a lesson to you —

PETER: It's time I got a look in.

DENIS: Well, I think it's a damned shame. (*He'll be losing his temper in a minute.*)

GEORGE: It's your own fault. You brought it on yourself.

DENIS: I didn't. I didn't! I never asked to be sent to College; I never asked to have all this money spent on me. I'd have been content to live here with the rest of you —

PETER: You were too clever for the like of us.

MRS GEOG: Different altogether.

DENIS: I wasn't.

AUNT ELLEN: To look at you standing there amongst them, Denis, 'tis easy seen how different you are.

DENIS: Yes, I'm different now, but whose fault is that? It's not mine. Who was it made me out to be so clever; who insisted on making a doctor of me, or sending me to Trinity? It was all of you. From the time I was a baby you treated me as if I was something wonderful, and now when you find I'm not what you thought I was you kick me out — across the sea to Canada, where you'll never hear of me again. You give me the education of a gentleman, lashings of money in my pocket, no wish denied me, and in the end you tell me I'm to be a labourer.

GEORGE: There's other work besides farming in Canada.

DENIS: It's unfair.

MRS GEOG: I won't let you go, Denis.

DENIS: Oh, I'll go fast enough, never fear. We all know what George is when he's made up his mind about a thing. He made up his mind I was to go to College to be a doctor, and I went.

Now he's made up his mind I'm to go to Canada, and I'll go. He's got the purse; he can do what he likes.

AUNT ELLEN: If you weren't a fool you wouldn't be saying these things; he might do great things for you yet if he had a mind to.

DENIS: I'm asking no favours from him. I'll not take a shilling from him. I'll get enough some other way to take me out of this; don't be afraid you'll be bothered with me. I'll go back to Dublin tomorrow.

MRS GEOG: Denis!

DENIS: I'll be free, anyway, from this to make my own life in my own way. I'm tired of other people managing it for me.

GEORGE: You're vexed with me now. Some day you'll be very thankful to me.

DENIS: I've no doubt I will. You're giving me a great opening. I'm tremendously obliged to you all.

MRS GEOG: It breaks my heart to hear you talk so bitter. And Delia — what'll Delia say at all to all this?

DENIS: Delia? Oh, you may be sure George has some plan in his head for Delia. She's to go to South Africa, I suppose, or maybe he's arranged to marry her himself.

GEORGE: I've no wish to part you. She can marry you and go to Canada if she's willing. I'll pay the passage for the two of you.

DENIS: Thank you for nothing. I'm asking no money from you, and I've no intention of asking Delia to come out and rough it in Canada. She wasn't brought up to that sort of thing.

PETER: John Duffy would give you money with her maybe. Enough to set the two of you up in Canada.

DENIS: I'm asking no favours from John Duffy or from any of you. I'll tell Delia the truth; tell her I'm being kicked out by my family because I'm good for nothing. I'll make an end of the whole thing. I'll write to Delia tonight, this very minute — I'll go back to Dublin in the morning; I'll not stay another night here.

AUNT ELLEN: This is hard for you, Denis, but maybe it's the best thing that could happen.

DENIS: That's it, Aunt Ellen; the best thing in the world for all of us. Peter will go out to you, Donough will marry Jane, Baby will go to Dublin; there'll be plenty of money for everything. Denis will be — well, it doesn't matter a damn where Denis will be. He'll be out of the way, at any rate. Babe, darling, get me a sheet of paper and an envelope.

MRS GEOG: My heart's broken between you all.

KATE: Don't take on, mother.

(BABY's *brought him the paper.*)

DENIS: Thanks, Babe; you're a jewel. Look out for yourself when you go to Dublin; all the fellows in Skerry's will be mad after you. There's something really fascinating about you. (*How bitter he is! Look at the toss of her head. They're watching him writing.* AUNT ELLEN's *got the girls round her; she's speaking in a low voice to them.*)

AUNT ELLEN: I don't think he should write that to Delia about his being turned out. Great laughing the neighbours will be having at us, and all the talk we made of his cleverness for the last twenty years.

KATE: There's truth in that, Aunt Ellen.

BABY: I'd be ashamed to be seen on the street for the next twelvemonth, and all we've been blowing about him.

PETER: There's that little loan I got partly on the good prospects of Mister Denis.

AUNT ELLEN: If you'll take my advice you'll give out that he's gone out to a good position in Canada. I had a brother there once, twenty-five years ago. He died without a child. No matter. Can't you say Denis has gone out to his cousins — that they're in a big way of business? That will save your face. (*A great idea, sure enough.*)

JANE: You're a great woman for schemes, Aunt.

GEORGE: It's a good idea. We don't want to be disgraced out and out.

BABY: People to laugh at me — 'twould make me mad.

AUNT ELLEN: Do you hear what we're saying, Denis?

DENIS: I do. It's nothing to me what lie I leave behind me. I don't care if they know the truth about me. But you can have your own way in this, too. I've told her I'm off to Canada in two days, and we can't get married. I'll put in a postscript to say I'm going out to a big position.

AUNT ELLEN: It's a pity you're so hasty. Delia is a good match; you shouldn't throw her away so smart.
(*He's got the letter done.*)

DENIS: There! Send Hannah down to Duffy's with it.
(JANE *goes to the door.*)

JANE: Hannah, come here a minute.

GEORGE: Before you send it, Denis, think again over what I've said. I know you're fond of Delia; I don't want to come between you. Marry her; I'll send you both to Canada, and I'll put a bit of money in your hand.

DENIS: You've washed your hands of me, George. You and Delia have got to take the consequences of it as well as I.

(*Here's* HANNAH *with an egg.*)

Take that note down to Duffy's, Hannah.

HANNAH: I will. There's your egg. 'Tisn't laid two hours, and Mrs O'Connell says she'll send you in one every day as long as you're here.

DENIS: I'll be putting no strain on her hens, Hannah. I'm off tomorrow.

HANNAH: Tomorrow! Yerra —

AUNT ELLEN: To Canada he's going, Hannah. To a grand position there with his uncle's eldest son.

HANNAH: Canada! For goodness sake! And is he not going doctoring?

AUNT ELLEN: This is better than doctoring. A great position he'll have. You can be off now. Tell everyone you meet about Denis.

HANNAH: I will to be sure, I'm delighted, Mister Denis; things have turned out so well for you. Delia Duffy will be burning the house down for pure joy tonight. I'll be off as fast as my legs can carry me. (*God knows that's not saying much. Still when she's got a bit of gossip she'll lose no time.*)

GEORGE: You're feeling bitter about this, Denis. I'm sorry for you. Will you believe me saying I think it's for the best?

DENIS: You don't care a damn whether I believe you or not. (*That's enough for* GEORGE. *He's going out.*)

MRS GEOG: Your tea's cold. Wait till I get you a hot sup. Will you have a bit of chicken?

DENIS: I couldn't eat anything. I wish you'd all leave me alone. You've got all you wanted from me. I'll be gone for ever in the morning.

MRS GEOG: You're beat out. You've a headache, maybe?

DENIS: I have.

MRS GEOG: The tea will do you good. I'll get them to make you a piece of hot toast. Kate or Baby, or one of you, run into the kitchen and make a piece of toast — quick.

BABY: I think it's time Denis learned to make his own toast.

PETER: I'm not going to make it for him anyway.

JANE: I've other things to do.

(*Off with them all.*)

MRS GEOG: Don't mind them. I'll make the toast for you. It will all come right.

DENIS: It's so unfair — so unfair; that's what I mind.

MRS GEOG: It is, it is. (*She's kneeling by the fire toasting bread.*)

DENIS: It was your fault first, mother. You made me out to be something great.

MRS GEOG: And aren't you? Is there a lad anywhere as clever as you? Sure, hasn't everyone the same story of your smartness, and they can't all be mistaken.

DENIS: They are.

MRS GEOG: Not at all. You'll get what you want in the end. You'll see.

DENIS: I want nothing at all now except to be let alone.

MRS GEOG: My poor boy... I never feel as if the others were my children the way you are.

DENIS: And I've been a bad son to you.

MRS GEOG: You haven't, you haven't. You've never given me a cross word. You mustn't go across the sea to Canada. What would I do without you, and what would poor Delia do?

DENIS: Poor Delia!

MRS GEOG: Every girl in the place is wild about you. They were mad that you'd never look at one of them only Delia Duffy. I never thought she was half good enough for you; I always hoped you'd marry a lady from the city, for all John Duffy has the Post Office and is Chairman of the District Council.... But you'd have got money with her.

DENIS: Well, that's all over now.

MRS GEOG: The toast is just done. Hold it a minute and I'll fetch the cup of tea. You can sit there and be taking it.

(*Here's* KATE *back. She has a piece of toast on a plate.*)

KATE: I made a piece of toast at the fire upstairs.

(*And* JANE *in the other door with another piece of toast.*)

JANE: Denis, will you — Oh, have you been making toast?

(*And* HANNAH's *head in at the door.*)

HANNAH: Have you the toasting-fork there, ma'am. Peter wants to make a piece of toast for Mister Denis.

DENIS: I want none of your toast. You can keep your bally toast.

(*But he's taking the piece his mother holds out to him.*)

CURTAIN

ACT II

The same room again later in the evening and GEORGE *and* PETER *sitting, talking.*

PETER: You think I should take it, then?

GEORGE: I do.

PETER: But supposing it fails?

GEORGE: Aunt Ellen will stick to it for a year or two, and by that time it will have failed or succeeded. If it's a success, you're game ball; if it fails you're no worse off than you are now, and there will always be foolish, contrary people starting them co-operative things; that class is as thick as thieves and lavish with the money; once you get well in with them they'll not desert you. Besides, you knowing all about shopkeeping, you'll be able to make things easier for the locals. Do you understand me?

PETER: I do.

GEORGE: Them co-operatives have never succeeded yet, but if they ever do — 'twould be bad days for us. I'd like to see you there for life, and yet 'twouldn't be well to be too successful.

PETER: Ah, there'll be some sort of a middle course. (*With a wink.*)

GEORGE: That's what's in my mind.

PETER: And Donough will marry Jane and come here in my place, and Baby will be up in Dublin, and Denis will be off our hands. Faith, it all fits together as neat as a puzzle.

GEORGE: And you could be giving an eye to Aunt Ellen's bit of land, and not letting her play puck with it with her contrary schemes, and in the end she'll leave it to you, why wouldn't she? She'll forget Denis when the salt water's between them.

PETER: He's been a weight on us for years; we're well rid of him. But all the same, I felt sorry for the poor fellow tonight.

GEORGE: Ah, he'll do first-class in Canada. Sure, all sorts does well out there. I'm only afraid of the mother having the life wore out of me fretting after him.

PETER: She'll get over that in time.

GEORGE: Well, she must. I'm not going back on what I said about Denis. Go he must.

(*Here's their aunt.*)

AUNT ELLEN: George, your mother wants you. She's above in her room.

GEORGE: Is she after going to bed?

AUNT ELLEN: She is not; she can't get this business of Denis out of her mind, the creature.

GEORGE: There's no use in her talking of it to me. My mind is made up; we're all determined. Denis must go.

AUNT ELLEN: Even so, a word from you might quiet her. Anyhow, she won't take rest till she sees you.

GEORGE: I'll go to her so.

(*He's gone. 'Tisn't likely there's anything he can say will quiet her.*)

AUNT ELLEN: You'd have to pity her. Denis was always her white-headed boy, and this is a blow to her. Well, we must all go through with it.... Tell me, are you coming out to Kilmurray?

PETER: I'm after talking it over with George; he advises me to go.

AUNT ELLEN: He's right. You'll never regret it. I suppose you know all about co-operation?

PETER: Divil a bit. But I can keep a shop.

AUNT ELLEN: That's all we want.

PETER: I'll leave you and the Committee to do the co-operating.

AUNT ELLEN: You'd better come back there with me tomorrow. The sooner you see the Committee the better. Not that there's a fear you won't get it, for I mentioned your name to them and they were agreeable; but it's best to make sure of them; you never know when they wouldn't turn round behind your back and put in an ignorant fellow — a fellow who couldn't weigh a pound of sugar — just because he was a relation of one of them. It's one of the curses of the country, giving positions to relations.

PETER: I agree with you, Aunt.

AUNT ELLEN: They're a jobbing, ignorant crowd out at Kilmurray.... There's a knock. Who can it be this hour of night?

PETER: Hannah's snoring this half-hour. I'll see who it is.

(*He's gone and here he is back and* JOHN DUFFY *with him.* JOHN *is one of the solidest men in Ballycolman, Chairman of the District Council, Chairman of the Race Committee, and a member of every Committee and every League in the village. He has three public houses and a grocery business and the Post Office, and a branch of the National Bank once a month, and a trade in old hens and eggs, and a terrible turnover in turkeys at Christmas.... Oh, a weighty man.... Yes, he buried the wife long ago; he's no child but* DELIA. *He's not looking in too pleasant a humour.*)

AUNT ELLEN: Oh, good evening, Mr Duffy; you're welcome. I was wondering who the knock might be.

DUFFY: 'Tis late for visits, but I slipped up to see George for a minute.

AUNT ELLEN: He's in the mother's room. Will you tell him, Peter?

(PETER*'s gone to tell* GEORGE.)

Will you sit down, Mr Duffy.... 'Twon't be long to Christmas now.

DUFFY: That's true.

AUNT ELLEN: You're looking well. How's Delia these times?

DUFFY: She's well enough. She got a great throw-over tonight.

AUNT ELLEN: Is that a fact?

DUFFY: Is Denis around?

AUNT ELLEN: He's not. He's gone to bed.

DUFFY: He's going from you, I hear?

AUNT ELLEN: He is indeed, poor boy. It's hard parting from him, but since it's for his advantage we wouldn't stand in his way.

(*Wouldn't anyone believe her the way she says it?*)

DUFFY: To be sure, to be sure.

AUNT ELLEN: I always said he was too clever to be a doctor. When you see the ignorant fellows that are turned into doctors, you can't believe, Mr Duffy, that it takes much wit to cut off a man's leg or to give him a bottle of medicine.

DUFFY: There's something in that.

AUNT ELLEN: Now in Canada he'll find an opening suitable to his smartness. A brother of my own went out there forty years ago and 'tis wonderful the way he got on.

DUFFY: Is it to his people Denis is going?

AUNT ELLEN: It is. He left a troop of sons and daughters after him.

DUFFY: And where do they live?

AUNT ELLEN: They? — Oh, they live in Saint Paul.

DUFFY: I thought that was in the States.

AUNT ELLEN: There's a place of that name in Canada, too. Do you suppose I wouldn't know my own brother's place?

DUFFY: I beg your pardon, ma'am; indeed I meant no such thing. He's in business, I suppose?

AUNT ELLEN: You may say he is, then. By all accounts he owns half the town.

DUFFY: Do you tell me? Denis will have a fine position so.

AUNT ELLEN: Oh, the best in the world. Nothing to do but superintending like, strolling about with his hands in his pockets making other people work, and putting money in the Bank all the time.

DUFFY: Bedad, that sounds a good life. Tell me, what class of business has your brother?
(*That's a facer!*)

AUNT ELLEN: A mixed business, Mr Duffy.
(*Good woman!*)

DUFFY: I see.
(*Here's* PETER *back with* GEORGE.)

GEORGE: You were wanting me, John?

DUFFY: I was.

GEORGE: If it's the fertilizer you're after, I didn't get it in yet. I have it ordered a fortnight or more.

DUFFY: 'Tisn't that at all.... This is great news about Denis.

GEORGE: Ay.

DUFFY: He's off to Canada?

GEORGE: He is.

DUFFY: Hannah was blowing about a fine place he's going to, and your Aunt was saying the same thing just now. It's a fact, I suppose?

GEORGE: That's true.

DUFFY: Lashings of money and nothing to do.

GEORGE: I believe so.

DUFFY: His cousins own the town?

GEORGE: They do.

DUFFY: 'Tis very sudden.

GEORGE: That's the way things come, John. Only this evening it was settled.

AUNT ELLEN: Of course, Denis being so clever, we always looked for something big to turn up for him.

DUFFY: Delia's in a state over it.

GEORGE: Ah, she needn't be. Indeed, we were all sorry about that, but it couldn't be helped. They were only children, John, and with Denis going off now there was no use going on with it. Delia's a nice little girl; she's too good for Denis —

PETER: That's a fact.

AUNT ELLEN: She'll take up with someone who'll be a deal more suitable.

DUFFY: They've been promised to one another for two years; so soon as he'd be a doctor they were to be married, and now in the heel of the hunt he gets a big position in Canada, he spreads his sails and away with him, leaving her behind. Faith, it looks to me as if you thought she wasn't good enough for him. (*Didn't I know he was near his temper.*)

GEORGE: Indeed, John, you're making a mistake. That's not the way with it at all. It's the other way about.

DUFFY: That's the way I look at it, anyway, and that's the way the neighbours will look at it.

GEORGE: Sure, it's not cross about it you are?

DUFFY: Oh no, not at all. There's nothing in the wide world a man likes better than to have his only child trampled on like dirt, to be left fooled, to be made a mock of by the countryside. Cross? What would make me cross? I never felt in a pleasanter temper than I do this minute.

PETER: You're talking strange.

DUFFY: The two of you will hear stranger talk than this before you've finished with the Duffys.

GEORGE: What do you mean?

DUFFY: I mean that Denis marries Delia, or else . . . .

GEORGE: He can't marry her.

AUNT ELLEN: Put that notion out of your mind, Mr Duffy.

DUFFY: Then if he won't marry her, I put the matter into the lawyer's hands tomorrow. £1,000 damages. (*Oh, my God!*)

GEORGE: John!

AUNT ELLEN: Mr Duffy!

PETER: You're raving!

DUFFY: Ay, you·think yourselves great people, don't you? You've a brother who's a gentleman, who is much too high up to get married to a Duffy. It's good enough for Delia to be thrown aside like an old shoe when the fancy takes you. She's not good enough to be brought to Canada, to the fine place there that . . . .

GEORGE: John, wait. I . . . .

DUFFY: But I'll show you you've mistaken your man. As long as Delia has a father by her she'll not be treated that way. I'll show you! The Duffys aren't people to be trampled on so easy. I've power to my back — and money — more money than you have — and, by the same token, I'll see a lump of yours before I'm done with you. I'll have the smartest lawyer in Ireland on my side. I got all Denis's letters off Delia tonight — oh, there's no doubt of my case. I'll beat you to the wall, I'll bleed you, I'll teach you the way to treat a decent, honest, poor girl who never did you a day's harm only demeaned herself mixing with low, sneaking people the like of the Geoghegans. Good night to you.

GEORGE: Stop, for God's sake, Mr Duffy. You don't know what you're talking about.

DUFFY: Faith, I do, only too well.

GEORGE: 'Tisn't true. All that about Canada isn't true.

DUFFY: Isn't he going there?

GEORGE: He is, but not to . . . .

DUFFY: That's enough about it.

(*He's going out, but* GEORGE *is holding him back.*)

GEORGE: Don't go. Look here, I'm telling you the truth now, the same as if you were a magistrate on the bench. He's going to no situation there; he's been kicked out of this because we're tired of paying his bills.

DUFFY: Do you expect me to believe that?

GEORGE: You must believe it. Aunt Ellen, tell him that what I'm saying is true.

AUNT ELLEN: It's true, every word of it. I've no cousins in Canada, my brother died unmarried, Denis will have to work like a labourer in Canada.

PETER: We're turning him out; he's a useless, idle fellow.

AUNT ELLEN: Delia's well rid of him; a burden he'd be to her.

GEORGE: She'll get a man twice as good before the year's out.

PETER: He's a waster.

GEORGE: No sense at all.

PETER: A gambler, betting all day on horses.

AUNT ELLEN: Cards and drink.

GEORGE: He has his mother's heart broken.

PETER: 'Tis a great escape Delia's having.

GEORGE: They'd be in the Union before they'd be a year married.

AUNT ELLEN: He's a disgrace to the family.

DUFFY: Well, what sort of a fool do you take me to be at all? Haven't I two eyes in my head? Don't I know Denis since the day he was born? Isn't he known to be the cleverest, smartest . . .

GEORGE: Not at all.

DUFFY: . . . lad in the countryside. Didn't you tell me yourself the way he swept all before him in the College in Dublin?

GEORGE: 'Tisn't true. Three times he's after failing.

DUFFY: Wasn't he going to be set up there in a big house?

PETER: Not at all.

DUFFY: Wasn't his aunt going to leave him all her money?

AUNT ELLEN: He'll never get a penny from me.

DUFFY: And now you'd like me to turn around and disbelieve it all. Ah, you're clever, but you're not clever enough for me.

GEORGE: You're making a mistake. Tonight things turned up.

DUFFY: They did; I know well they did. Canada turned up, a big position turned up, plans and schemes you made to throw us over. I see your game. Tell me George, is St Paul the name of the place Denis is going to?

GEORGE: No.

(*Look at* DUFFY *turning on the aunt.*)

DUFFY: Didn't I know you were lying, ye old brazen thing, the way I wouldn't be able to trace him to bring him back to marry my daughter. But I don't care a damn where he is going to. You're right, Delia's well quit of him; she's well quit of the whole troop of the Geoghegans — but I want that £1,000 and I'll have it too.

PETER: It's the truth we're telling you, Mr Duffy. The rest was all lies.

DUFFY: I know well it's liars you all are.

(*Here's* DONOUGH; *he's excited-like.*)

DONOUGH: I couldn't go home till I'd congratulated you about Denis. All the people at the concert were talking of it. It's over railways he'll be, I'm told; a sort of railway king.

GEORGE: Oh, my God!

DUFFY: Do you hear that?

DONOUGH: George, my mind's made up; I'm going with him. When he has all that power he'll be able to do something for the man that's going to marry his sister. I'm tired of slaving on here and no nearer marrying Jane than I was five years ago. Now I'll have her out to me before the autumn. What day is he sailing?

AUNT ELLEN: Don't mind what the people are saying, Donough. There's not a word of truth in it all.

DONOUGH: Isn't Denis going to Canada?

AUNT ELLEN: He is, but not....

DONOUGH: Well, then, what's to hinder me going along with him? 'Twill be a queer thing if he doesn't contrive to get me into a good job out there.

GEORGE: He'll do nothing of the sort.

PETER: Put the idea out of your head.

DONOUGH: Why so?

DUFFY: Listen here to me, Donough; I'll tell you the way it is. This family's too high up in themselves for the like of you and me. We're not class enough for them, do you see? The Geoghegans are a great people, the Duffys aren't good enough for them at all. We've been thrown over; Delia's not a fit match for my brave Denis. You'll be the next to go; it couldn't be expected that Jane Geoghegan would marry Donough Brosnan. They have plans of marrying Jane to a lord.

DONOUGH: What's that you say?

GEORGE: Don't mind him, Donough.

DONOUGH: I will mind him.

GEORGE: You can marry Jane tomorrow for all I care. Duffy's mad.

DUFFY: Mad? Take care what you're saying, George Geoghegan. There's a law against slander and abuse as well as against breaking a promise of marriage. Here's my final word to you: Denis marries Delia and takes her with him to Canada.

GEORGE: He can't.

DUFFY: Or he finishes his course in Dublin and marries her when he's a doctor, the very minute he's qualified.

GEORGE: He can't.

DUFFY: Then I bring an action. £1,000 damages. You can take your choice. I'll give you ten minutes to yourselves to talk it over. I've got to go and see Magner for a minute. I'll be back for an answer. Mind, I mean every word I say. The marriage or an action. That's my final word to you, you pack of schemers!

(*He's off — what a slam he gave the door!*)

AUNT ELLEN: He's a terrible man.

GEORGE: That's a nice fix we're in.

PETER: What the divil can we do now?

DONOUGH: I don't understand what it's all about.

GEORGE: We're kicking Denis out to Canada because he's a useless, idle, extravagant fellow, and Duffy has an idea that he's going out to some big place there, and is mad he won't marry Delia.

DONOUGH: Is that the way it is? I never had much belief in Denis.

GEORGE: I wish to God you could get Duffy and the rest to be of the same mind. There's no one in the village will believe the truth.

DONOUGH: Sure, there's nothing harder to believe than the truth.

PETER: But what are we going to do?

GEORGE: Let me think. My head's bursting. What was it Duffy said? Either marry her and take her to Canada, or go through with College; or else the breach of promise . . . . I won't send him back to College; I'd rather have the breach — 'twouldn't cost me more in the end. Maybe Denis might be ten years in Dublin or twenty years missing his examinations and spending money. Oh, where would it all come from? . . . But £1,000 to go to Duffy, or £500 itself — we'd be ruined; we'd never get it back from the shop.

DONOUGH: Yerra, let Duffy bring the case against Denis and bankrupt him. What matter?

GEORGE: Bankrupt him! Do you think I'm the one to stand by and see a Geoghegan broken by a Duffy or anyone else? I'd sooner die in the Union. There's but the one thing for it. Denis must marry her; he must take her with him to Canada.

AUNT ELLEN: He'll do that all right; sure he's mad to marry her.

GEORGE: Call him down here, Peter.

AUNT ELLEN: He's gone to bed I think.

GEORGE: Pull him out of bed, then. This must be settled before Duffy comes back. He'll put the case into the lawyer's hands tomorrow if we don't.

PETER: I'll call him. (*He's gone.*)

AUNT ELLEN: It's a terrible upset we're in.

GEORGE: It was all your fault with your schemes for saving the family's good name. If we'd told the truth from the first, this wouldn't be on us now. (*He's turning on her.*)

AUNT ELLEN: That's a queer thing to say to me, George. Small respect you're showing me.

GEORGE: I don't know what I'm saying.

AUNT ELLEN: It looks like it indeed. Anyway, the truth's a dangerous thing to be saying in a little place like Ballycolman.

DONOUGH: It will be all right. Denis will marry Delia, and there'll be no more about it.

GEORGE: I won't have an easy minute till the pair of them are married and gone. Oh Donough, it's an awful thing to be the head of a family. Since the father died I've not had a minute's rest, pulled this way and that way, this one wanting to get married, another going into business, Baby flying up to Dublin, Denis doctoring — many a time I wished I was born an orphan.

AUNT ELLEN: God forgive you.

GEORGE: It's true, Aunt Ellen. Look at the life I've led between you all, and no one ever thinking maybe I'd want to get married, or have a bit of fun, or spend a bit of money. For two pins I'd throw the lot of ye over tomorrow and sail away out of this for ever.

AUNT ELLEN: Yerra talk sense, George; that's no way to be behaving.

GEORGE: There's no escape for me. I'm caught like an old cow with her head in a stall.

(*Here's* PETER *back with* DENIS. *It was no lie saying he was in bed, look at his striped pyjamas and his elegant dressing gown.*)

DENIS: What do you want me for? Haven't you bothered me enough this evening without hauling me out of bed?

GEORGE: Denis, old Duffy has been here raging mad. He threatens a breach of promise unless you marry Delia. You'll have to do it. You'll have to marry her at once.

DENIS: What? Marry Delia?

GEORGE: Yes, and take her to Canada along with you.

DENIS: Oh!

AUNT ELLEN: I knew you'd be delighted. 'Twas breaking your heart parting from her.

DENIS: And what are we to live on in Canada?

GEORGE: You'll find plenty to live on.

AUNT ELLEN: A man's lost without a woman out there, they say. You'd read on the papers the great scarcity of women there is in Canada.

PETER: That's so; she'll be a great addition to you.

AUNT ELLEN: Father Murphy would marry you tomorrow when he knows the hurry you're in.

DENIS: I see.... Listen here to me. Haven't I agreed to everything you've planned for me all my life through. Tonight I agreed to go to Canada because it's your wish; I agreed to break with Delia. Now you want me to take Delia off to Canada, without a position, without a place to go to, with a few pounds in my pocket that wouldn't keep us for a month. Put the idea out of your head; I'll not do it. There's things I'll submit to myself, but I won't ask Delia to share them.

GEORGE: Do you mean to tell me you don't want to marry Delia? You don't care about her?

DENIS: I do care about her. That's why I won't marry her.

GEORGE: That's crazy talk. You'll do all right in Canada.

PETER: You won't be there a week before you'll have a big position.

DONOUGH: You're sure to do fine.

GEORGE: A clever lad like you will get on fast.

DENIS: You hadn't much opinion of my cleverness an hour ago. I'll have to rough it and take my chance with all the others, and as soon as I've made a place for myself I'll marry Delia; but I'll not ask her to share the roughness and poverty you're sending me out to.

GEORGE: Denis don't turn on us like this.

DENIS: You turned on me bitterly tonight, George. You've kicked me out, you've wrecked my life, you've made me give up Delia.

GEORGE: But I want you to marry her now.

DENIS: And I won't. You know why.

GEORGE: I'd give you a few pounds going to Canada.

DENIS: I won't take them.

GEORGE: If you went back to College —

DENIS: I won't go back to College.

AUNT ELLEN: In the name of God, what do you want?

DENIS: I want to be let make my own life in my own way. I want to be let alone and not bothered. (*He's going towards the door.*)

GEORGE: Where are you off to?

DENIS: To bed, of course — and to Canada.

GEORGE: Will you marry Delia?

DENIS: No. (*And he's gone.*)

DONOUGH: Wait — Denis — (*He's gone after him.*)
(*Poor* GEORGE. *You'd have to pity him.*)

AUNT ELLEN: And Duffy will be here in a minute for his answer.

PETER: Well, it's the breach of promise now, and no mistake.

GEORGE: We're ruined, we're ruined!

AUNT ELLEN: Yerra, not at all. Maybe when the fit of anger passes John Duffy will think better of what he said tonight. But we must stand up to him boldly; don't let on we're afraid of him.

PETER: Maybe he'd come to terms.

GEORGE: I wouldn't demean myself making terms with him. Let him bring us into the courts. I'll face him; I'll not have it said I was afraid of him.

AUNT ELLEN: That's right.

GEORGE: A Geoghegan's as good as a Duffy any day.

AUNT ELLEN: And better.
(*There's a knock.*)
Glory be to God! there he is.

PETER: I suppose I'll have to let him in. 'Twouldn't do to pretend we're all gone to bed.

GEORGE: I'm afraid of no man. Open the door. 'Tis terrible, oh, 'tis terrible! Why did I ever open my lips tonight about Denis?... I'm wondering... I'm wondering, Aunt, if you spoke to Duffy yourself tonight? You used to be good friends long ago, I've heard it said. I... I....

AUNT ELLEN: To be sure I'll speak to him; a woman can often come around a man. Ye only heat him.

GEORGE: I'll have nothing to do with compromises and settlements, and it's no surrender, as they say in Derry, but — but — do your best for me. Whisht! He's coming. I'll be up to speak to the mother.

(*And he slips out one door as* PETER *and* DUFFY *come in the other.*)

DUFFY: Well, ma'am, I'm back. Where has George gone to?

AUNT ELLEN: He slipped up to speak to his mother. Peter, go and look for him.

(*Isn't she cute the way she got rid of* PETER?)

Won't you sit down?

DUFFY: I'd sooner stand. Two minutes will give me my answer, I suppose.

AUNT ELLEN: Take it easy while you have a chance.... John Duffy, you're a clever man; I don't know a cleverer.

DUFFY: I'm obliged for your good opinion, ma'am.

(*How stiff he is.*)

AUNT ELLEN: That story of Denis being good for nothing is true, but it suits you not to believe it, and you're right. I'd do the same in your case.

DUFFY: You would?

AUNT ELLEN: I would so. Oh, I always gave in you were one of the smartest men in the country.... You're looking to getting a deal of money out of this action?

DUFFY: I am.

AUNT ELLEN: I wonder will you. They're queer, chancey, uncertain things, breach of promise cases. Great expense, a troop of lawyers, terrible harrying in the witness-box and maybe twenty pounds at the end of it all, or the case dismissed. And Delia such a nervous little girl, I wonder you'd like to drag her through the courts.

DUFFY: Don't be afraid for Delia, ma'am. A thousand pounds will cover a deal of blushes.

AUNT ELLEN: A thousand pounds! You'll never see the quarter of it, no, nor a hundred pounds. It's the foolish people who go looking for money in a breach of promise case. The wise ones settle it up between themselves — and you were never a foolish man, Mr Duffy.

DUFFY: I'm foolish enough, anyway, not to let my name be trampled in the dirt. It doesn't suit me to have Delia treated as if she wasn't good enough for a Geoghegan.

AUNT ELLEN: 'Tis a pity. She'll hardly get married so. The lads are shy of having anything to say to a girl was in a breach of

promise case — afraid they'd be the next to be hauled up....
What good will that do either of you? A little bit of money
now slipped into your hand without bother or lawyers would
be more value to you. A clever man would settle the whole
thing for fifty pounds.

DUFFY: Would he indeed?

AUNT ELLEN: You know well the Geoghegans are a weak family.
If you got a couple of hundred pounds damages itself, who
knows would you ever be paid? But it doesn't reflect well on
me to have my nephews dragged into Court. Come, Mr Duffy,
if I gave you fifty pounds would you withdraw the case?

DUFFY: I've got my senses still, thank God. Fifty pounds? Keep
it.

AUNT ELLEN: That's not a civil way to be answering me — and
yet we were good friends once — John.

DUFFY: We were.

AUNT ELLEN: I often think of those old days — ah, I suppose
you've forgotten them long ago. But we were good friends.

DUFFY: 'Twasn't my fault we weren't closer than friends.
(*After all, he's sitting down and near her too.*)

AUNT ELLEN: I remember. Those days are gone long ago....
You'd have given me anything I asked then.

DUFFY: I would.

AUNT ELLEN: Do you remember the day you walked twelve
miles to get a red ribbon I'd set my mind on having for the
races?

DUFFY: I do.

AUNT ELLEN: And now I'm offering you fifty pounds, and
you throw it back in my face as if I was an old hen-woman
at a fair.

DUFFY: Fifty pounds is no money at all.

AUNT ELLEN: Sixty, then ... seventy .... Ah, John, you couldn't
refuse me ... for the sake of old times ....

DUFFY: A lot you're talking of old times. Look here, Ellen, are
you in earnest? Do you want the case stopped?

AUNT ELLEN: I do so.

DUFFY: Then there's a way you can do it.

AUNT ELLEN: Tell it to me.

DUFFY: You can do what I asked you to do when we were boy
and girl together.

AUNT ELLEN: Mr Duffy!

DUFFY: Why not? Give me a hundred pounds down, and promise
me you'll marry me before Shrove, and I'll let Denis and the

Geoghegans go to the divil.

AUNT ELLEN: I could never do it.

DUFFY: You were near doing it fifteen years ago, after I buried the wife.

AUNT ELLEN: I've lived my own life always, I'm too old to change. I wanted freedom. I wanted to live like the birds, I wanted to do what I pleased with my own money.

DUFFY: You've had your freedom, and what have you made out of it? Nothing at all. You've run after crazy schemes, goats and the like: your farm is gone to waste; you're getting on in years, soon you'll be an old woman, Ellen, with no one to look after you, only relations craving for your money. You'd better have me, I'll take care of you, I'll look after you, you'll have all the freedom you want. When you were a girl, Ellen, you were too proud to look at me, and I married Honora Reilly to spite you. After she died on me I asked you again, but you wouldn't have me. You're the only woman I ever wanted. You made me mad tonight with your talk of old times. You must marry me, you must! Never will you regret it . . . .

AUNT ELLEN: I couldn't, John. I'm old. I'd like to be free.

DUFFY: Good night, so.

AUNT ELLEN: Why are you going?

DUFFY: What use is there in me staying?

AUNT ELLEN: But what about the case?

DUFFY: I'll see the lawyer in the morning.

AUNT ELLEN: You're a hard man. You always get what you want.

DUFFY: I didn't get the one thing I wanted in all the world.

AUNT ELLEN: If I gave you a hundred pounds without the promise?

DUFFY: 'Twouldn't do me.

AUNT ELLEN: Why do you want to marry me?

DUFFY: Contrariness, I suppose.

(*He's kissed her, glory be to God!*)

AUNT ELLEN: Stop, John! You should be ashamed of yourself.

DUFFY: You'll have me. I see you will.

AUNT ELLEN: You're taking a lot for granted.

DUFFY: I'm taking you, anyway. (*He's kissed her again!*)

AUNT ELLEN: You're a terrible man.

DUFFY: Why the divil didn't you let me do that thirty years ago, when we were boy and girl together? I made an offer at it one time, and you slapped me across the face.

AUNT ELLEN: It's what I'd like to do to you this minute.

DUFFY: You may then. (*Look at him sticking his face out to her.*)

AUNT ELLEN: Get along with you!

DUFFY: Cripes! I'd like to get drunk, I'd like to pull the house down, I'd like to go bawling singing through the streets of Ballycolman!

AUNT ELLEN: I hope you'll do nothing of the kind, a respectable man like you, with a grown daughter and a wife interred.

DUFFY: Don't remind me of her. I'm twenty years old — not a minute more.

AUNT ELLEN: If you keep shouting like that you'll have George down.

DUFFY: Faith, that reminds me.... I'll draw up a paper and you can sign it. (*He's always an eye to business.*)

AUNT ELLEN: What are you asking me to sign?

DUFFY: A promise to pay me a hundred pounds down, and that you'll marry me before Shrove, provided I drop the case against Denis.... Have you your cheque-book handy?

AUNT ELLEN: It's here in my bag.

DUFFY: Make out a cheque so for me for a hundred pounds.

AUNT ELLEN: It's a whip of money.

DUFFY: Sure, it's not going to pass out of the family. I'll spend it on stocking the farm.

AUNT ELLEN: You're a terrible man.... I suppose you must have your way. (*She's writing him a cheque, it must be a fact that she's in love with him.*)

DUFFY: Sign there, now.

(*She's doing that too. He's got the cheque and the paper signed, and into his breast pocket they go.*)

AUNT ELLEN: For the love of goodness don't breathe a word of this to the Geoghegans. They'd have my life for making terms with you. I'll find my own way later of telling them about the marriage.

DUFFY: I'll not open my lips. And it would suit me better if they thought I withdrew the case of my own free will. Isn't it like a story on the pictures, Ellen, the way you and I have come together at the end of all. (*More love-making. Look at his arm round her waist.*)

AUNT ELLEN: Leave go of me; there's someone coming.

(*It's* GEORGE, *and his Aunt's slipped out. She's in a flutter and no wonder.*)

GEORGE: I'm sorry for leaving you so long, Mr Duffy. I was speaking to my mother and that young rascal of a brother of mine. It's no use trying to make him see reason; you might as well be talking to a deaf man.

100

DUFFY: Is that so?

GEORGE: My aunt was speaking to you?

DUFFY: She was.

GEORGE: I hope you're feeling in a more reasonable way?

DUFFY: Oh, I've reason enough on my side.

GEORGE: There's no use expecting Denis to marry Delia; he'll not do it. What we've got to do, Mr Duffy, is to settle our little differences the best way we can.

DUFFY: That's a fact.

GEORGE: I'm glad to see you taking that view. What use is there going into court? Five minutes friendly talk is better than all the lawyers in the Four Courts .... Come, John, we were always good friends — what will you take to drop the case?

DUFFY: To ... ? Five hundred pounds. (*Tch! Tch!*)

GEORGE: I mean in earnest.

DUFFY: I'm speaking in earnest.

GEORGE: I'll give you two hundred.

DUFFY: Put your hand there. There's one condition I make: not a word of this to your family, or anyone. I'd rather have it thought that I withdrew the case myself.

GEORGE: It will suit me, too, to be quiet about this. The family would be mad with me for going behind their backs. My aunt was all for fighting you to the bitter end.

DUFFY: Was she indeed?

GEORGE: Don't mind a word she was saying; she's a cranky old schemer.

DUFFY: Would you believe me telling you she came near striking me tonight?

GEORGE: She did? Don't mind her, John; she didn't mean a word she said.

DUFFY: Faith, there's things she said tonight I'll hold her accountable for .... Tell me, when will you let me have the money?

GEORGE: I'll write a letter to you tonight promising to pay it in six months' time, provided you don't bring up the case. I'll have to look about for the money.

DUFFY: That'll do me. But if I haven't the letter in the morning I'll start with the case.

GEORGE: Oh, you'll have it, never fear.

(*Here's poor* MRS GEOGHEGAN.)

MRS GEOG: Is that Mr Duffy's voice?

DUFFY: Good night to you, ma'am.

MRS GEOG: Is it true what I hear that you're making a set against

101

my poor Denis, that you're going to bring him into the Courts?

DUFFY: That's so.

GEORGE: Don't go into it now, mother. I've been talking it over with Mr Duffy. By tomorrow morning he's likely to see matters in a more reasonable way.

DUFFY: I'm a generous man, ma'am. (*You are!*)

MRS GEOG: I know you are. I'll say no more, only leave it to God and yourself.... Would you oblige me by taking a note down to Delia?

DUFFY: Certainly, ma'am.

GEORGE: What's that, mother?

MRS GEOG: Only a letter of goodbye from my poor Denis. There's a note for yourself, too, Mr Duffy.
(*She's half whispering, she doesn't want* GEORGE *to hear, but he's writing the note to* DUFFY *in the corner of the room.*)

DUFFY: Thank you, ma'am. (*It's a thick letter; he can't help himself from opening it.*)

MRS GEOG: Are you going to bed, George?

GEORGE: I have to write one letter first.
(*Look what* DUFFY's *pulling out of the envelope. Notes! Bank notes . . . !*)

DUFFY: .... May the divil ....

MRS GEOG: What's the matter, Mr Duffy?
(*She's afraid* GEORGE *will notice and her finger's on her lips.*)

DUFFY: Oh, nothing at all, ma'am, nothing at all. I'll be going.

MRS GEOG: I hope business is good by you these times?

DUFFY: Business? Oh, business ma'am is good; never better, never better. Well, be the .... Good night to you both.
(*He's gone. Well, well, such strategy and manoeuvring — such lying as you might call it.*)

CURTAIN

ACT III

The scene is the same but it's morning and BABY *singing at the piano.... Yes, a lovely voice, 'twas the nuns taught her.... What's that she's singing? "Because God Made you Mine", one of them religious songs I suppose. Look at poor* KATE *dusting the room. She's no singer.*

KATE: That's lovely, Baby. You've a great turn for music.

BABY: I have, then. I love them passionate songs. There's some like comics, but give me a song with passion in it. It goes through me like. I suppose I'm queer.

KATE: Why wouldn't you like them? Myself, I could never tell one tune from another, but I'd listen to you all day.

BABY: Whisper here, Kate. I had a letter from Maggie Clancy this morning, from Dublin. She wants me to go up to her before Christmas.

KATE: And will you?

BABY: I will so. Then I'll be able to start at the classes the very minute Christmas is over.

KATE: Where'll you get the money?

BABY: George got twenty pound for sheep yesterday; the money's upstairs. He's promised it to me; and maybe I could coax a few pounds out of mother.

KATE: I suppose you're longing to be off.

BABY: God knows there's wings in my heart to be gone out of this. I could never stay on here the way you did, never seeing a bit of life or having a chance.... Are you sorry you didn't get married that time?

KATE: Oh, Babe, often I lie awake thinking of it. Not that we were such friends; twice only I saw him; but he was a big, powerful, hairy man, and to have a place of my own and not to be depending always on other people — even though they're your own family.

BABY: I know, I know; 'tis hard on you. Maybe you'll get a chance of marrying again.

KATE: Yerra, no; I'm too old. Ah, where's the use in talking of it? (*Here's the mother.*)

103

MRS GEOG: Have either of you seen Denis?

BABY: We didn't.

KATE: I gave him a bit of breakfast very early — 'twasn't more than half-seven, I think, and he went out and I didn't lay eyes on him since.

MRS GEOG: And now it's close on twelve o'clock! Oh, Kate, do you think is there anything after happening to him?

KATE: Yerra, what would happen to him?

MRS GEOG: What mightn't happen after all the work there was last night? Shipped off to Canada, parted from the girl he loves, many a man has thrown himself into the river for less.

KATE: Ah, not at all.

BABY: There was a grand song I used to sing one time about a girl drowned herself for love, but I never had a song about a man destroying himself for a girl. Anyway, Denis is the sort takes good care of himself. You needn't fret about him.

MRS GEOG: God grant you're right. But all the same I wish you'd walk up street and see is there e'er a sign of him.

BABY: I might do that. Listen here, mother. I'm off to Dublin in a day or two.

MRS GEOG: You are?

BABY: I'll want clothes and the like, going to Dublin. I suppose you won't grudge giving me a bit of money?

MRS GEOG: Money? Where would I get money?

KATE: Sure, the child would want a couple of pounds anyway.

BABY: There's no need to be saving it for Denis any longer.

MRS GEOG: I see what's in your mind the same as if I was sitting inside you. You've grudged Denis every penny he ever got. The poor boy, he's no friend in the world but myself. Maybe he's lying cold and dead now by reason of the way he's been treated in this house by his own flesh and blood, but that's nothing at all to you so long as you can skeet out of this to Dublin. All his life it's been the same story: hindered at every turn, denied any little thing he had set his heart on, and for all that the cleverest of you all. I haven't got any money, and if I had it isn't to you I'd give it.

(*And with that she's gone.*)

BABY: If I wasn't so cross I'd want to laugh at the notion of us denying Denis anything!

KATE: Well, we all treated him hardly enough last night.

BABY: I believe you're soft on him still. I believe we all are in our hearts, only we daren't let on.

(*Here's* GEORGE.)

GEORGE: Are you there, Baby? Did you take the money?

BABY: I did not. Where is it?

GEORGE: In my box. At least it was; it's not there now.

BABY: Do you mean it's stolen?

GEORGE: Ah, who'd steal it? I must have put it in some other place. But it's queer. I'm certain it was there I put it. I'll have another look.

(*He's gone again. Aren't they a worry to him the whole flock of them?*)

BABY: 'Twould be a nice thing if, after all, the money was gone.

KATE: George brought it down to the shop maybe.

(JANE's *coming in now, and a paper in her hand.*)

JANE: You're after vexing the mother with your talk of going to Dublin.

BABY: Why should it vex her? She was wild for Denis to go, and now she's mad with me for following his example.

JANE: Of course, a boy is different.... You've your mind made up?

BABY: I'm off a Monday, if I can get the money.

JANE: Monday. I wish you'd wait and see me married. I ran across to Peg Turpin's this morning for a minute. She lent me this. Look here, it's full of the queerest, grandest things ever you saw.

BABY: Is it Weldon's you have?

JANE: No. A better paper — "Vogue". Peg's sister sent it her from Dublin.

(*Tch, tch! Look at them all round it like wasps round a jam-pot.*) What would you think of that one?

BABY: To be married in?

JANE: Yes.

KATE: Wouldn't you feel ashamed-like walking up the chapel in it?

JANE: I would not.

BABY: It's elegant, elegant! That now with tan shoes and white gloves — only I don't like the hat. 'Tis too quiet for a wedding. You should have something flashier — a big feather, or one of them scarlet seagulls.

KATE: For God's sake look over the page.

BABY: Well, of all the...!

JANE: It's extraordinary the things they put in those fashion papers.

KATE: I'd drop dead if I had that on me.

BABY: It's not so outlandish when you've looked at it for a while.

"This simple, girlish frock" — that's what's written under it. It should suit me, so. Would you fancy me in it?

KATE: You'd look lovely in anything, Babe. But I'd be in dread Father Murphy would speak of it from the altar if you paraded Ballycolman in that rig-out.

BABY: Do you think I'd waste it on Ballycolman? It's in Dublin I'd wear it.

JANE: There's a blouse below at Peg's I've set my heart on. 'Tis lace from here to here, stripes of green velvet, gold buttons — oh, 'tis gorgeous!

(*Here's* AUNT ELLEN.)

AUNT ELLEN: Is there no sign of Denis?

JANE: He's not been here, I hope to goodness nothing's happened to him.

BABY: You're as bad as mother. She has him killed and buried . . . . Look, Aunt, what would you think of me in that?

AUNT ELLEN: Show . . . . Wisha, Babe, you'd never disgrace us going about like that!

BABY: It's elegant. And Jane has a lovely one here picked for her wedding.

AUNT ELLEN: Are there wedding dresses there? Show me.

BABY: I believe Aunt Ellen is thinking of getting married!

(*Listen to them all laughing.*)

AUNT ELLEN: How smart you are! . . . What about that one, girls? Supposing — supposing I was getting married.

BABY: Sure, that's an opera cloak, Aunt.

(*Look at* DUFFY *coming in. He's looking pleased with himself.*)

DUFFY: Good morning to you.

BABY: ⎫
JANE: ⎬ Good morning, Mr Duffy.
KATE: ⎭

DUFFY: Good morning, Ellen. I hope you're good.

AUNT ELLEN: I am, thank you.

DUFFY: Were you thinking over what I said to you last night?

AUNT ELLEN: To tell you the truth, I never thought of it since.

(*God forgive her!*)

DUFFY: You didn't?

AUNT ELLEN: Never once.

BABY: Her mind's full of the one thing only at the present minute, Mr Duffy — dresses, wedding dresses, no less. It's my belief she's going to get married on the sly.

AUNT ELLEN: Hold your tongue.

DUFFY: Wedding dresses? Is that what you're at? Oh, that's all right.... However, I didn't come here to talk the fashions; I wanted to see George for a minute.

KATE: He's above. I'll call him.

JANE: Come on across to Peg's, Babe, till you see the blouse I was telling you about.

(*The three of them are off with themselves. They'll spend the rest of the morning talking fashions at Peg's.*)

DUFFY: So you've fixed on the dress already?

AUNT ELLEN: I haven't. But if I've got to be married, I may as well be married decently.

DUFFY: Oh, never fear, we'll make a smart thing of it.... Do you know, Ellen, Easter's terrible late this year.

AUNT ELLEN: Is it? But what matter? I always think it's nicer late.

DUFFY: But a late Easter makes a late Shrove. I looked at the calendar before I slept last night. Holy Star, I could hardly believe my eyes. I don't think there was ever such a late Easter in the memory of man.

AUNT ELLEN: What matter?

DUFFY: Christmas, I'd have said if I'd known; and I think Christmas it must be, Ellen.

AUNT ELLEN: What? Marry you before Christmas? I'll do no such thing.

DUFFY: I can't wait. You must.

AUNT ELLEN: I tell you, you must wait.

DUFFY: Peg will make you a dress in a week.... If you won't, I'll have to tell George about the bargain you made.

AUNT ELLEN: You wouldn't do such a thing after you promising.

DUFFY: A man in love you know....

(*Here's* GEORGE *and the mother.*)

MRS GEOG: Mr Duffy, did you see Denis?

DUFFY: I didn't. He wasn't over at my place. Delia's in bed, sick.

MRS GEOG: The creature!... I hope, Mr Duffy, you've come up to tell us you've changed your mind about the breach of promise? I'm sure you couldn't wish to be hard on us, old friends as we are.

GEORGE: To be sure, Mr Duffy will be reasonable.

AUNT ELLEN: You're all talking as if the man was something terrible.

DUFFY: Well, I've been thinking things over.... I've a strong case to go on, there's no one can say I haven't. I've justice on my side, my good name to keep up, the honour of my poor mother-less girl, and — and all that. But, after all, quarrelling among neighbours is a bad thing. Your poor father, George, was a good friend of mine, and for his sake, and because it's Delia's wish, and because I'm a peaceable Christian man, I'm going to withdraw the case.

MRS GEOG: The blessing of God on you for that word!

GEORGE: Thank you, John.

DUFFY: Mind you, it's a great loss to me. I'm letting a deal of money go from me, and I suppose there'll be people who'll say behind my back — aye, and up to my puss, maybe — that the Geoghegans bested the Duffys. But I don't care. I'll bear all that for the sake of the goodwill I have for the family.

MRS GEOG: You won't be without your reward.

GEORGE: Shake hands, John. You've spoken like a man.

MRS GEOG: If ever I wronged you in my thoughts, Mr Duffy, may God forgive me and reward you as you deserve.

DUFFY: I'm looking for nothing ma'am. I'm glad I was able to do this for you. And now I must be going back to the Post Office. The Inspector might be here this morning.

GEORGE: Wouldn't you have something before you go?

DUFFY: No, thank you, George. Seldom I touch anything.

GEORGE: Ah, a small drop . . . . Come, John?

DUFFY: Well, just a mouthful.

GEORGE: A drop for you, Aunt?

AUNT ELLEN: No, thank you, George.

GEORGE: You're like myself; you touch nothing. You'll have some, mother?

MRS GEOG: A small drop — for Mr Duffy's sake. Here's long life to you, Mr Duffy.

DUFFY: Well, here's luck to . . . .

(*It would make you thirsty to watch them. Would we have time to slip out for a — Whisht! Here's* DENIS *and* DELIA.)

MRS GEOG: Denis! Where were you? I thought you were gone from us.

DENIS: Not at all. You don't get rid of me quite as easily as that. Good morning, Mr Duffy.

DUFFY: Morning.

MRS GEOG: Sit down, Delia. Would you take a glass of wine?

DELIA: No, thank you, Mrs Geoghegan.

DENIS: You might as well. Drink success to me in Canada, and all that sort of thing.

DELIA: Oh, I'll do that.

(*They're all trying to make up to her.*)

MRS GEOG: Don't fret over this, alanna. It will come all right in the end, I'm sure. Maybe in a year or two Denis will be able to come back and marry you.

DUFFY: I thought you were sick.

DELIA: I'm better.

DUFFY: You look it.

DELIA: You seem sorry.

DUFFY: You'd better come along home now. The Inspector's likely to come this morning, and 'tis you know about them postal orders that went astray on us.

DELIA: I'll come in a minute.

MRS GEOG: She wants to see a little of Denis before he goes, small blame to her.

DUFFY: Ay, he'll have other things to do in future besides love-making.

DELIA: Indeed, yes. I suppose, Denis, our love-making has come to an end?

DUFFY: That's a sensible girl. I thought maybe you'd be for not giving him up.

GEORGE: I'm sorry, Delia, we had to come between the two of you, but there was nothing else for it.

DELIA: I'm sure you only did what was right, George.

DENIS: As a matter of fact, I haven't given Delia up.

DUFFY: But you must.

GEORGE: You can't get married, you know.

AUNT ELLEN: You're off to Canada tomorrow.

DENIS: Yes, yes, I know all that. George, I've been thinking things over. What you said last night was true. I've been a bad brother to you, it's right for you to turn me out. The only thing that makes me unhappy is the case that Mr Duffy threatens against us.

GEORGE: That needn't bother you.

DENIS: It does. It's likely to draw a lot of money out of you.

GEORGE: Hush! Listen here....

DENIS: All my life through I've sacrificed myself to you; I've done all you wished me to; I'll go through with it to the end. Forgive me for what I said last night. I've seen I was wrong. I wrote another letter to Delia last night; I saw her early this morning, and we talked the matter over. Don't let the weight of the breach of promise be on your mind a minute longer. Mr Duffy will never bring it.

DUFFY: How do you know I won't, young man?

DENIS: Because, Mr Duffy, Delia and I were married half an hour ago.

(*Well, glory be to God!*)

DUFFY: Ye...? It's a lie.

DENIS: I beg your pardon; it's true.

DUFFY: You couldn't be married so smart.

DENIS: Father Murphy had heard the story of my going to Canada, and he was quite ready to marry me. I'm so glad, George, I've done what you've wished me to do.... Excuse me for a few minutes.

(*He's gone out. Where's he gone to?*)

DUFFY: How dare you — how dare you!

(*He's in a temper. No wonder.*)

DELIA: Father!

DUFFY: Ruining me — ruining me, that's what you'd like to be doing. Hadn't I my fortune made? Wasn't I settled for life? Look at here! A letter from George giving me two hundred pounds provided I don't go on with the case.

MRS GEOG: George!

AUNT ELLEN: George, how could you!

GEORGE: I didn't, I didn't!

DUFFY: Look at here again — twenty pounds in notes from Mrs Geoghegan to let the case drop, to put nothing in the way of the two of you.

GEORGE: That's the twenty pounds I missed this morning. Give them here; they're mine.

AUNT ELLEN: Ann, I'm surprised at you!

DUFFY: And look at this. A hundred pounds from Aunt Ellen and a promise to marry me before Shrove. And now I suppose it's no better than waste paper.

MRS GEOG: Ellen, I'm amazed at you, thinking of getting married at your age!

GEORGE: Aunt Ellen, after what you said!

DELIA: Quiet yourself, father.

DUFFY: 'Tis easy to say, "Quiet yourself!" I never thought you'd turn on me like that, Delia — the only child I ever had!

DELIA: Sure, it's pleasing you I thought we'd be. Last night you were fit to be tied at the notion of my not getting married.

DUFFY: I thought he had spirit enough to throw you over. But the Geoghegans are a mean-spirited lot; they haven't even the courage to jilt a girl.

AUNT ELLEN: Well, thank God, I'm free of my promise and have courage enough to jilt you, Mr Duffy.

(*There's a stab!*)

DUFFY: Do you hear what she says, Delia? That's your doing....

I've your hundred pounds, anyway, and I'll not give it up, not if you bring me into a court of law. And I've your twenty pounds in notes, ma'am; I'll not part with them.

GEORGE: They're not hers; they're mine.

DUFFY: Faith, they're mine now.

GEORGE: For Baby they were meant. Do you know, mother, I could have you put in jail for a thief?

MRS GEOG: And what about the two hundred pounds you squandered unknown to any of us?

GEORGE: And you, Aunt Ellen, after all you said about putting a bold face on it, no surrender, and the like....

MRS GEOG: Yes, indeed, you were very brazen, engaging yourself to be married like that!

GEORGE: Look here, Mr Duffy, give me back that letter I wrote to you.

DUFFY: I will not.

AUNT ELLEN: Give me back my cheque.

MRS GEOG: I'd be thankful for that twenty pounds.

DUFFY: There's been trickery and underhand dealing here. I'm not inclined to part with these in a hurry.

GEORGE: Trickery? Underhand dealing? You're a nice one to talk of trickery when you had us all tricked up to the eyes last night, and making me promise not to say a word of it to anyone! And I suppose you had Aunt Ellen bound the same way. And mother robbing me, and Aunt Ellen betraying me behind my back — Is it thieves and traitors I'm dealing with?

AUNT ELLEN: And what about yourself, George?

DELIA: Look here, all of you, what's the use going on like this, scolding and attacking each other? Too smart you've been all trying to be, and Denis and I have shown you up. Can't you make peace now? Can't you....

DUFFY: Will you hold your tongue, girl! Enough trouble you've made already. One certain thing is — after this morning's work I'm done with you — done with you. You can leave the house today; not a shilling will you ever get from me.

GEORGE: And I say the same about Denis. We're quit of him now for ever. I tell you it's very soon, Delia, you'll repent of the deceitful way you acted today.

DELIA: You can spare your words, George, and you, too, father. Denis and I aren't asking help from any of you. We can get on very well without you. Denis has got work; he can support his wife, and no thanks to any of you.

DUFFY: Is he after getting an appointment?

MRS GEOG: I knew something good would turn up for him.

GEORGE: What is it, Delia?

DELIA: Here he is himself; he'll tell you.

(*In the name of goodness will you look at him! 'Tis overalls he has on him and trousers with a string and a muffler round his neck and an old greasy cap. What at all can have happened?*)

MRS GEOG: For goodness sake! Denis!

AUNT ELLEN: Where in God's name did you get the clothes?

DENIS: Larry Hogan lent me them.

DELIA: I've been telling them, Denis, that you've got work. Tell them what it is.

DENIS: I haven't much time. I want a bite of something before I go. (*He's looking at his wrist watch.*) I'm due in ten minutes. By the way, you might keep this watch, Delia; it's hardly suitable to my employment.

(*He gives it to her.*)

GEORGE: Where are you going?

DENIS: Oh, not far; don't fret, George; not as far as Canada; not farther, in fact, than a hundred yards from the shop door.

GEORGE: What do you mean?

DENIS: Well, as we came up the street from the chapel after being married, one of the men working on the road where the steam-roller is was taken ill. I saw he was pretty bad and ordered him off to hospital. The foreman was cursing at being left short-handed; I offered myself in the sick man's place. I'm to go down there after dinner hour at one o'clock . . . .

(*What the —!*)

Delia is going to see if we can get two rooms in one of Nolan's cottages. I'll send up for my clothes this evening. You'll be glad to see me starting to work at last, George.

GEORGE: You're — you're mad.

DUFFY: You'll be working on the street?

DENIS: Yes, on the street. I hope in a day or two we'll have worked up as far as the Post Office, Mr Duffy.

DUFFY: Oh, my God!

MRS GEOG: Denis, Denis, you mustn't do it! George, speak to him, speak to him!

GEORGE: Denis boy, don't do it. Hard as we were on you, we wouldn't like to drive you to that.

DENIS: My dear old chap, don't worry about me. I assure you, I don't mind. Ballycolman or Canada, it's all the same to me. In fact I prefer Ballycolman. I like being amongst friends.

GEORGE: Friends! Think what everyone will say of you, and what sort of a name will they put on us to say we drove you out on the road!

DENIS: Oh, let them say what they like. Mother, give me a bit of bread and a drink of milk. I must be off, or I'll lose my job. And you might put some tea in a can.

MRS GEOG: I'll not. You to be working, Denis! It's a disgrace we'd never get over.

DUFFY: Delia, speak to him; make him hear reason.

DELIA: Why should I? You told me straight a minute ago we needn't look to you for help. We've got to live. Do you think Nolan's have a room?

DUFFY: Delia, Delia, do you want to break my heart? A Duffy to be in one of Nolan's little houses! Look at here — let the two of you come and live with me.
(*He's almost crying.*)

GEORGE: Come and live here.

AUNT ELLEN: Come and live out at my place.

DENIS: No, thanks. I want to be independent. I want to be working.

GEORGE: We'd get you something decent to do.

DUFFY: A job will turn up for you. Amn't I Chairman of the District Council? I'm sure you know enough doctoring to be a tuberculosis officer... or....

DENIS: No, I don't.

GEORGE: Think of something, Aunt Ellen. You were always a woman for schemes.

AUNT ELLEN: Denis, I always favoured you; you were always my pet. Come out to Kilmurray; manage the shop there. It's a hundred and fifty a year in your pocket, and I'll leave you the farm when I die.

DUFFY: Do, Denis!

MRS GEOG: Do, like a good boy.

GEORGE: For the mother's sake.

AUNT ELLEN: Don't be pussy with us, Denis.
(*Look at him smiling and shaking his head.*)

DUFFY: Look at here: I'll give you this if you will. There's twenty pounds.

DENIS: Keep it, Mr Duffy.

DUFFY: Here's your aunt's cheque for £100 — 'tis endorsed and all.

AUNT ELLEN: Take it, Denis, take it.

DUFFY: George, will you give him that £200?

GEORGE: I will. Anything to save us from this.

113

DENIS: I don't want it.

DUFFY: Then what in the earthly world will tempt you?

DENIS: I only want to be able to do what I like with my own life — to be free.

DUFFY: Free?... Bedad, isn't he like old Ireland asking for freedom, and we're like the fools of Englishmen offering him every bloody thing except the one thing?... Do Denis, do like a darling boy, go out to Kilmurray and manage the shop.

DENIS: I don't know that much about shopkeeping.

GEORGE: Yerra, that's the best reason you could have for going. Sure, 'tisn't a real shop, only one of them co-operatives. The sooner it bursts the better.

DENIS: You'd like to force me to do this just the way you forced me to do everything else — to go to Dublin, to go to Canada, to give up Delia. Will I never be free from you?... If I go — but mind you, I don't say I will — Delia will have to look after the shop. I won't.

DUFFY: Now, Delia, be a good girl; say you will.

DELIA: Denis, we're beaten; we'll have to go, we'll have to give in to them. But don't fret yourself; I'll look after the shop; you'll never be asked to do a hand's turn in it.

GEORGE: God bless you, Delia.

DELIA: Listen here, George. Don't flatter yourself that shop's going to fail. It's not. It's going to best you all — you can make up your mind to that.

GEORGE: Begob, I wouldn't wonder if it would, with you at the head of it.

DUFFY: Isn't she a Duffy?

DELIA: There's not one of you here have ever understood Denis. He's been straitened and denied all his life through, but I'm going to give him what he wants now.

DENIS: Do you think Kilmurray is what I want?

DELIA: An easy life, no responsibility, money in your pocket, something to grumble at — What more do you want?

AUNT ELLEN: Maybe we'll get you something better later on, Denis. And anyway you'll have the farm when I die.

DUFFY: Ellen Geoghegan, what sort is the farm likely to be the day you die, and you treating it the way you do? Listen here: isn't it your sacred and solemn duty to those two helpless young creatures to take care you leave it to them in good condition?

(*That's right.*)

AUNT ELLEN: Maybe so.

DUFFY: To do that you've got to marry me.

AUNT ELLEN: I'm free of my promise; I'd rather keep free.

DUFFY: You daren't. Not with the responsibility that's on you now. Suppose you squandered the farm?

AUNT ELLEN: You frighten me! I suppose, for Denis's sake, I'll have to have you so.

DUFFY: That's the woman! And maybe in the end of all you won't get the farm, Denis, my boy.

AUNT ELLEN: What are you saying?

DUFFY: What's to hinder us having a son of our own?

AUNT ELLEN: Mr Duffy, I'm surprised at you. I didn't think you could be so coarse.

(... *Yes, she does have a very delicate mind.*)

DUFFY: I'm sorry, Ellen; I'm sorry. Still you never know what mightn't happen.

MRS GEOG: Ellen, if that day ever comes to you — and I pray that it will, — take my advice, go up to Dublin and see Sir Denis. He's an old man, but he's hearty yet, I'm told, and ....

DUFFY: No, no, ma'am. One whiteheaded boy is as much as this family can support. We're not going to rear another.

MRS GEOG: Well, thank God, everything's well settled. I'm dying to tell the others; they'll be delighted.

GEORGE: Begob, I clean forgot them!

AUNT ELLEN: Peter will have to stay on here.

GEORGE: Jane can't get married.

AUNT ELLEN: Baby can't go to Dublin.

GEORGE: How is it we all forgot them?

AUNT ELLEN: Thinking all the time of Denis we were.

GEORGE: What in hell are we to do? ... There's a noise in the street .... It's them coming .... What are we to say to them? They'll have my life.

MRS GEOG: Quiet yourself, George. They'll be all delighted when they hear the way Denis is settled for life. I'll talk to them. Leave it to me.

GEORGE: Faith, I'll do that with a heart and a half. I'll see you later, John.

(*He's glad to go.*)

MRS GEOG: Don't take it hardly, Denis. There are worse things than a shop and a farm and £320 in your hand, and when all's said and done it's better than working on the roads.

DENIS: I'm not going to grumble, mother, where's the use? I've always had to do what you all made me do, and I suppose I may as well go on with it. I can't fight you all ....

MRS GEOG: That's my brave darling boy. (*There's kissing!*) Oh, Delia, take care of him; he's not strong at all.

DELIA: I'll look after him. Give me the money, Denis, I'm going to put it in the bank. George must make me out a promissory note. While I'm at the bank, Denis, change your clothes. This afternoon we'll drive out to Kilmurray. I want to look at the shop.

(*That's the girl will manage him.* GEORGE *is sticking his head in the door.*)

GEORGE: They're coming!

MRS GEOG: I'm ready for them.

(*Here's* KATE, JANE, BABY, DONOUGH *and* PETER, *all in together in great excitement; they all talking together.*)

ALL: What's this we're after hearing — that Denis and Delia have got married?

BABY: Is this a fact?

MRS GEOG: It's quite true, thanks be to God, Denis is married, he's going out to Kilmurray to manage the shop, we're after giving him £300 and more.

ALL: What? What's that you say?

MRS GEOG: I knew you'd all be delighted.

ALL: Delighted!

BABY: I suppose this means I can't go to Dublin?

MRS GEOG: Not at all, you'll go — some day — never fear.

BABY: Some day!

JANE: Does this mean I can't marry Donough?

MRS GEOG: Not at all. You'll marry him — some day.

PETER: And what about me?

MRS GEOG: You'll be all right — some day.

ALL: Well, I think it's a shame.

MRS GEOG: Shame? Think shame to yourselves! What sort of unnatural children have I got at all? Would you grudge your brother the one little bit of luck he's had in all his life? Look at him sitting there with the girl he loves and he after marrying her and not one of you would as much as wish him joy.

JANE: I'm sure, Denis, I have nothing against you. I hope you'll be happy only —

BABY: May you be happy — some day!

PETER: Good luck to you.

AUNT ELLEN: Girls, look here, I've a plan in my mind for you all. After I'm married —

ALL: After you're what?

(*They think she's mad.*)

DUFFY: After we're married.

BABY: That's the boldest plan she ever made. After you're married? Wisha, God help you, John Duffy.
(*And she's right.*)

CURTAIN

CRABBED YOUTH AND AGE

A little comedy

To
Sarah Purser
Her friends will know why

CHARACTERS

MRS SWAN, a widow
MINNIE SWAN ⎫
EILEEN SWAN ⎬ her daughters
DOLLY SWAN ⎭
GERALD BOOTH
CHARLIE DUNCAN
TOMMY MIMS

The first performance of this play was given at the Abbey Theatre, Dublin, on November 14th, 1922, with the following cast:

Mrs Swan	HELENA MOLONEY
Minnie	CHRISTINE HAYDEN
Eileen	MAY CRAIG
Dolly	EILEEN CROWE
Gerald Booth	GABRIEL J. FALLON
Charlie Duncan	P.J. CAROLAN
Tommy Mims	TONY QUINN

The Play was produced by the Author.

Time: Last Sunday night. [Early 1950s — Editor.]

The scene is a comfortably furnished sitting-room; there are easy chairs, a couch, a bright fire, a piano and a good deal of bright electric light.

There are two doors in the room, one of which leads to the dining-room. This door is ajar and the sound of a table being cleared can be heard, punctuated by talk and laughter; in this talk and laughter a woman's voice is predominant.

In the sitting-room sit the three Miss SWANs *and Mr* GERALD BOOTH, *a good-looking young man, not quite ordinarily dressed; there is a touch of something artistic about him; he might possibly write poetry. The Miss* SWANs *are in the attitude of listening to him with great attention.*

MINNIE: (*the eldest* SWAN) Yes, Mr Booth, go on. What happened next?

GERALD: (*continuing the narrative*) Well, then at the beginning of the second act there is a beautiful scene between the Queen and the Pretender, and Rudolf comes in all dressed in dark crimson and —
   (*There is a burst of laughter from the next room; he stops.*)

MINNIE: (*encouragingly*) Yes, Mr Booth? Do go on.

EILEEN: (*the second* SWAN) It's so interesting, it's fascinating. Isn't it, Dolly?

DOLLY: (*the youngest*) Ripping.

GERALD: Where was I?

MINNIE: Rudolf had just come in.

GERALD: Oh, yes. Well, he starts to tell all about the plot against the King and —

MINNIE: Against the *King*?

DOLLY: I thought it was against the Queen and What's-his-name.

GERALD: Of course; I mean against the Queen, and she and the Pretender . . . and the Queen . . . and Rudolf . . . and . . . and . . . .
   (*He tails off. His thoughts are evidently with the people in the next room.*)

MINNIE: Yes? Yes?

GERALD: Where was I?

MINNIE: (*tartly*) Dolly, do go and shut that door. We positively can't hear ourselves speak.

(DOLLY *gets up.*)

GERALD: (*rising*) Allow me.

MINNIE: No, no, please go on with the story. I want to know what happened next. Shut — that — door, Dolly.

(DOLLY *does so.*)

GERALD: I should really be giving your mother a hand to clear the table.

MINNIE: She has Charlie and Mr Mims to help her. I should think the three of them could manage.

(*Even through the closed door a burst of laughter is heard.*)

GERALD: Isn't she wonderful? I don't know anyone like her.

DOLLY: (*coming back to her seat*) I'm supposed to be quite like her.

GERALD: Oh yes, of course, but —

MINNIE: There's a slight difference in age, you mean?

GERALD: No really, I don't. I never think of your mother's age. I suppose she is middle-aged but she doesn't seem to be — not that she has the mind of a girl — what I like is her kind wisdom and then her delicious sense of humour. (*A burst of laughter is heard.*) Listen to that! No girl could laugh like that.

MINNIE: (*swallowing something*) Couldn't she?

GERALD: I think I ought to send those chaps in here. I don't know what they're up to; they can't be all this time clearing away.

MINNIE: Oh, let them alone. They'll all be back presently. Do go on telling us about the play. It must have been too wonderful.

GERALD: All right. Where was I?

MINNIE: You were — where was he, Dolly?

DOLLY: Second act.

EILEEN: And there had been a beautiful scene between the Queen and her lover and then — then it seemed rather mixed.

GERALD: (*laughing*) Yes, I'm afraid it was. (*Rising*) Look here, we'll get Mrs Swan to tell you the rest when she comes back; I get things mixed but she'll remember exactly and make it a thousand times more vivid and interesting than I can. Shall I make her come back now?

MINNIE: Oh, please —

GERALD: The others can finish washing up.

(*He is gone. His entrance into the next room is greeted with a shout of welcome. There is a moment's pause, the three Miss*

SWANs *look at each other, then* MINNIE *gets up and shuts the door into the dining-room with decision.*)

MINNIE: I'm simply not going to stand it any longer.

EILEEN: We can't do anything.

MINNIE: Yes, we can. Don't be ridiculous, Eileen. It's absurd for three healthy, grown-up women to sit round helplessly while this sort of thing goes on. It must be put a stop to.

DOLLY: Hear, hear. But how?

MINNIE: By a little plain speaking.

EILEEN: Oh, no, no. I hate plain speaking.

MINNIE: There's a time when it is necessary. It's necessary now. Mother has simply got to behave herself.

EILEEN: You talk as if she was something — something dreadful.

MINNIE: Well, isn't she? Here we are, Sunday night, three young men to supper, nice food, fire, piano, comfortable chairs, three young women. Puzzle: find the young men. Answer: in the kitchen with mother. *(Man's woman)*

DOLLY: Washing up.

MINNIE: Is that right, is it fair, is it decent?

EILEEN: I don't think *you're* decent. Talking of young men like that. It's — it's quite vulgar.

MINNIE: I'm not a bit ashamed of myself. Surely we sisters can talk out straight to each other. It's not that we're in love with these particular men — I loathe Tommy Mims — but the same thing happens no matter who comes. Some day someone will come to the house whom we do love, I mean someone will come whom one of us might love if we were given a chance, but we'll never get to know him, he'll never get to know us. He'll be so busy listening to mother, helping mother, adoring mother, that he'll never notice that mother has three daughters.

DOLLY: Yes, it's simply rotten.

EILEEN: I believe that when the right man comes he won't notice mother at all: he'll have eyes and ears only for you, or for Dolly, or — for me.

MINNIE: Don't you flatter yourself, my dear. Mother gets 'em every time at the first shot.

EILEEN: *(pained)* Oh, you *are* vulgar.

DOLLY: Give her her due, I don't believe mother means to monopolise them; after all, she *is* attractive. She's nicer than any man I ever met.

MINNIE: But do we ever meet any men? We see them in the distance with mother, that's all. I'm tired of looking at men through a telescope.

123

EILEEN: Ah, wait till the right man comes —

MINNIE: Oh, love at first sight and all that sort of thing! I know. But I'm not going to trust to that. It's too chancy. Besides, it's not simply that I want to get married. I want to get to know some men, I want to have some men friends. No, my mind is made up. I'm going to have it out with mother now, this very minute. (*She goes to the door and listens.*) I don't hear them ... they must have gone to the kitchen. Ah, they're coming back to the dining-room. (*She opens the door.*) Mother! (*There is a sound of voices and laughter from the dining-room.*) Mother!

MRS SWAN: (*off*) Yes, Minnie?

MINNIE: We want you for a minute, can you come?

EILEEN: Oh, not *we*.

MRS SWAN: (*off*) Yes, dear, certainly.

MINNIE: (*at the door*) No, Charlie, I don't want you ... nor you, Tommy, just mother by herself for a minute. You can go on and wash up.

(MRS SWAN *comes in, a pleasant-looking middle-aged woman simply dressed.*)

MRS SWAN: What is it Minnie? Why did you interrupt us? Charles was just telling me such an amusing story. I've never known him in better form.

MINNIE: I expect so.... We want to talk to you very seriously.

MRS SWAN: What is the matter? Has anything dreadful happened?

MINNIE: Nothing more dreadful than usual. Sit here. (MRS SWAN *sits down.*) Now, mother, will you please to look at us?

MRS SWAN: Look at you?... Well, you all look very pretty.

MINNIE: Here we are — your three daughters. I'm nearly thirty, Eileen is twenty-six, Dolly is twenty-four. Don't you think it is time some of us got married?

MRS SWAN: Yes, I do hope you'll all marry. When the right man comes along you —

EILEEN: That's what *I* say.

MINNIE: All kinds of young men come along and how are we to know — how is *he* to know — that he's the right one?

MRS SWAN: Well, I suppose.... I really don't quite know what you mean, Minnie.

MINNIE: (*dramatically*) Where are tonight's young men?

MRS SWAN: That's like the beginning of a song. (*She sings softly:*)
    "Where are the boys of the village tonight?
    Where are tonight's young men?"

MINNIE: Well, where are they?

MRS SWAN: Washing up, I hope.

MINNIE: And how are we to know whether the right man is washing up.

MRS SWAN: All men are right when they are washing up. But, seriously, they were so kind, they know that Ellen is out and they wouldn't allow me to wash up by myself. They'll be back here in a few minutes.

MINNIE: Yes, they'll come back to you...

DOLLY: And sit by you...

MINNIE: And talk to you...

DOLLY: And you'll sing...

MINNIE: Duets with that odious Tommy Mims...

DOLLY: And talk poetry with Mr Booth and cap Charlie's dull stories.

MINNIE: They'll be as jealous as cats about you and flatter you and love you, and talk to us — when common politeness forces them to talk to us — about you...

DOLLY: And tell us how wonderful you are...

EILEEN: How charming...

MINNIE: How young...

DOLLY: How witty.

MRS SWAN: My dears!

MINNIE: Oh, we admit that it's all quite true, you *are* charming and young and witty. But we're tired of being told it. I want someone to tell me that I'm all these things.

MRS SWAN: I left Gerald behind. Didn't *he* tell you?

MINNIE: Of course he didn't. And the manoeuvring you had to do to get him to stay at all, and then he talked most of the time about you and bolted — literally bolted — in less than five minutes.

MRS SWAN: Is that my fault? If you three girls can't amuse one young man — well, I give you up, or rather I don't give you up; I keep you for life, worse luck.

DOLLY: Worse luck? Do you want to get rid of us?

MRS SWAN: Of course. I want to see you all happily married. I want a little rest. Do you think I never get tired of trying to be nice to your friends, trying to make them feel at home?

DOLLY: But you're too nice to them.

MRS SWAN: Nonsense. Anyone would think from the way you speak that I wasn't an old woman, that I dressed myself up, that I — I — oh, it's too absurd. I don't like your young men, I much prefer older men, men of my own generation.

MINNIE: (*grimly*) I never see you with them.

MRS SWAN: Do you want me to fill the house with old fogies, as you'd call them? I make these stupid young men welcome for all your sakes. I'm trying my best to bring you together, so that you can get to know each other. Didn't I try all during supper?

MINNIE: Yes, that's what's so humiliating, you make me feel a fool dragging me into the conversation by the hair of my head. I simply go dumb.

MRS SWAN: Why should you go dumb? You ought to have plenty to talk about. I gave you a better education than I ever had. You go to the theatre every week — I never was at a theatre till after I was married — you go to concerts —

DOLLY: You can't talk about music.

MRS SWAN: I can.

MINNIE: Oh, yes, *you* can; you can talk about anything under the sun and make it interesting and attractive and amusing. But we can't, not when you're there at least, and you always *are* there, or if you're not the young men aren't there either. I don't blame you really and I don't blame the poor boys, only we don't get a look in and we're growing old and it's dreadful to be always sitting in the background. I suppose we're not very clever or pretty or attractive, but perhaps if we were given a chance —

DOLLY: Yes, that's what we want, a chance.

MRS SWAN: But, darlings, what can I do?

MINNIE: You could remind them sometimes that you're old enough to be their mother.

DOLLY: And that every dog has its day.

MRS SWAN: But I don't pretend to be a year younger than I really am. You can't say that I'm anything wonderful to look at, or that I dress beautifully — this old black dress, could anything be simpler? I don't paint my face, I don't even powder my nose, as everyone seems to do nowadays. I'm just a plain middle-aged widow. It's not as if I wanted to marry again.

DOLLY: Ah, if you only would.

MRS SWAN: Dolly!

DOLLY: Well, you want us to marry; why shouldn't we want you to marry?

MRS SWAN: You want to get rid of me?

DOLLY: Not more than you want to get rid of us.

EILEEN: No, no, mother, we don't.

MRS SWAN: You're going very far, Dolly.

DOLLY: Sorry.

MINNIE: I wanted plain speaking tonight, mother.

MRS SWAN: (*thinking it out*) Yes... perhaps I was wrong, but when your father died I wanted to be everything to you, to share your work and your play. I taught you your first lessons, when you went to school I learnt at home all the things you were learning — things I was never taught when I was a girl. Yes... perhaps that was wrong, it means that I've everything that you have except your youth, and then I have my experience which perhaps makes up....

MINNIE: And here we are.

MRS SWAN: (*getting up*) I shall leave the field entirely free for you all. I must think it out. I can't have you feeling that I am standing in your way. I don't think it true, but you mustn't even imagine it. You can come and say good night to me on your way to bed. I shan't be asleep.

MINNIE: Mother, don't be hurt, please don't think that —

MRS SWAN: I *am* a little hurt, Minnie, I won't deny it, but I must think it all out. I hope you'll have a pleasant evening.
(*She goes out by the other door.*)

EILEEN: That's the sort of thing plain speaking always leads to. I think I'll go up to her. I can't bear to think of her going to bed at this hour — nine o'clock — like a naughty child.

MINNIE: You'll do nothing of the kind. You'll — ssh! Here they are.

(GERALD BOOTH, CHARLIE DUNCAN *and* TOMMY MIMS *come in.* CHARLIE *and* TOMMY *are simple, good fellows.*)

CHARLIE: Only one cup broken tonight, Mrs Swan — oh, I thought she was here.

MINNIE: Sit down, everyone.

DOLLY: Sit here, Mr Booth. You were washing, too?

GERALD: No, hanging.

DOLLY: Hanging?

GERALD: Cups.

DOLLY: Oh!

EILEEN: Sit here, Mr Mims.

TOMMY: I'll not sit there, that's Mrs Swan's special place I know.

MINNIE: You can take it tonight, she's not coming back.

GERALD:
CHARLIE: } Not coming back?
TOMMY:

MINNIE: No, she's gone to bed.

GERALD:
CHARLIE: } Bed?
TOMMY:

MINNIE: Yes, she felt rather tired.

DOLLY: A slight headache, you know. Have you been playing much golf lately, Mr Booth?

GERALD: But I hope it's nothing serious.

CHARLIE: She seemed as right as rain ten minutes ago when we were clearing away.

MINNIE: No, it's nothing serious, a mere trifle.... What shall we do? Cards? Music? What would you like, Charlie?

CHARLIE: She does too much, that's the truth. Always on the go. It's a marvel to me how she keeps it up. I've told her a thousand times —

TOMMY: So have I.

CHARLIE: But it's no use. And then she reads half through the night.

GERALD: But that's what keeps her so wonderfully vivid and up-to-date. French, Italian, German, it's all the same to her. She's kept up with all Hauptmann's later work and that's no joke I can tell you.

CHARLIE: And yet she finds time to go to football matches on Saturday afternoons. Why, she was able to put me right about that score with —

MINNIE: Yes, she's wonderful. But you haven't answered my question, Charlie, cards or music?

CHARLIE: Oh, not *music*! Why, Mrs Swan's room is just over this, isn't it?

MINNIE: Yes, of course, I forgot. Cards, then? What shall we play? "Pop-corn"?

TOMMY: Oh, *no*. "Pop-corn" is so noisy.

CHARLIE: Something very quiet — if we play at all.

GERALD: I think it's rather brutal to play anything with her lying ill over our heads. I believe we ought all to go home and leave the house absolutely quiet. Probably even our talking disturbs her.

TOMMY: Yes.

CHARLIE: (*getting up*) You're quite right. We ought to go.

MINNIE: No, no, please. It's only quite a slight headache, I assure you.

GERALD: Then if she gets a good night's rest she'll be all right in the morning, so we'll steal away —

DOLLY: Oh, Mr Booth, she'll be vexed if you go.

GERALD: We can't help that, Dolly. We must think of her health before everything.

(MRS SWAN *comes in. The men swoop at her.*)

CHARLIE: }
TOMMY: }   How are you?

GERALD: I'm so sorry. I didn't know you weren't feeling fit. Why didn't you tell us?

MRS SWAN: It's nothing, nothing to make a fuss about, quite a trifle. But I'm better in bed, I think — Minnie thinks so — but the light in my room has gone out, the bulb must be broken. I want to get another.

CHARLIE: I'll take this one from the piano lamp.

MRS SWAN: Oh, you won't be able to play without that.

CHARLIE: Of course we won't play *tonight*.

GERALD: (*very serious*) I want you to tell me exactly what is the matter. Is it a headache?

MRS SWAN: Yes, but very slight.

GERALD: And what else? I'm not a medical student for nothing, you know.

MRS SWAN: Oh, just general tiredness and — and a feeling that I ought to be alone.

GERALD: I thought so. I know exactly what will put you right in an hour.

MRS SWAN: What is it?

GERALD: A wonderful stuff my mother uses. It's absolutely harmless, half sedative and half tonic. I'll get it for you. (*He starts to go.*)

MRS SWAN: Now?

GERALD: The sooner the better.

DOLLY: Oh, not tonight, Mr Booth.

GERALD: Certainly. (*He looks at his watch.*) I'll just have time to get home, get the stuff and be back here by eleven. My last bus isn't until 11.15.

DOLLY: Oh, Mr Booth! Oh, mother!

MRS SWAN: No, I positively forbid you, Mr Booth, I'm not really ill. It's just — you must remember that I'm not a young woman — I'm really rather old, older than any of you think. I'm not like all you young people.

CHARLIE: Rubbish. You're the youngest thing here.

TOMMY: I can never think of you as old.

MRS SWAN: Ah, but I am. What were you doing in 1924, Mr Mims?

TOMMY: 1924? I'm afraid I don't know. I wasn't born till the early thirties.

MRS SWAN: Exactly. Well, I was *married* in 1924. Now you see the difference there is between us.

129

DOLLY: How dreadfully old-fashioned it sounds, doesn't it, Mr Booth?

GERALD: Yes, fascinatingly pre-war.

MINNIE:
EILEEN: } Mr Booth!
DOLLY:

MRS SWAN: (*unconsciously settling down on the sofa*) Yes, it *was* rather a lovely time — those summers before the dreadful war. We went to London for our honeymoon, it was March, 1924. We arrived from Ireland early in the morning and Jack brought me to a theatre that night — my very first theatre, my very first play — and what a play. (*For a few seconds she is lost in reminiscence.*)

THE MEN: Yes, yes?

MRS SWAN: One of the most wonderful plays ever written and it was its very first night. By the greatest luck Jack managed to buy two tickets which had been returned, they were in the stalls, lovely seats, right in the centre and we could look up and see the author but we didn't want to look at him — only at the marvellous play and the wonderful actress.

GERALD: What was the play?

TOMMY:
CHARLIE: } What actress?

MRS SWAN: Sybil Thorndike, "St. Joan" and Mr and Mrs Shaw sitting together in a box. I remember that after the first interval Mrs Shaw's hands were full of violets, someone must have given her masses and masses of them.

THE MEN: Ah!

MRS SWAN: And that evening had a funny little sequel, for a couple of days later, in the Strand, I asked my way of a middle-aged gentleman and then I stared at him and gasped, and he said "Yes, it is," and ran away — and it was Bernard Shaw. And the last night we spent in London — Jack knew that when he'd paid the hotel bill he'd have just a ten-pound note left over so he said, "Let's blow it on one last grand spree," and we did. We didn't go to a theatre, we dined very late, a glorious dinner, champagne and everything and we went to a very smart night-club. We danced and danced (I had a five-pound note of my own Jack didn't know of and I can assure you we needed it before the evening was over) and there was such a nice young man there with kind twinkling eyes and something so odd and attractive about him, he was enjoying himself no end and I knew I had seen his face in the papers but I couldn't place him,

suddenly it came to me in a flash — the Prince of Wales! That's what he was then, Edward the Eighth to be, I do hope he's happy with that Mrs What's-her-name. And another time —
(MINNIE *coughs significantly,* MRS SWAN *stops.*)

THE MEN: Go on.

MRS SWAN: No, no, I was forgetting, I — I must go to bed. I'm not well at all, I'm not as young as I once was, you know. Good night, everyone. Have you got the lamp for me, Charlie?
(*She has got up.*)

CHARLIE: Oh, I say, must you really go?

MRS SWAN: Yes, I really must. Some other time I'll tell you of my youthful adventures. You must talk to the girls tonight and make adventures for yourselves.

TOMMY: You don't look ill.

MRS SWAN: I feel ill, I feel worse.

GERALD: Then I'm off for mother's medicine. I'll be back before eleven.
(*He dashes from the room.*)

MRS SWAN: (*calling after him vainly*) Mr Booth, Mr Booth! Oh, I'm so sorry he should have troubled. The lamp, Charlie.... Now please no one else is to stir. I don't want any fuss made, and play the piano if you want to, it won't disturb me and I like to know that you are enjoying yourselves. Good night, everyone. Thank you, Charlie.
(*She takes the lamp and goes.*)

CHARLIE: I'm glad Booth has gone for that stuff. I wonder whether we ought to get a doctor. He's only a medical student.

DOLLY: He's practically a doctor; he's only got his final to do.

MINNIE: Do sit down — or, Eileen, you play a waltz. I want Mr Mims to show me that queer new step. I can't get my feet round it.

EILEEN: Right-o.
(*She sits at the piano and plays a few bars.*)

MINNIE: Will you, Mr Mims?

TOMMY: (*very serious*) I don't think I could — tonight. Look here, has she a hot-water bottle?

MINNIE: Mother?

TOMMY: Yes.

EILEEN: A hot-water bottle in September!
(*She defiantly plays a chord.*)

TOMMY: The season doesn't matter when you're ill. I'm going to fill one for her, I know where they are. I won't be five minutes.
(*He rushes out.*)

131

EILEEN: (*in a sepulchral voice*) Two gone!

MINNIE: Well, Charlie, perhaps *you'll* sit down quietly and entertain us; you needn't speak above a whisper if you don't like.

CHARLIE: There's something in the wind, Minnie.

MINNIE: Is there?

CHARLIE: I don't believe your mother is really ill. If she was you'd all be fussing like anything.

DOLLY: It's very slight.

MINNIE: She's tired.

CHARLIE: And bored with us?

MINNIE: Well, perhaps a little.

CHARLIE: I thought so. I wonder why.

MINNIE: She was saying tonight that she preferred older men, men of her own generation.

CHARLIE: (*aghast*) Did she say that?

MINNIE: Yes. Didn't she, Dolly?

DOLLY: Rather!

CHARLIE: I suppose it's only natural.

MINNIE: Of course.

CHARLIE: Coming here three times a week — and every Sunday, gassing about football and taking her to the pictures.

MINNIE: Neither are quite in her line, are they?

CHARLIE: No, how dense of me not to see it before. But I'm beastly stupid you know; I always think that when I'm awfully fond of people they are, of course, equally fond of me. I have sometimes wondered in a vague sort of way how she could put up with such an obvious chap as I am, but I was stupid and hoped — hoped — (*he chokes a little*).

MINNIE: Charlie, what's the matter with you?

CHARLIE: (*getting up, he seems years older*) I'll go now, of course.

DOLLY: Charlie!

MINNIE: You mustn't, you mustn't.

CHARLIE: Imagine her going to bed — at nine o'clock — to avoid me! Will you tell her, if she asks why I went — but I suppose she won't — that it was just my stupidity and vanity that kept me from realising. And of course if she ever wants me I'll come like a shot — but she won't want me — but if there's anything I can ever do for her, you'll tell me, won't you, Minnie? I'm not clever, but you can trust me and — and — I'd do anything in the world for your mother, and — and — oh, damn it all —

(*Blinking back his tears, he goes quickly out.*)

DOLLY: Now!

EILEEN: Plain speaking. All three gone!

DOLLY: (*acidly*) Never mind, Eileen, Mr Mims will be back in a minute with mother's hot-water bottle. I think we'll leave him to Minnie, she's so fond of him.

MINNIE: (*going quickly to the other door*) Mother! Mother!

DOLLY: We'll have to admit, my dear, that we're three very dull young women and be satisfied with the crumbs that fall from mother's table.

MRS SWAN: (*appearing*) I can't get this light to work.

MINNIE: Quick! Call Charlie back, he's leaving because he thinks you don't like him. He's not gone yet, I haven't heard the front door bang; he's probably crying — in the hall. Quick!
(*She hurries her across the room and out.*)

DOLLY: And, as Minnie says, it's not as if we particularly liked any of these men. They're none of them worth all the trouble we've gone to.

EILEEN: Mother is nicer than the three of them put together. Still, I do believe that one day the right man will come and —

MINNIE: I don't believe he'll ever come. I don't believe he'll ever recognise me. The older mother makes herself out to be and the more ill she makes herself the more she seems to attract them. If we ever want to have a life of our own we must go away from her.

EILEEN: Leave mother? Oh, I couldn't.

DOLLY: On the chance of picking up some stupid man? Not likely.

MINNIE: No, as mother says, she has us for life.
(MRS SWAN *leads* CHARLIE *in.*)

MRS SWAN: You silly, silly fellow.

CHARLIE: And you really do like me?

MRS SWAN: The idea of you running away in a huff like that. I've a right to be very angry with you. What do you mean by it? And you never told me if you were going to take me to the pictures on Tuesday or Wednesday. I suppose you want to run away from that engagement, too?

CHARLIE: Oh, no. Oh, Mrs Swan!

MRS SWAN: Well, Tuesday or Wednesday?

CHARLIE: Tuesday *and* Wednesday, please.
(TOMMY *comes in with the hot-water bottle.*)

TOMMY: I wasn't long, was I?... Hullo, not in bed yet?

MRS SWAN: The light in my room is broken, I can't get it to work, and there are no candles in the house.
(GERALD *comes in, breathless.*)

GERALD: Such a piece of luck, Mrs Swan; I hadn't gone fifty yards from the gate when I met Thompson — the chemist at the corner, you know — I told him what I wanted and when he heard it was for you he turned back and opened his shop and gave it to me. He'd do anything for you, he says. But you know you ought to be in bed.

MRS SWAN: (*feebly*) The light in my room —

TOMMY: Look here, tuck her up on the sofa; we'll get you candles later on.

GERALD: Yes, good idea. (*To* DOLLY.) Would you get me a glass of water, Miss Swan?

DOLLY: Certainly. (*She goes out.*)

GERALD: (*To* EILEEN.) And a rug — if you can find one.

EILEEN: (*hurrying out*) Certainly.

GERALD: Now you're to lie down on the sofa and rest yourself.

MRS SWAN: But I'm not ill and you're not to go away — any of you.

GERALD: Of course you're not ill and none of us are going away, we'll stay and talk quietly. Now just do as you're told.

(EILEEN *comes in with rug.*)

Thank you, Miss Swan. Now, Mrs Swan, tuck your feet up, put the hot-water bottle there, Tommy.... Yes, that's it.

(DOLLY *comes in with a glass of water;* GERALD *takes it from her.*)

Thank you, Miss Swan. Now, Mrs Swan, take two of these tablets and get them down with a sip of water.... (*She does so.*)

That's it.

(*He has her on the sofa, wrapped in the rug, the bottle at her feet.*)

Now we'll talk very quietly, and in less than no time you'll fall asleep, and when you wake up you'll be as bright as a button. Or, better still, I'll read you to sleep. May I?

MRS SWAN: If you like.

GERALD: But would you like me to?

MRS SWAN: You know I always love your reading.

GERALD: Good. Tommy, put out all the lights except this low one. (TOMMY *does so.*) What are the books on that table, Charlie?

CHARLIE: (*looking at them*) A German book — I can't read its name — and a poetry book — oh, Yeats.

GERALD: That will do splendidly. Give it to me. I'll sit here on a cushion. Sit down everyone.

(*They all settle themselves.* GERALD *sits on the ground near* MRS SWAN's *head, the other men are grouped near her in the circle of soft light. Somewhere in the dark background the* Miss SWANs *have found alighting places.*)

GERALD: Which poem shall I read?

MRS SWAN: Whichever you like. If you like it I am sure I shall.

GERALD: (*turns the pages, then reads:*)
   "I would that we were, my beloved,
    White birds on the foam of the sea."

(*There is a soft sigh from the background.*)

MRS SWAN: What is it? Is anything the matter, Minnie?

MINNIE: Nothing, mother darling, we're all right.

DOLLY: Quite all right.

EILEEN: Please go on, Mr Booth; it's beautiful.

GERALD: "I would that we were, my beloved,
    White birds on the foam of the sea —
    We tire of the flame of the meteor
    Before it can pass by and flee."

MRS SWAN: Stop! Mr Booth, your medicine is wonder-working.
(*She jumps off the sofa and runs across the room and switches on all the lights.*)
I want light, I want music, I want dancing!

THE MEN: Mrs Swan!

THE GIRLS: Mother!

MRS SWAN: Yes. I'll take no refusal. Wake up, Minnie, you are dropping to sleep. Come along, Dolly, Eileen!

EILEEN: I don't dance.

MRS SWAN: Well, move back the sofa, clear the floor.

GERALD: (*to* MRS SWAN) You shouldn't, you'll knock yourself up again.

MRS SWAN: Not I. Come along, clear the floor, Charlie, Mr Booth, Mr Mims; get your partners.
(*In a moment the floor is cleared.* MRS SWAN *sits at the piano and plays a bar or two.*)
What do you want? A waltz? A two-step?

TOMMY: There's that new step in the half-time that Miss Swan wanted me to show her; *you* know it, I showed it to you yesterday.

MRS SWAN: Oh, that? Don't you know it, Minnie?

MINNIE: No, I can't get it right, somehow.

MRS SWAN: It's as easy as winking. I picked it up in no time.

TOMMY: Let's show it to her, Mrs Swan.

MRS SWAN: Shall we?

TOMMY: Yes, come on.

MRS SWAN: But I can't dance *and* play.

TOMMY: Miss Eileen can play. (*To* EILEEN) Will you? "Catch your cabbage", please.

EILEEN: Of course; get up, mother.
(*She takes her mother's place at the piano.*)

MRS SWAN: And we must have more tea at once, lots of tea — and whiskey for the men. Run and get some quickly, Dolly.

DOLLY: Yes, mother. (*She goes out.*)

MRS SWAN: Now, Tommy — I beg your pardon — Mr Mims.

TOMMY: Oh, please, make it Tommy.

MRS SWAN: Very well, Tommy. Watch us, Minnie; start away, Eileen.
(*They begin to dance.* CHARLIE *and* GERALD *sit on the sofa with* MINNIE *between them. Their eyes are fixed on* MRS SWAN. *After a moment they speak together.*)

CHARLIE: }
GERALD: } Wonderful! Isn't she wonderful?

MINNIE: Yes, indeed.

CHARLIE: She's got the step perfectly. I must try it with her when Tommy is finished.

GERALD: No, it's my turn next.

CHARLIE: Watch her, Minnie.
(DOLLY *appears at the door carrying a tray with a decanter and glasses on it. She stands there unnoticed watching the dance.*)

GERALD: She's a poem herself.
        "He made the world to be a grassy road
          Before her wandering feet."

MINNIE: Mr Booth —

GERALD: Hush! Don't break the spell ... wonderful ... wonderful ....

CHARLIE: Wonderful.

CURTAIN

THE BIG HOUSE

Four scenes in its life

To
Rutherford Mayne
of the Ulster Players
this play of County Cork

THE SCENES

SCENE I. The drawing-room at Ballydonal House. A November morning, 1918.

SCENE II. The dining-room at Ballydonal House. A June evening, 1921.

SCENE III. The same. A February night, 1923.

SCENE IV. A corner of the garden early the next morning.

CHARACTERS

In the order of their appearance.

ATKINS
REV. HENRY BROWN
CAPTAIN MONTGOMERY DESPARD
KATE ALCOCK
ST. LEGER ALCOCK
VANDALEUR O'NEILL
MRS ALCOCK
ANNIE DALY
THREE YOUNG MEN

The first production of "The Big House" took place on September 6, 1926, in the Abbey Theatre, Dublin, with the following cast:

Atkins	P.J. CAROLAN
Rev. Henry Brown	MICHAEL J. DOLAN
Captain Montgomery Despard	F.J. McCORMICK
Kate Alcock	SHELAH RICHARDS
St. Leger Alcock	BARRY FITZGERALD
Vandaleur O'Neill	TONY QUINN
Mrs Alcock	EILEEN CROWE
Annie Daly	RIA MOONEY
	ARTHUR SHIELDS
Three Young Mèn	J. STEVENSON
	WALTER DILLON

The Play was produced by the Author.

SCENE I

The large drawing-room at Ballydonal House. The room must give the impression of size, on a small stage one of its sides must not be seen but should be "masked" by a large Chinese screen. At the back are two large windows, they can be either Georgian type or mock-Gothic, there are heavy curtains on them. On the side of the room which is seen is a door up stage and, lower down, a fireplace. A profusion of furniture, some good, some bad, profusion of small unimportant pictures, photographs, china on the walls; the effect of all being a comfortable room containing the vestigia of generations, the mid-Victorian vestigia prevailing. There is a bright fire and bright sunshine outside the windows. It is about ten-thirty on a November morning, 1918. The room is empty. A door on the unseen side of the room opens and the voice of ATKINS, *the butler, is heard.*

ATKINS: Mr Brown to see you, sir.
   (MR BROWN *appears round the screen, a middle-aged, bearded clergyman.*)
BROWN: (*looking round the room*) Atkins! Atkins!
ATKINS: (*coming back but still unseen*) Did you call, sir?
BROWN: Mr Alcock isn't here.
ATKINS: (*coming into sight round the screen and looking round the room. He is a small stout man of sixty-five, his gait is a little rolling, his voice a little thick, he is obviously a little drunk.*) I beg your pardon, your reverence, he was here a minute ago. (*He crosses to the door above the fireplace, opens it and looks into the next room. He shuts it again.*) There's no one in the small drawing-room but Captain Despard. I'll send looking for him.
BROWN: Thank you.
ATKINS: He'll likely have walked out to the yard to see do they understand about the bell.
BROWN: What bell?
ATKINS: The big bell, Father — your reverence, I mean — the yard bell. It's to be rung at eleven o'clock and it's not been rung these twenty years.

BROWN: I see. Part of the celebrations?

ATKINS: But indeed he needn't be bothering. I have Paddy O'Reilly tutored in the bell. He's to be there since ten o'clock, the rope in his hand, the cook's alarm clock hanging on the wall in front of his face and on the stroke of eleven he's to start bell-ringing, ring for a quarter of an hour and then walk into the kitchen for the bottle of stout the master's after ordering for him.

BROWN: I see. Well, it's a great day.

ATKINS: It is, Father.

BROWN: You'll be expecting your grandson home now. Is he still in Salonika?

ATKINS: He is. When he couldn't get through them Dardanelles he gev up and he's sitting in Salonika ever since.

BROWN: He's been luckier than some.... Will you try and find Mr Alcock? I can't wait long, I have a lot to do this morning.

ATKINS: I will, your reverence. There's the papers — this morning's "Constitution" and Saturday's "Irish Times". We don't get it till the morning now since the second post was cut off, bad luck to it. But I suppose it's the same way at the rectory.

BROWN: It is indeed.

ATKINS: Ah well, please God now the Germans are bet we'll have posts and sugar and everything back the way it used to be long ago. Will I bring you a glass of sherry while you're waiting?

BROWN: No, thank you.

ATKINS: You'll excuse me for asking, Father — your reverence, I mean — I forgot you were so mad for the temperance. I'll have the master for you now as fast as I can get him. (*He ambles out.* MR BROWN *opens the "Irish Times" and glances at it. From the door above the fire enters* CAPTAIN DESPARD, *twenty-five years old, in uniform, he limps a little. He stops on seeing* BROWN.)

BROWN: (*going to him, holding out his hand*) How d'ye do? You are Captain Despard, I'm sure.

DESPARD: Oh — ah — yes.

BROWN: My name is Brown, I'm the parson here. St. Leger — Mr Alcock — told me you were coming here.

DESPARD: Oh — yes.

BROWN: You've been having a nasty time with your foot, haven't you? Is it better?

DESPARD: Nearly all right. I hope I'll be able to go back in another week or ten days.

BROWN: But fortunately there'll be nothing to go back to.

DESPARD: Nothing?

BROWN: No war. Only half an hour more of it, thank goodness.

DESPARD: I doubt if it's as over as people think it is.

BROWN: But President Wilson's terms —

DESPARD: Those damned Yankees — beg pardon — but this Armistice business is a bad mistake, we should have marched through to Berlin.

BROWN: Hm! But if we get all we want without losing another man or killing another man —

DESPARD: Oh, losing! Killing! It's not a picnic.

BROWN: No, indeed, it isn't.... You were very good to poor Reginald. It made a great difference to Mrs Alcock to know there was a friend with him when he died.

DESPARD: There wasn't much I could do.

BROWN: Still, it made a difference. Have you ever come across her other boy, Ulick?

DESPARD: Only once. A rather quiet dull sort of chap, isn't he? Not like poor old Reg.

BROWN: No, he's very different from Reginald.... I suppose you have no idea where Mr Alcock is?

DESPARD: I haven't seen him since breakfast.

BROWN: Atkins is supposed to be looking for him, but Atkins is a little — well, he started to celebrate early.

DESPARD: Atkins? Oh, that's the butler. Why, he started to celebrate last night. You should have seen him handing round the soup. It was a marvel, but not a drop spilled.

BROWN: Poor Atkins. It's his one failing.

DESPARD: Typically Irish old fellow, isn't he?

BROWN: I hope not.

DESPARD: Oh, but he's a delightful old chap. And the rest of it doesn't seem to be so awfully Irish.

BROWN: The rest of it?

DESPARD: Well, the house itself, the way it's run, and — and everything.

BROWN: Do they read "Castle Rackrent" in the trenches?

DESPARD: (*staring*) I don't think so, never heard of it. What do you mean?

BROWN: Nothing. I withdraw my insinuation. I started by thinking how blunderingly English your conclusions were. I beg your pardon. Second thoughts make me give you credit for exceedingly sharp penetration.

DESPARD: Oh, thank you.

BROWN: I'm sure you're thinking that we haven't known each other long enough for me to say that sort of thing to you. But here in the country fresh acquaintances are so rare that I've got into the impolite habit of taking short cuts. You must forgive me.

DESPARD: Oh, rot. There's nothing to forgive. I suppose I was a bit taken aback by your talking of my penetration. What the dickens have I penetrated?

BROWN: Mr Alcock told me you have never been in Ireland before. You've been in this house for a day and two nights and in that short time you've put your finger on the great fact that it is not typical. It isn't. It's a protest against the type.

DESPARD: The type being?

BROWN: Not quite what you think it is. Not always slovenly and ramshackle. The difference doesn't lie in the obvious things you've seen, it's not that this room is clean and decent and comfortable. Irish country houses frequently are that, it's not that your dinner was eatable and your bath hot —

DESPARD: Oh well, Irish hospitality — it's traditional, you know.

BROWN: But is St. Leger traditional, is Kate — Miss Alcock?

DESPARD: She's a jolly fine girl.

BROWN: You won't realize how fine until you see the others!

DESPARD: What others? She's the only daughter.

BROWN: I mean the types. Without an idea. With no culture. Ignorant. Don't know whether the portraits that hang in their dining rooms are eighteenth-century masterpieces or photogravures, don't know if the silver they use every day is old Irish or modern Brummagem. Don't know the history of their own family, don't know Irish history. Have nothing but a few religious prejudices and very good health. Can't even grow decent flowers.

DESPARD: Well, they're great sportswomen, Irish sportswomen are traditional, you know.

BROWN: That's the least Irish thing about them, your real Irishwoman despises sport, she thinks its only use is keeping the men out of mischief. And the Irish gentleman! Ignorant. Asleep. Look at their libraries. A splendid collection of eighteenth-century classics, twenty volumes of sermons of the early nineteenth century — after that nothing. They're divorced from all reality.

DESPARD: Oh, I say!

BROWN: Absurd of me to blaze out like this, isn't it? But I know what I'm talking about. My name's as common as dirt, but I'm from County Wexford, and County Wexford Browns fancy themselves. They came over with your people once upon a time. I'm attacking my own class. And I'm extraordinarily interested in watching this house and the fight it's making.

DESPARD: Fight? What the dickens is it fighting for?

BROWN: Its life.

(KATE ALCOCK *comes in, her arms are full of Michaelmas daisies.*)

Ah, Kate! Good morning.

KATE: Mr Brown! I haven't a finger. Aren't they lovely? They're lasting so long this year. What a morning. Such sunshine. You've made each other's acquaintance?

BROWN: Yes.

KATE: You've heard the great news of course? Aunt Kat wired to father from London first thing this morning, we knew at breakfast time.

BROWN: Miss Doyle at the Post Office made no bones of sharing the news, the whole village knew it before you did and she sent a messenger to the rectory on a bicycle.

KATE: Well, I don't blame her. Can you believe that the horrible thing will be killed dead at eleven o' clock, in less than half an hour?

BROWN: Captain Despard doesn't believe it will be killed.

KATE: Oh, soldiers are such optimists. Where's the boss?

BROWN: He's being looked for.

KATE: You're coming to dinner tonight, I hope. With this news it's going to be a celebration.

BROWN: That's what I called in to say. Alice's cold is almost gone, and she'll be delighted to come, for, as you say, it will be an occasion.

KATE: It's only ourselves, you know, not a dinner-party.

BROWN: Gracious, we didn't expect a dinner-party. When were you at a dinner-party last, Kate? Here, in County Cork, I mean?

KATE: Mother and I were counting up the other day. Not since the first winter of the war when those people took Knock for the shooting. They were awful bounders, but they did manage to gather fifteen people for a dinner party.... My goodness, Monty, you're going to have a dull time of it here .... I told the boss it was cruel to invite you.

DESPARD: You forget. I invited myself.

KATE: Well, on your own head be it. We tried having Colonials here for their leave, men, you know, who had no relations or friends to go to. The South Africans didn't mind much, but the Australians always, after one day, sent themselves telegrams recalling themselves to the front.... I must get some more vases. Here's the boss.

(MR ALCOCK *comes in,* KATE *goes out.*)

ALCOCK: Henry!

BROWN: Good morning, St. Leger. I couldn't let you know yesterday whether Alice would be well enough to come over tonight. I've come now to tell you that she can.

ALCOCK: Good. You've heard the news?

BROWN: Yes.

ALCOCK: In our quiet way we're going to let things rip tonight, I depend on Captain Despard to make things lively.

DESPARD: Don't expect too much from me.

ALCOCK: Oh, I've another string to my bow. (*To* BROWN.) I've just been down to that place you don't approve of — the wine-cellar.

BROWN: Atkins has been looking for you.

ALCOCK: I didn't see him, and I should have thought his feet would have turned instinctively in that direction. If anyone knows the way to the cellar he does. I haven't been there for six months or more but, thanks to Atkins, it's like Mother Hubbard's cupboard. You know all we take — a little claret at dinner, my small whiskey before I go to bed — but Atkins! My dear Despard, that old chap has an unerring palate. I bought a couple of dozen of cheap Burgundy, not bad at all, but cheap, I thought I'd buy him off with them. He tried one bottle but then concentrated on my best Pommard, and there's only one bottle of brandy left. He seems to have a conscience about champagne, it is sacred in his sight and you shall have plenty of it tonight.

BROWN: You can leave my name out of it.

ALCOCK: Hang it all, the night of the Armistice you must make an exception. Mrs Brown is T.T., but I'm sure she'll drink her glass tonight like a good 'un.

BROWN: I wouldn't put it past her. Women seem to be able to square their consciences in a way we can't.

ALCOCK: By the way, I'm glad I've seen you beforehand. Tonight *is* an occasion and we'll drink a toast — the King and Victory. But not a word. No speeches or anything like that. Mary's feeling it a bit, of course. I know Reg is very much in her mind and if we once started to say things anything might happen.

BROWN: You needn't be afraid, I won't want to say anything, I couldn't trust myself. I'll be thinking of Dick.

ALCOCK: Of course. (*To* DESPARD.) He lost his only boy at Gallipoli. Such a splendid chap.

DESPARD: Rotten luck.

BROWN: When did you hear from Ulick?

ALCOCK: Yesterday. Fit as a fiddle. Only a few lines, things had been pretty strenuous of course.

BROWN: I wonder how soon you can expect him back.

ALCOCK: His mother has set her heart on having him for Christmas.

ATKINS: (*Unseen*) Mr O'Neill.

(*A gawky common-looking young man comes in.*)

ALCOCK: Hallo, Vandaleur.

VANDALEUR: (*in a very marked brogue*) Good morning, Alcock. Good morning, Mr Brown.

ALCOCK: Mr O'Neill, Captain Despard. (*They shake hands.*)

DESPARD: How d'ye do?

VANDALEUR: I hope ye're well. (*To* ALCOCK) I was riding in this direction and me mother asked me to leave in a note, she and the gerr'ls want Mrs Alcock and Kate to go over to tea next week. Here it is. 'Tis a bit crushed I'm afraid.

ALCOCK: (*ringing the bell*) I'll get it sent to Mary. Will you wait for the answer? Sit down.

VANDALEUR: (*sitting*) Thank ye .... Me fawther's sick.

BROWN: I'm sorry to hear that. Is he seriously ill?

VANDALEUR: I don't know .... I sold the black mare.

ALCOCK: Oh, did you get a good price?

VANDALEUR: Rotten.

BROWN: I'll go over and see your father this afternoon.

VANDALEUR: Ye needn't then.

BROWN: I can quite easily go, and if he's ill —

VANDALEUR: Sure he went to Cork by the morning train.

BROWN: Oh! Will he be back tonight?

VANDALEUR: Well, he was going to the doctor, and it would depind on what he said whether he'd end up the day in the hospital or in the County Club, but I think meself he'll be for the club.

BROWN: Oh! (*Enter* ATKINS.)

ALCOCK: Take this to the mistress please, and tell her that Mr O'Neill is waiting for the answer.

ATKINS: Yes, sir. (*He takes the note and goes.*)

ALCOCK: Well, this is a great day, Vandaleur.

VANDALEUR: Indeed, 'tis wonderful weather for this time of year.

ALCOCK: I wasn't thinking of the weather.

VANDALEUR: There was a great turn-out for Dicky Smith' funeral a-Choosday, why weren't you there?

ALCOCK: I meant the war — the Armistice.

VANDALEUR: Oh, to be sure. Is it to be today or tomorrow?

ALCOCK: Within an hour.

VANDALEUR: Fancy that now. I suppose they'll fire off a big gun like or ring a bell.

DESPARD: Were you fighting?

VANDALEUR: I was not. (*To* ALCOCK.) I met Michael Dempsey on the avenue and he was telling me that you have some sheep sick and that one's after dying on you.

ALCOCK: Yes, Kate's in a great stew about it. But I've written to the vet and I heard from him this morning. He's going to wire this morning and let me know if he can come today or tomorrow

VANDALEUR: Is it the fella from Knock you mean?

ALCOCK: Yes.

VANDALEUR: He's a bloody bad vet. He lost me a mare and a foal last year. I'd rather have the district nurse than that fella When they told me at home 'tother day that a cow was sick "Send for Mrs Maguire," says I. "Send for Mrs Maguire." That' all I'd say. Wasn't I right, Captain?

(DESPARD *merely looks contemptuous.*)

BROWN: Well, I hope the cow survived.

VANDALEUR: Of course she did, she's lepping round giving gallon of milk. 'Tis all a cod, inspectors and departments and tillage What the divil do the lads that make the regulations know about tillage? They wouldn't know the difference between wheat and oats.

ALCOCK: Well, we don't want to starve.

VANDALEUR: There's plenty to ate in this part of the country.

ALCOCK: But in the towns, in England —

VANDALEUR: Ah, let them go to the divil.

(MRS ALCOCK *and* KATE *come in.*)

MRS ALCOCK: Good morning, Van. Will you wait a minute while write a note to your mother? I won't be long.

VANDALEUR: Sure there's no hurry. Good morning, Kate.

KATE: Good morning, Van. Sit down, don't mind me, I'm only doing these flowers.

VANDALEUR: (*sitting*) Flossie and Maggie and Helana and Gertie sent you their love.

KATE: Please give them my love.

VANDALEUR: (*after a pause*) Sissy sent you her love too.

KATE: Give my love to Sissy.

ALCOCK: (*To* DESPARD.) Do you feel up to a stroll?

DESPARD: I'm afraid not. I've got to rest my foot as much as possible.

VANDALEUR: Are you after hurting your foot?

DESPARD: Yes.

ALCOCK: He got a nasty knock in France.

VANDALEUR: France?

DESPARD: There happens to be a war on there.

VANDALEUR: Sure I know.... Jerry Mangan's not the better of the fall he got, yet.

KATE: Oh, did he get a fall? I hadn't heard.

VANDALEUR: Lepping a small bit of a fence on that old red mare of his. Sure he's the rottenest rider in the country.

ALCOCK: I wish I had a horse to offer you, Despard, the only beast in the stables is the old carriage mare.

KATE: I'm sure the Goods or the O'Sullivans would lend him a horse.

VANDALEUR: Sure me fawther would lend him one. What about Prince Chawming?

DESPARD: (*shortly*) No, thank you.

VANDALEUR: He's quiet but a good goer and a very handy lepper.... You know him, Kate?

KATE: Yes.... Have you any flowers left, Van?

VANDALEUR: I don't know. 'Tis the gerr'ls looks after the flowers.

MRS ALCOCK: (*getting up*) There, Van. Now don't forget it in your pocket.

VANDALEUR: I won't, Mrs Alcock. Me mother sent you her love.

MRS ALCOCK: Thank you.

VANDALEUR: And so did the gerr'ls. At least I didn't see Helana when I was leaving, but I'm sure she would have if I had seen her.

MRS ALCOCK: Give them all my love and say I'm looking forward to seeing them next week. How's your father?

VANDALEUR: Sick.

BROWN: Are you in a great hurry, Van, or will you walk down the avenue with me?

VANDALEUR: Sure I'm in no hurry.

BROWN: Well, unfortunately, I am, so if you don't mind we'll be off now. I want to talk to you about the graveyard at Kilbeg. Good bye, Mrs Alcock, till this evening.

MRS ALCOCK: Seven-thirty. I'm so glad Alice is better, make her wrap up well.

ALCOCK: I'm sending the brougham for you at seven o'clock
Now don't start to protest, it's all been arranged.

BROWN: It's very kind of you. The little walk really wouldn't hav
done her any harm.... *Au revoir.*

(BROWN *goes to the door, while* VANDALEUR *awkwardly an*
formally shakes hands with everyone. He finishes wit
DESPARD.)

VANDALEUR: You're sure you won't have Prince Chawming?

DESPARD: Certain.... Thanks.

BROWN: Come on, Vandaleur. (*They go out.*)

KATE: Go on, Monty, say it. Don't spare our feelings. "What
lout!" Or was it something worse, something unprintable?

DESPARD: In present company "lout" will have to do. Who is he
A farmer's son?

KATE: (*laughing*) Farmer's son! Vandaleur O'Neill!

ALCOCK: If family counts for anything he gets full marks. /
quarter of him is Irish — the best old Irish, the other three
quarters are successive English invasions. Compared to hin
we're second-rate interlopers. His father is first cousin and hei
to Lord Rathconnell, but the father is drinking himself to death
he won't last a twelvemonth longer. Van doesn't drink, Van wil
be the next lord.

DESPARD: That clodhopper?

MRS ALCOCK: Poor boy, it's not his fault, and he's really a goo
boy.

ALCOCK: No, it's not his fault, it's his wicked old father and hi
foolish mother. He was sent to a preparatory school in Englan
at the end of the first term he refused to go back, and his fathe
and mother gave in. That's all the education he ever had. He ca
just sign his name, I suppose he can read. He's lived at hom
ever since with his father and mother and his five sisters.

KATE: Flossie and Sissy and Maggie and Gertie and "Helana"
And we've got to have tea with them all next week. Why di
you say we'd go, mother?

MRS ALCOCK: My dear, what could I do? Mrs O'Neill asked m
for *any* day next week. I couldn't say I was engaged for th
whole week, that's simply unbelievable in Ballydonal.

KATE: I don't mind Van, I like poor Van. It's the "gerr'ls", as h
calls them. What day did you say you'd go?

MRS ALCOCK: Wednesday.

KATE: Thank God.

MRS ALCOCK: Why?

KATE: I've two committees that afternoon.

MRS ALCOCK: I don't believe it.

KATE: It's quite true. Poultry Society and Library.

MRS ALCOCK: You and your committees!

KATE: They're better than tea with the O'Neills.
  (ATKINS *appears.*)

ATKINS: There's a lad of the O'Flynns wishful to speak to your ladyship.

MRS ALCOCK: Who?

ATKINS: One of the O'Flynns from the cross.

MRS ALCOCK: Are you sure he doesn't want the master?

ATKINS: He asked specially for your ladyship.

MRS ALCOCK: All right, I'll come. (ATKINS *goes.*) Atkins is drunk, St. Leger. He always ladyships me when he's drunk.

ALCOCK: Yes, my dear.

MRS ALCOCK: Can't you do something? Can't you speak to him?

ALCOCK: Not much use while he's drunk. And I suppose there is some excuse this morning.

MRS ALCOCK: If there wasn't you'd invent one. You're too easy-going.

ALCOCK: He's been here for more than forty years.

MRS ALCOCK: Will you do what I've been asking you to do for the last twenty years? Will you get him to give you his key of the cellar?

ALCOCK: My dear, that would hurt his feelings.

MRS ALCOCK: What about *my* feelings? Captain Despard will go back to England talking about us being so Irish. And I'm not Irish, Captain Despard, thank God. I'm a Hampshire woman, a respectable Hampshire woman, in exile, with a drunken Irish butler, and now I've got to go and talk to a "lad of the O'Flynns". Even after living here for twenty years I won't understand half of what he says. I suppose he wants a bottle of medicine for his old grandmother, or he wants to sell me a rabbit he's poached a hundred yards from our own front-door. (*Half vexed, half amused, she goes out.*)

DESPARD: Mrs Alcock's quite wrong, I'm enjoying myself immensely.

ALCOCK: Ah, but that's just what you mustn't do. You mustn't "enjoy" us as if we were a comic story or a play. My wife would like you to take us as seriously as you'd take any country-house in England. She tries — she's tried for twenty-five years — to keep us serious, but always at our most proper moments Atkins or a lad of the O'Flynns keeps breaking in. You remember Dr. Johnson's friend?

DESPARD: (*not remembering*) Yes, oh yes.

ALCOCK: There's a great deal to be said for marrying out of your race. I like every now and then seeing Ballydonal through her foreign, hostile eyes. A touch of Hampshire does us no harm, keeps us from becoming like the O'Neills.

KATE: They married the foreigner, as you said yourself, but it didn't save them.

ALCOCK: True, it doesn't always work.

DESPARD: It's all part of what the padre was saying — that you're not the type.

ALCOCK: Oh, Brown talks a lot of nonsense. I keep telling him that we *are* the type, people like the O'Neills are the dreadful variants.

DESPARD: Is the padre himself up to type?

ALCOCK: He's a gentleman by birth and education — no, I'm afraid he's no longer the typical Irish parson. I believe you can be ordained now without having been to college — to what you and I would call a college. And the priests are as bad. Old Canon Maguire, who was here for forty years, was a travelled, cultivated gentleman, it was a pleasure and an honour to have him to dinner, but he's dead and gone and the new parish priest — impossible — a barbarian.

KATE: I'm sure priests are like soldiers. Didn't Bernard Shaw say that there are only two kinds of soldiers — young soldiers and old soldiers? There are only three kinds of priests, young, old and middle-aged. The old are, as father says, charmers, the middle-aged are rather dreadful generally, but I adore the curates, especially the Republican ones, they're such splendid workers.

DESPARD: Kate!

ALCOCK: Yes, she's hand-in-glove with them. The other day I came round a corner of the road, between here and the village, and I found a curate sitting on a pile of stones giving my daughter a lesson in Irish while she mended a puncture in his bicycle.

KATE: Well, he had cut his hand; I didn't want him to get the cut full of dirt. And he was a very old friend, a great pet, he got into trouble with the bishop in 1916.

DESPARD: About what?

ALCOCK: (*dryly*) Not theology!

KATE: (*airily*) Drilling and guns and a plan to blow up a military barracks.

DESPARD: Oh, no! Good God!

KATE: A fact.

DESPARD: Are the Protestant curates as bad as that?

KATE: Worse. They play tennis.

(MRS ALCOCK *comes in.*)

MRS ALCOCK: You must come, St. Leger, the boy is trying to get at you through me. Something about a brother of his who's been arrested. One of those Sinn Feiners, I think. He wants you to write "a bit of a note" to somewhere or someone, he's not sure to whom.

ALCOCK: Oh, these notes! Do you want a character, Despard, for some brother or cousin of yours whom I have never seen? I shall be delighted to give you one, I am a past master in the art of describing and praising the unknown. I'll come, Mary.

KATE: (*to him as he goes out*) Any wire from the vet?

ALCOCK: No, nothing so far.

(MR *and* MRS ALCOCK *go out.*)

KATE: Poor father!

DESPARD: Why poor?

KATE: Oh, I don't know.... Yes, I do. It's not his *métier*, all this.

DESPARD: This?

KATE: Notes to magistrates, sick sheep and general rural uplift. His place is in the music room, at his piano.

DESPARD: Does he play the piano?

KATE: Does he play —? Why, it's what he does do, much too well to be quite respectable in an Irish country gentleman. He was never intended for Ballydonal, he was in the Foreign Office, but his elder brother broke his neck hunting, and so he had to come back here.

DESPARD: Yes, it's no sort of a life for him or for you.

KATE: Oh, I'm not like father, I love it.... There's something I want you to tell me — how soon do you think we may expect Ulick home, not on leave, for good and all I mean? Supposing this armistice means peace, how soon is he likely to be able to get clear of the army?

DESPARD: Awfully hard to say. Three or four months perhaps, if he pushes hard.

KATE: Oh, he'll push like the dickens... December, January, February... he might be home in March.

DESPARD: Of course he might get some leave before then. Your mother told me he's due leave.

KATE: Yes, he hates fighting so much that he has a sort of conscience about pressing for leave and allows himself to be passed over. But if the war is over he'll have no conscience, he'll move heaven and earth to get out of the army.

DESPARD: To come and live here?

KATE: Yes ... And you go back to the law, I suppose?

DESPARD: Not if I can help it. I'll move heaven and earth to stay in the army.

KATE: You like it so much, Monty?

DESPARD: It's taught me what living is.

KATE: It seems to me like four years stolen out of life.

DESPARD: Yes, I know, it's been hard on girls, not much fun and all the men away.... Do you remember, Kate, what I said to you that night in London, the night before I went back to France?

KATE: I'm sure we all said a lot of silly things.

DESPARD: I said a lot of things to you, but I didn't say one thing.... I don't believe it's right for a chap to get engaged — married perhaps — when there's a war on. It's not fair to the girl. That's why I didn't ask you to marry me.

KATE: Oh, there were lots of other reasons. Feminine ones. That pretty Scotch girl, for instance.

DESPARD: Lulu Mackenzie? Nonsense. I liked you better than all the others rolled together.

KATE: That's only because I was Reggie's sister, your best friend's sister.

DESPARD: No, really. Do you remember Billie Dale? Vulgar little chap, but he had a knack of hitting the nail on the head. Well *he* said to me that night, "Monty, the little Irish girl has all the others beaten to a frazzle."

KATE: That dreadful Mr Dale!

DESPARD: As dreadful as you like, but it's God's truth.

KATE: To begin with, I'm not particularly little, I haven't gray eyes and long dark lashes, I don't speak with a fascinating brogue —

DESPARD: Your voice —

KATE: Stop! I remember you telling me that your favourite play was *Peg o' my Heart*. Well, I'm none of your Pegs. I don't go about with an Irish terrier under my arm, I don't much like dogs, I've no April moods, I don't go from tears to laughter in a moment, I don't believe I've cried once in ten years.

DESPARD: You're charming!

KATE: Much you know what I'm like! You've only known me in London spending a giddy fortnight there, on a holiday and consequently exactly the opposite of what I really am. I'm quite different here. Before you were out of your bath this morning I had fed my hens, when I've finished these flowers

I'm going to garden till lunch — not a lady-like snipping off of dead flowers, really hard digging with a spade, forking dung probably. After lunch I go to the creamery for a committee meeting. I ride to the committee. I don't ride there on an unbroken pony, bare-backed, with my hair flying, I ride on a bicycle, a rather old and dirty bicycle, and I wear a rather old and dirty tweed coat and skirt. After the meeting I go to a poultry lecture, after the lecture to an Irish class. I'll have to leave the class early because you're here, and dinner tonight is an affair. If you weren't here I wouldn't be home in time for dinner, and I'd have tea and bread and jam when I came back. That's the real me, the me I like to be.

DESPARD: Yes, because you've never had the chance to be anything else.

KATE: I think I could have been other things.

DESPARD: You can be other things now.

KATE: Monty, are you asking me to marry you?

DESPARD: Of course.

KATE: I wish you wouldn't.

DESPARD: I can't help myself.

KATE: Oh, yes, you can. It's all sentimentalism, pegofmyheartiness.

DESPARD: You liked me in London. Don't you like me here?

KATE: It's different here, you're not part of my life here, you're part of the London holiday — a very nice part, Monty.

DESPARD: Make London your life, have Ballydonal for holiday.

KATE: Ah, there's Ulick.

DESPARD: What the devil — beg pardon — what has your brother got to do with it?

KATE: Everything.

DESPARD: Everything?

KATE: He's like me; we think Ballydonal *is* life, our life. Of course, as long as Reggie was alive he was the eldest and he'd inherit, but he hated the country, he went straight from school into the army; he'd never want to live here. We planned that Ulick should rent the place from him or live here as sort of manager-agent. Ulick's all father isn't, a born farmer, a born public man, but he didn't depend merely on his instincts; he spent five years learning the newest and best ways of farming, and I've learnt lots of things you'd think silly and dull about poultry and milk and vegetables and bees, we were just ready to start here together — Ballydonal Limited — and then this horrible war came and upset everything, and I've been carrying on as best I could and Ulick's been drilling and marching and breaking his heart to be back, but now the war's over and Reggie's dead and —

DESPARD: Well?

KATE: I don't see why I shouldn't say it, even to his best friend. I'm glad Reggie's dead, glad he died like that, honourably, with letters after his name and mentioned in despatches and all that sort of thing. You knew him well, better than I did probably, and you knew he was handsome and popular, and that he gambled too much and drank too much and got himself mixed up in at least one very shady affair —

DESPARD: Reg was a bit reckless, but there was no harm in him. Just Irish high spirits.

KATE: Just Irish dissipation. Just what has tumbled the big houses into ruins or into the hands of the big graziers or into the hands of the Roman Catholic Church. Vandaleur O'Neills! Not poor Van himself, but the generations of your Irish high spirits that have gone to the making of Van. Reggie wouldn't have cared if he had dragged Ballydonal down. But Ulick and I do care — tremendously. We're going to hold our heads above water, hold Ballydonal above water, proudly and decently.

DESPARD: Milk and hens and turnips! It seems a poor ambition.

KATE: Oh, it's not milk for milk's sake exactly. Everything's mixed up in it, the country, the people, the whole thing.

DESPARD: Good Lord, you're not a Nationalist, are you?

KATE: I thought fervent Nationalism was part of the make-up of your little gray-eyed Irish girl.... But no, I don't think I'm a Nationalist, I don't bother about politics, they crop up sometimes at committee meetings and are a great nuisance, and that's all I know about them.

DESPARD: But you learn Irish.

KATE: Yes. You learnt Latin.

DESPARD: I had to. It was part of the make-up of my career.

KATE: Irish is part of my make-up. I don't like it much; I don't suppose you liked Latin much. Ulick's better at it than I am; he really likes it, he even has managed to keep it up in spite of the war; he'll fit perfectly into the Ballydonal picture.

DESPARD: Hasn't it occurred to you that Ulick may marry? Where would you come in then?

KATE: I wouldn't come in, I'd go out.

DESPARD: So you'd much better marry me. I believe we'd make a good thing of marriage. I'd understand you. After all, my grandmother was Irish — from Ulster.

KATE: Ulster!

DESPARD: That's where I get my sense of humour from.

KATE: I see .... These Irish grandmothers!

DESPARD: Think it over, give me a chance. I'm here for a week anyway.

KATE: If I answered you now, Monty, I'd say "no". If you want me to think it over you must wait until I've seen Ulick.

DESPARD: I don't see the necessity of talking it over with him.

KATE: Oh, maybe I won't talk it over with him, but I just want to see him, see him here, and — and — oh, I do like you very much, Monty, but to live and work here with Ulick — !

DESPARD: Ten to one after France and the army this place will seem so desperately slow that he'll chuck it after a year.

KATE: If you only knew him! ... Why, he comes here sometimes — I don't mean on leave — that's the only really Irish bit of me, I see him sometimes when he's not here at all.

DESPARD: What? Do you mean a ghost? Is this place haunted?

KATE: Sometimes. By Ulick. The night he enlisted he came, he stood on the gravel outside the hall-door, he looked so sad, so very sad. And twice I've seen him in the library standing at the bookcase where all the farming books are. And then only three nights ago.

DESPARD: Where?

KATE: I was coming back from the village, it was dusk, I had pushed my bicycle through the gate between the park and the grass-garden. I was closing the gate when I saw him coming up the drive towards me. He was walking very fast and he was looking very happy. He passed me, and I said "Ulick", I couldn't help it, he seemed so real. By that time he was on the hall-door steps, he turned round, gave me a smile and was gone.

DESPARD: By Jove!

KATE: That was just when the Armistice had begun to seem inevitable. He was dreaming it all over, you see, he was dreaming he was home. And you think he'd chuck it! How he's managed all this time to keep himself from deserting — !

DESPARD: He must be a rum chap. Well, everyone to their taste. But if you're right and he does stick here he'll be certain to marry. It will be part of his programme; he'll marry one of O'Neill's sisters.

KATE: Monty, your Irish grandmother has given you a revolting imagination.

(MR ALCOCK *comes back, the others separate a little self-consciously.*)

DESPARD: It's such a ripping morning, I think, foot or no foot, I must go out for a bit. I'll go and put on a pair of stronger shoes. May I come and watch you gardening, Kate?

KATE: Certainly. (*He goes.*)
Well, what did young O'Flynn want?

ALCOCK: Oh, just a note to the R.M. at Carrig. His brother has got himself into a bad mess, I'm afraid. He was suspected of being mixed up in that raid for arms at Carrigmore, and now three shotguns were found in the mattress of his bed.

KATE: What an uncomfortable place to put them. Did you give his brother the note?

ALCOCK: Of course . . . . I like Despard.

KATE: Do you?

ALCOCK: Don't you?

KATE: Oh, yes, quite.

ALCOCK: You saw a good deal of him in London last spring, didn't you?

KATE: Yes, he was staying with Aunt Kat for his leave, and then he got measles, and that kept him there longer so we saw a lot of each other.

ALCOCK: I know he was a great friend of Reggie's but Reggie never told us much about him. Who are his people?

KATE: Oh, the usual respectable English people with public-school temperaments. They think they're very poor, we'd call them quite rich.

ALCOCK: He's been a barrister, hasn't he? He'll go back to it after the war, I suppose?

KATE: Darling, don't try and be diplomatic. Have him into the library and ask him his income and his intentions. They are both entirely honourable. As you most obviously suspect — he wants to marry me.

ALCOCK: And you?

KATE: Am not at all sure that I want to marry him, and am not going to be rushed.

ALCOCK: I'd like you to marry, Kitty.

KATE: Thanks.

ALCOCK: That's the worst of living here. You meet no one you could, decently, marry.

KATE: I don't think I want to get married at all. I'm quite happy here, especially now Ulick's coming home.

ALCOCK: Ulick must marry, of course. You wouldn't be so happy then.

KATE: That's what Captain Despard threatened me with.

ALCOCK: I think if you really like Despard you'd be wise to take the chance of getting out of all this. Ballydonal's no life for an unmarried woman.

KATE: It's my life. I don't like marrying out of my life, out of my class — I don't mean that in a snobbish way, I'm sure the Despards are as good as we are — but they're different, they're English.

ALCOCK: You're half English yourself.

KATE: The English half of me seems swamped.

ALCOCK: How can you, if you stay here, marry into your class? Who is there to choose? Vandaleur?

KATE: No, not poor Van.

ALCOCK: There's not another house left within visiting distance except Carrigmore, and there are only two old women there. Get out of it, get away. You've done your duty by Ballydonal splendidly in Ulick's absence; now that he's coming back, quit.

KATE: Are you going to quit?

ALCOCK: Your mother would like to, but I think I'm too old to change. But, gracious, I'm going to quit in all kinds of other ways. My mind is full of letters of resignation.

KATE: From what?

ALCOCK: Everything. Every blessed committee and board I'm on. The Old Age Pensions, the Creamery, the Library, the District Council, the Hospital, the Select Vestry, the Diocesan Synod, the Agricultural Show, and all the other fifty committees. Ulick must take my place on them all. The moment he comes back I retire. I'm going then to play scales, nothing but scales, for a month.

KATE: Disgusting self-indulgence.

(ATKINS *comes in.*)

ATKINS: (*presenting a telegram*) The boy is waiting in case there's an answer.

ALCOCK: (*taking it*) Thank you. This will be from the vet. (*A loud bell is heard.*) By Jove, we were forgetting! (*He looks at his watch.*) Eleven o'clock! Thank God.

KATE: (*raising her arms with a gesture of relief*) Oh, at last, at last.

ATKINS: He's ringing it too slow, the young divil. Wait till I talk to him. (*He hurries out.*)

KATE: We can begin to live again.

ALCOCK: Poor Reginald!

KATE: Yes, poor old Reg. (*They are silent for a little.*)

ALCOCK: Imagine London and Paris, how the flags must be flying and the bells ringing.

KATE: And imagine poor Berlin.

ALCOCK: I don't want to think about that. I spent such happy years there long ago — and Vienna too. Oh, well, they must be glad it's over. But they won't be junketing.

KATE: I'm glad we're here and that it's quiet. I'm so slow, I'll only take it in by degrees. I couldn't throw down my work now and start ragging. It wouldn't mean anything to me. I'll take a week to realise.

ALCOCK: The sunshine and your gay flowers will help us to take it in.

KATE: Yes. Michael Dempsey says — oh, the vet, when is he coming, I promised to let Michael know the moment we heard.

ALCOCK: I forgot. (*He opens and reads the telegram,* KATE *has turned away.*)

KATE: I searched all through the sheep-book again last night, and I know a lot of things it's *not*, but I'm blessed if I know what it *is*. Michael persists in calling it a "blasht". Well, is he coming today? (*She turns and looks at her father, he looks at her strangely.*) What is it?... My darling, has anything happened?

ALCOCK: (*with difficulty*) Ulick.

KATE: Ulick? (*She snatches the telegram.*) "His Majesty deeply regrets... of wounds." Ulick? But the war is over.

ALCOCK: The eighth... three days ago.

KATE: Dead?... Ulick?... (*She begins to laugh hysterically.*) Listen to the bell, listen to the bell!

ALCOCK: My dear!

KATE: Victory! Victory!

ALCOCK: It *is*. For King, for Empire. That's what matters.

KATE: Damn King and Empire. They don't matter, not to us.

ALCOCK: (*his arm round her*) Hush, my dear, hush.

KATE: (*breaking from him*) I won't hush. Why should I? Ulick's life was here, here. All he loved, all he worked for.

ALCOCK: We must try and be proud —

KATE: (*passionately*) Never. Never in this world. I'll never be proud of it, I'll never pretend that it was anything but stupid and hateful. You and your King and your Empire! Much good they ever did Ulick, or me, or you.

ALCOCK: Stop, Kate, stop —

KATE: Stop your damned bell then.

(MRS ALCOCK *hurries in, she goes straight to her husband and throws her arms round his neck.*)

MRS ALCOCK: Do you hear it? Peace! Victory!

ALCOCK: Yes, yes, dear. (*Over her shoulder to* KATE.) Kate, please.

(KATE *goes out.*)

MRS ALCOCK: Isn't it wonderful? But — so silly of me — I feel I want to cry.... It's Reggie, my poor dead Reggie.

ALCOCK: Of course, dear, of course.

MRS ALCOCK: But I won't cry, I won't cry. I'll be proud of my dead, I'll think of my living. I'll think of Ulick.

ALCOCK: Yes... Ulick....

MRS ALCOCK: Won't Ulick laugh at us when he hears that we rang the poor old bell?

ALCOCK: (*leading her to the sofa*) My dear... I have something to tell you.

MRS ALCOCK: Yes, but listen to the bell, it's ringing faster now, Paddy is ringing it *con amore*; he must be thinking of his beloved "Masther Ulick".

ALCOCK: I want to tell you.... (*He stops.*)

MRS ALCOCK: Yes?

ALCOCK: I have had a telegram from the War Office.

MRS ALCOCK: About Ulick?

ALCOCK: Yes, about Ulick.

MRS ALCOCK: He's coming back? When?

ALCOCK: No. He's never coming back.

MRS ALCOCK: Never? What do you mean?... What do you mean, St. Leger?

ALCOCK: My poor darling.

(*She stares at him, tries to say something, can't. His arm is round her and as he draws her to him the curtain falls. The bell is ringing quite merrily by this time.*)

CURTAIN

SCENE II

The dining-room at Ballydonal. An evening in the latter part of June, 1921. Dinner is over, everything has disappeared from the table except dessert — a dish of strawberries. MR *and* MRS ALCOCK *are sitting at the table, he wears a dinner jacket.*

MRS ALCOCK: A few more strawberries, St. Leger?

ALCOCK: No, thank you.

MRS ALCOCK: Just two or three — this big one. There are plenty left for Kate. (*She helps him to a few.*)

ALCOCK: Thanks. Take some yourself.

MRS ALCOCK: I never remember having them so early as this, and so sweet.

ALCOCK: Of course the weather is exceptional.

MRS ALCOCK: Yes. Brady says if we haven't rain soon these will be the last as well as the first. I wonder why weather is so difficult. It seems as if no weather was just the right weather. The roses are hardly worth the picking, they fade in a few hours.

ALCOCK: I love it. I love the heat. Do you remember that June in Rome — ninety-four or ninety-five, was it? — the heat and the roses?

MRS ALCOCK: I remember. But even then the weather was wrong for the children, and I had to take them up to that horrible place in the hills.

ALCOCK: ... How long ago it seems.... Like a different existence....

MRS ALCOCK: Yes.... It's nine years since we were abroad. Couldn't we manage to go this summer, even for a few weeks? There are such cheap trips again. I don't care how I go. I'll be a Polytechnic — whatever that means — or a Free Churcher, I'll stay at the scrubbiest *pensions*, I'll submit to being shown the Eiffel Tower from a charabanc — anything to get away.

ALCOCK: Isn't your sister going next month? Go with her.

MRS ALCOCK: Not without you.

ALCOCK: I can't.

MRS ALCOCK: What good does your staying here do?

ALCOCK: I'd be miserable away.

160

MRS ALCOCK: You're miserable enough here in the middle of it, we're both miserable. Imagine the relief of being in a country whose politics mattered nothing to us.

ALCOCK: I don't believe I'd find it any relief. I'd always think I might have been able to do something if I'd stayed.

MRS ALCOCK: You know you can't do anything. You can only wring your hands. It's much better to wash your hands of the whole thing.

ALCOCK: You're almost making an epigram.

MRS ALCOCK: Am I? I know I'm talking common sense. I know that we're living in a community of criminal lunatics and that the sooner we get out of it the better.

ALCOCK: I'll wait till I'm put out.

MRS ALCOCK: Burned out?

ALCOCK: Yes ... or starved out — that seems more likely.

MRS ALCOCK: (*with a sigh*) Sometimes I envy the O'Neills. Kate had a letter today from Sissy O'Neill. They are with some relations in London and having a wonderfully gay time. Everyone makes no end of them because they've been burned out of the ancestral home. If London only knew what the ancestral home was like!

ALCOCK: Such an ugly house.

MRS ALCOCK: Such a filthy house. Mrs O'Neill once told me that the drawing-room carpet had never been up in *her* time — and I believe her.

ALCOCK: I suppose the Irish refugees will soon become as *distingués* as the Russians. I understand that all the Russians are counts and princesses, all the Irish will be the descendants of kings. I can see the O'Neills having quite a success. I can see chivalrous young Englishmen laying their hearts at the large feet of Flossie and Helana.

MRS ALCOCK: I can't quite see that. Englishmen at least know a pretty girl when they see one; no one could call those red-faced O'Neills pretty.

ALCOCK: Being burned out will have paled their cheeks. Kate, unburned, wouldn't have a look-in beside them, so, not to spoil her chances of matrimony, I'll stay.

MRS ALCOCK: Don't talk rubbish. What good can you do? Your being here didn't save poor Maggie Leahy this afternoon.

ALCOCK: (*sighing*) No.

MRS ALCOCK: All this murder has got to be put down ruthlessly. *You* can't be ruthless, so you'd better not be here while it's being put down.

161

ALCOCK: Ah, you admit it was murder.

MRS ALCOCK: I admit nothing of the kind. Maggie's death was an accident — a most distressing one — but the ambush last night was murder pure and simple.

ALCOCK: I envy you, you have a wonderful power of discrimination.

MRS ALCOCK: Right is right and wrong is wrong.

ALCOCK: Agreed.

MRS ALCOCK: There are the eternal verities.

ALCOCK: No doubt there are, but what are they?

MRS ALCOCK: You refuse to recognise them when you meet them, when they're as plain as the nose on your face.

ALCOCK: Oh, of course, England is right and Ireland is wrong, the Republicans commit murder, the Black and Tans commit — accidents.

MRS ALCOCK: That's stupid — and unkind. I'm not as crude as that.

ALCOCK: Forgive me, my dear. I'm all on edge. Maggie Leahy's death seems the last straw. Let's talk of something else, something quite off the point — avalanches or irregular French verbs.

MRS ALCOCK: I suppose I'm on edge too, that's why I say we both want a holiday.... Shall we have coffee here on the chance of Kate coming in?

ALCOCK: Yes.

(MRS ALCOCK *rings.*)

Even if I'd go away, Kate wouldn't.

MRS ALCOCK: Kate, more than either of us, should go away. I'll try again to persuade her to go. The horrible affair this afternoon may have shaken her nerve.

ALCOCK: After all — though one would never have wanted them to come, all these horrors I mean, though one would have done everything in one's power to stop them — now that they're here it's all, in a sense, enriching. I mean Kate's life has been a richer, graver life than if she'd just played games and danced herself into matrimony. I don't believe she'd change places with her London cousins.

MRS ALCOCK: More fool she then. They're all married, at least they will be next month when May marries, and Kate won't even go over to be bridesmaid! I've no patience with her.

(*Enter a parlourmaid* — ANNIE.)

We'll have coffee here, please, Annie.

ANNIE: Yes, ma'am.

MRS ALCOCK: I suppose Miss Kate hasn't come in yet?

ANNIE: I haven't seen her, ma'am.

MRS ALCOCK: I wish she was safely home.

ALCOCK: There's been nothing fresh about poor Mrs Leahy?

ANNIE: I'm told the husband is nearly demented.

ALCOCK: Poor fellow, no wonder! But it's not true, is it, that the baby was shot too?

ANNIE: I don't think so, sir. But of course I'd put nothing past them Tans.

MRS ALCOCK: Bring us the coffee, please. Is cook keeping something hot for Miss Kate?

ANNIE: Yes, ma'am .... Father Doyle says they're a disgrace to civilisation. (*She goes out.*)

MRS ALCOCK: I don't trust that girl. Sly, like all Irish servants.

ALCOCK: Oh, I don't think so. But I must say I miss poor old Atkins. I often wish I hadn't pensioned him off. I met him in the village yesterday, he looked so extraordinarily well, I was strongly tempted to bring him back here with me.

MRS ALCOCK: He's well because he hasn't the run of the cellar. A week here and he'd be as bad as ever.

ALCOCK: For all he'd find in the cellar now! I wonder if my grandfather is turning in his grave.

MRS ALCOCK: Why should he?

ALCOCK: Oh, we must seem shockingly degenerate. No hunters in the stables, no swilling of claret, no card-playing. In this part of the country the eighteenth century lasted right down to the seventies, society even in my father's time was like one of Balzac's provincial novels .... Well, if grandfather upbraids me in the next world I'll retaliate by upbraiding him for stripping this room of its pictures. There was a Romney there, just opposite to me, my father remembered it as a child, and my great-granduncle hung over the fire — a dashing portrait of him in his admiral's dress with a sea-fight in the background, and they and all the others were sold to a little Jew in Limerick for a few beggarly pounds — they didn't even pay grandfather's racing debts.

MRS ALCOCK: It was shameful of him to strip the house the way he did.

ALCOCK: I'm afraid I can't take a very high line about it. I grumble because he left me so little that *I* can sell. I really must get money somewhere.

MRS ALCOCK: It made me simply furious this morning when I was walking back from the village and the Goods flashed past me in their motor choking me with dust. To think of all the rent they owe us! And their car isn't a Ford either, oh dear me no, some very expensive make Mrs Brown told me. Is there no way of making them and all the others pay?

ALCOCK: None.

MRS ALCOCK: I call them common thieves.

ALCOCK: Well, we can console ourselves with the thought that either the Republicans or the Black and Tans will commandeer their car one of these days.

(ANNIE *comes in with the coffee, which she puts before* MRS ALCOCK *and goes out.*)

ALCOCK: (*taking his coffee from* MRS ALCOCK.) Thank you.... Aren't you having any?

MRS ALCOCK: I don't think so.

ALCOCK: Why not?

MRS ALCOCK: It would keep me awake.

ALCOCK: It never used to. Aren't you sleeping well?

MRS ALCOCK: Not very — lately.

ALCOCK: Ah! lying awake imagining you hear the tread of strange feet on the gravel, a hammering on the door, a rattle of petrol tins, there's a click of a revolver, a scratch of a match, a —

MRS ALCOCK: Don't, don't, St. Leger, *please!*

ALCOCK: My dear, are you really frightened?

MRS ALCOCK: Terrified.

ALCOCK: I had no idea.... You really lie awake — ?

MRS ALCOCK: Listening. Till the light comes. Thank God the nights are short.

ALCOCK: How long has this been going on?

MRS ALCOCK: Since the spring. No, always.

ALCOCK: Always?

MRS ALCOCK: Never as bad as now, of course, but I've always felt strange, felt afraid.

ALCOCK: Good God! You've never got used to Ballydonal?

MRS ALCOCK: Never quite used.

ALCOCK: It's always seemed a little foreign, a little queer? My dear Mary, why didn't you tell me?

MRS ALCOCK: Oh, it's nothing to fuss about. I can stand it, I've stood it for more than twenty years. But I feel — just for the sake of sleeping again — I'd like to spend a month or two in some very dull London suburb; Ealing, I think, for choice.

(KATE *comes in very pale and tired.*)

My dear, how late you are, I was getting anxious. Do they know you're in? Mrs Moloney is keeping something hot for you.

KATE: I came in the back way. Mrs Moloney knows. She's sending me up some tea.

MRS ALCOCK: Oh nonsense, you must have some dinner.

KATE: I couldn't, mother, really. I couldn't eat anything. (*She sits at the table.*)

MRS ALCOCK: Just a little soup?

KATE: No really, thanks.

(ALCOCK *goes to the sideboard and pours something into a glass.*)

ALCOCK: Here, drink this.

KATE: What is it?

ALCOCK: Whiskey.

KATE: Oh, no, I couldn't, I don't want it —

ALCOCK: Now, no nonsense. Drink it down.

(*She does so. Suddenly she's afraid she's going to cry and gets up and goes to the window and stands looking out with her back to the room. Her mother is about to go to her.*)

ALCOCK: (*in a low voice*) Let her alone, she'll pull herself together.

MRS ALCOCK: (*low*) She shouldn't have gone, we shouldn't have let her.

KATE: (*turning round*) I'm sorry. I'm all right now. (*She comes and sits down at the table.*)

ALCOCK: Do you want to talk, my dear, or would you rather be all alone?

KATE: I don't mind.... It was very dreadful but I don't think she can have suffered, Dr. Hennessy is sure it was instantaneous. She was sitting on the bank by the road with the baby in her arms, Pat was working in the field behind her. He never heard the lorry till it came round the corner from the cross. They only fired two shots he says. One of them hit her in the breast, I don't know how the poor baby escaped.

ALCOCK: But — but — the whole thing seems incredible.... Were they blind drunk?

KATE: Nobody knows. I suppose they're in an awful state of nerves and fury after the ambush last night. Father Doyle is afraid they'll burn the village tonight.

ALCOCK: He was there — at the Leahys' cottage, I mean?

KATE: Yes, and Mrs Brown came. Mr Brown is away until tomorrow. Mrs Brown was splendid with all the children — six of them, imagine, and all so young. Pat was useless, simply blubbered like a child. Mrs Murphy's taken the baby, its arm got bruised when poor Maggie fell off the bank.

MRS ALCOCK: Can we send down anything? Food?

KATE: I think they've everything. I'll bring down a lot of flowers tomorrow, Maggie liked flowers. (*Enter* ANNIE *with the tea.*) Thank you, Annie. (ANNIE *goes.*)

MRS ALCOCK: Take a few strawberries, Kate. The first this year.

KATE: Thanks. (*But she doesn't take any.*)

MRS ALCOCK: (*pouring her out some tea*) That will do you good.

KATE: Don't bother about me, I'll be all right. Go to the drawing-room, mother, please, I'd rather you would.

MRS ALCOCK: I'd like to stay and see you eat a good tea.

KATE: I'll do that all right. Please don't wait, do go.

MRS ALCOCK: Will you promise me to eat something?

KATE: Yes, I promise.

MRS ALCOCK: And if you feel you'd like something more substantial, you've only got to ring the bell and Mrs Moloney will send you up something nice.

KATE: Yes, I know.

MRS ALCOCK: And you'll come to the drawing-room when you've finished?

KATE: Yes, I'll come. I won't be long.

MRS ALCOCK: Come, St. Leger. (*She goes.* ALCOCK *follows her as far as the door and turns back.*)

ALCOCK: I don't like leaving you, Kitty.

KATE: I'm all right now. I was silly for a minute.

ALCOCK: Well, no wonder.

KATE: "And no one but the baby cried for poor Lorraine, Lorree." That's been running in my head all the evening. So silly, for we all cried.... I suppose I'll see some meaning in it some time. Of course we read of much worse horrors in the war, but to see it — and she was my nurse — a friend really — I gave her her wedding dress, do you remember? and the first baby was called after me.

ALCOCK: Yes, and Pat's father was gardener here for thirty years. They're really part of the family, one of ourselves.

KATE: (*sombrely*) No, that's just what they're not.

ALCOCK: Not?

KATE: Not us, we're not them. That was the awful thing I realised this evening. There I was in that cottage with the neighbours and Father Doyle and Dr Hennessy and I knew Maggie better than any of them, and I — I was an outsider.

ALCOCK: What do you mean?

KATE: Just what I say. An outsider. Something outside, different, away from them.

ALCOCK: When death is in question one feels, of course, that religion makes such a difference.

KATE: Yes, there was religion to make me feel outside but lots of other things too; education, I suppose, and tradition and — and everything that makes me me and them them. Between us and them, like the people in the Bible, there was a "great gulf fixed".

ALCOCK: I know no one who has made less of the gulf than you, Kitty. Your democracy shocks your mother.

KATE: (*impatiently*) Oh, yes, I threw a bridge across the gulf and ran across it and called Pat, Mick, and Larry by their Christian names, and hobnobbed with priests and creamery managers and Gaelic teachers — but it was only a bridge, the gulf remained and when the moment came they instinctively forced me to stand on the farther side. Oh, it wasn't only tonight I've felt it. I've been conscious of it ever since I've been conscious of anything, but I thought it could be broken down.

ALCOCK: Your politics aren't extreme enough.

KATE: It's not that. They could forgive me for not being an out-and-out Republican. There's something deeper, something that none of us can put into words, something instinctive, this "them" and "us" feeling.

ALCOCK: History.

KATE: I think I'd like it better if they hated us. That at least would make me feel that we had power, that we counted for something; it's very hard to forgive toleration.

ALCOCK: And it's hard for us not to seem to patronise.

KATE: I don't patronise, I never have. I sit on committees like every ordinary member. I sit with schoolchildren at the Gaelic classes because I'm such a dunce at Gaelic. We're as poor as mice, we don't keep up any style. We're as Irish as most of them, we're honest and hard working.

ALCOCK: I suppose they feel —

KATE: "They, they, they!" Why should there be any "they"? I was made to feel in that cottage this evening that I had shot Mary, and yet they know perfectly well that I've no sympathy with the Auxiliaries.

ALCOCK: You're overwrought, my dear. You're exaggerating very much.

KATE: No, I'm not. What I'm saying is true, and you know it is. Van O'Neill is an ignorant clod, Father Doyle compared with him is a paragon of culture, but you're uncomfortable when Father Doyle comes here, you're not speaking your full mind to him, he's not speaking his full mind to you, but you're quite happy and easy with poor ignorant Van.

ALCOCK: I've known Van all his life.

KATE: I've known the people in the village all my life. I've worked with them, quarrelled with them, loved them, but at the end of it all I find myself — just different.

ALCOCK: Maybe it's right we should be different.

KATE: How can it be right? I want to be the same.

ALCOCK: You'll never be that.

KATE: Why not?

ALCOCK: It will be always "them" and "us".

KATE: I feel sick and discouraged.

ALCOCK: And your mother feels frightened.

KATE: Frightened? Of what?

ALCOCK: Everything. She says she's never felt quite at home here.

KATE: Yes, it must be worse for her — no, it's worse for me with the Irish side of me tormenting me. Let's give up, chuck up the sponge.

ALCOCK: Kate!

KATE: We're "going, going, going —" like a battered old piece of furniture at an auction. Let's smash the hammer down ourselves and cry "gone".

ALCOCK: Yes, go, Kate, go. You and your mother.

KATE: And you?

ALCOCK: No, no, I can't go yet.

KATE: Yet? What worse are you waiting for?

ALCOCK: I don't know.

KATE: I know. It's your devilish pride.

ALCOCK: I don't think so.

KATE: It's your devilish pride.

ALCOCK: No, no. It's — somehow I'd feel it physically impossible to go just now.

KATE: Yes. You're devilishly proud.

ALCOCK: Nonsense.... Your mother will be wondering where I am. I'd better join her. Come to the drawing room as soon as you can.

KATE: All right.

(ALCOCK *goes out. Left to herself* KATE *drinks a little tea disheartedly. A minute later* ANNIE *comes in.*)

ANNIE: (*planting an egg on the table*) Mrs Moloney sent this up, miss.

KATE: Oh, thanks, thank Mrs Moloney.

ANNIE: Aren't you cold with the window open, miss?

KATE: I don't think so.

ANNIE: There's a terrible breeze blowing in. (*She half closes the casement window.*)

KATE: It's getting very dark, isn't it, or is it very late?

ANNIE: 'Tis like as if there was going to be a storm, or thunder maybe. (*She is going out.*)

KATE: (*suddenly and decisively*) Annie!

ANNIE: Yes, miss.

KATE: Shut the door. Come here. I want you to tell me something.

ANNIE: (*wonderingly*) Yes, miss?

KATE: If the Black and Tans burn the village tonight will we be burned out the next night?

ANNIE: Oh, miss!

KATE: Will we?

ANNIE: Such a thing to say!

KATE: Will we, will we?

ANNIE: Sure how could I say?

KATE: I know you can't say definitely "yes" or "no". But you can tell me whether you think it's likely. Your brother — well, I know what he is as well as you do — is he likely to look on us as a suitable reprisal?

ANNIE: (*vaguely*) Miss!

KATE: He burned the O'Neills.

ANNIE: (*with contempt*) Ah, sure, the O'Neills!

KATE: Exactly. That's what I want to know. Will there be any difference made between them and us? Will all the master has done for the district count for anything?

ANNIE: Everyone has a great respect for the master and for yourself too, miss.

KATE: I know. But how much respect? Enough to save us? I'm only asking as a matter of curiosity; if you tell me they will burn us I shan't do ảnything about it — as a matter of fact there's nothing to be done — but I just want to know.

ANNIE: I don't know why you ask me, miss.

KATE: I don't know why I shouldn't ask you. We've known each other ever since we were children; you know as much about what's going on in the village as any girl in it. I suspect that you know more than any girl. I want a straight answer to a straight question.

ANNIE: Ah, don't bother your head about such things, miss.

KATE: I see.... You won't answer me.... You're probably

right not to. Thank you, you needn't wait. Thank Mrs Moloney for sending me the egg.

ANNIE: Yes, miss. (*She goes out.*)

KATE: (*to herself*) A great gulf fixed. (*She remains brooding, she makes no attempt to eat anything but drinks a little tea. The door opens,* DESPARD *appears in the uniform of the Auxiliary Police.* KATE *doesn't stir, they look at each other silently for half a minute.*) Why have you come? I told you not to.

DESPARD: (*thickly, rather drunkenly*) Professionally.

KATE: What?

DESPARD: Professionally. In the discharge of my duties.

KATE: Do you mean you're stationed here — in Ballydonal? I thought you were in Gormanstown?

DESPARD: Left. Why don't you read my letters?

KATE: I told you why.

DESPARD: Forgot. Shockin' memory.

KATE: I don't correspond with Auxiliaries.

DESPARD: No?

KATE: And I don't want them in this house.

DESPARD: No?

KATE: So will you please go?

DESPARD: This wonderful Irish hospitality! And I've come such a long way today, all the way from County Limerick.

KATE: Limerick?

DESPARD: Yes. The hell of a distance, but, as you were about to remark, lovely day for a drive.

KATE: Why? Why do you come?

DESPARD: Pleasure — and a duty. Pleasure to see you, duty to drop across and tell Ballydonal what we think of it.

KATE: To tell — ? You — ? I understand. How many of you are there?

DESPARD: Cars an' cars an' cars.

KATE: You're going to burn the village, I suppose?

DESPARD: Don't know. Depends.

KATE: Depends on whether you're drunk enough. You're drunk now but not very drunk.

DESPARD: You are going it, Kate.

KATE: What do you want here, in this house?

DESPARD: Stayed here once. Finding myself passing your gate felt it was only commonly polite to call on you.

KATE: Passing the gate... were you on the road between this and the village about four o'clock this afternoon?

170

DESPARD: No. Only just arrived.

KATE: Ah!

DESPARD: Why d'you ask?

KATE: Nothing.

DESPARD: My chaps searching your yard.

KATE: Searching the yard? In the name of goodness, for what?

DESPARD: Anything in trousers that might be hiding in loft or coach-house. Said I'd wait for them here. Damned rude, Kate, you might ask me to sit down or have a drink — *and* have a drink I mean.

KATE: (*getting up*) Take your men away, Captain Despard, take them away. You'll scare mother out of her wits. I give you my word of honour we're hiding no one in the house or in the yard.

DESPARD: Your word! My dear Kate! I said to the driver as we passed your gate "Taylor" (that's his name), "Taylor, that's Ballydonal House and there's a girl there who's as damned a little Sinn Féiner as any I know. Stop the car, turn round —"

KATE: Captain Despard —

DESPARD: Monty, Kate, Monty. This standoffishness, so uncalled for, unexpected —

KATE: Will you please, for the sake of the good friends we were once, go quietly away?

DESPARD: Remarked before — wonderful Irish hospitality, traditional. Well, I've learned not to wait to be asked. (*He sits down and pours himself out some whiskey.*)

KATE: (*reaching for the decanter*) Please, please, Monty —

DESPARD: Hands off! The dust of these roads. You wouldn't grudge an old friend a drink. (*He drinks.*) As you remarked, we were good friends. (KATE *moves towards the door,* DESPARD *gets between her and it.*) Where are you going?

KATE: To mother.

DESPARD: No. No warnings. Not allowed. You stay here, see? My business keep you here. House must be searched.

KATE: How ridiculous.

DESPARD: (*suddenly blazing out*) Yes, damned funny, like the ambush last night. Frightfully funny joke for the fellows who went west.

KATE: You know perfectly well we had nothing to do with the ambush.

DESPARD: Not guts enough. 'Scuse my language. But true. Whiners, that's what you are. "Why doesn't the Government.... Must establish law and order.... But Black and Tans are rather naughty." Compromise, conference, save your bacon. Wow, wow.

(KATE *turns away from the door and walks to the other side of the room.* DESPARD *goes back to the table and drinks again.*) Your father used to brag of his cellar, I remember. How's the old boy?

KATE: (*turning round*) You realise that if you burn the village as a reprisal we'll probably be burned as another reprisal?

DESPARD: Unfortunate. Got to think of the murder of those chaps. Must punish. Must make Ballydonal squeal.

KATE: It was strangers did it, no one from this village.

DESPARD: Yes, always the naughty boys in the next parish. Heard that tale too often. Cuts no ice.

KATE: Monty, if I could bring those poor men back from the dead I'd do so, believe me I would. But they've been avenged. This afternoon a poor woman sitting by the road nursing a baby was shot dead by some Auxiliaries who were passing in a lorry. Won't you take that as your vengeance, and let the village alone?

DESPARD: Spying. I know these women.

KATE: She wasn't spying, she was only a poor labourer's wife sitting in the sunshine with her baby. I've known her all my life, she was my nurse when *I* was a baby.

DESPARD: Your nurse?

KATE: Yes. How would you feel if it had been your nurse.

DESPARD: Damnable.

KATE: Yes, damnable. It's all damnable, Monty, you and us and everything, but it won't be so damnable if because poor Maggie is dead you turn round your cars and go quietly home.

DESPARD: Home? What the hell d'you mean?

KATE: Home to Limerick.

DESPARD: Limerick? Home? Up Garryowen! More Irish than the Irish, you see.

KATE: Go home altogether, back to England, and we can be friends again.

DESPARD: Friends? Only friends?

KATE: Good friends.

DESPARD: I'd do a lot for you, Kitty.

KATE: I know you would. Do this.

DESPARD: Damn me, we will be friends again, Kitty, damn me, we will. Give me a kiss and say you forgive and forget.

KATE: Oh, Monty, nonsense.

DESPARD: It's not nonsense. It's God's truth. Say you forget and forgive, kiss me and say you'll marry me and I'll spare the damned village.

KATE: Rubbish.

DESPARD: How rubbish?

KATE: This is County Cork, not third-rate melodrama.

DESPARD: What d'you mean?

KATE: You're behaving like the hero — or the villain — in a cheap novel.

DESPARD: You're damned superior.

KATE: You're not.

DESPARD: Won't quarrel with you, improves you to lose your temper. I'll kiss and be friends.

KATE: I won't.

DESPARD: Oh, yes, you will . . . . Come here.

KATE: Don't be silly.

DESPARD: (*going to her*) I mean it. Kiss me.

KATE: No.

DESPARD: Kiss me, you — (*He struggles with her, overpowers her, kisses her violently, repeatedly, suddenly he softens, grows tearfully tender.*) Kitty, Kitty, Kitty.

KATE: Monty, poor Monty.

DESPARD: (*crying*) Kitty, Kitty.

KATE: (*soothing him*) Hush, hush.

DESPARD: It's hell, Kitty, it's hell.

KATE: I know, I know.

DESPARD: You can't know how hellish.

KATE: My poor Monty.

DESPARD: The hot nights — that awful little barracks, the rotten chaps that are there, and never knowing when — who —

KATE: Yes, yes, I know.

DESPARD: It wasn't like this in France. I wish I were back there, I'd give my soul to be back there.

KATE: Get out of it. Give it up. Go back to England.

DESPARD: (*shaking himself free of her*) I'll see it through. The lice! We'll give 'em as hard as they give us and just a little bit harder.

(MR ALCOCK *comes in.*)

ALCOCK: Your mother is wondering — Good gracious!

KATE: It's Captain Despard, father.

DESPARD: Evening, Mr Alcock, how are you? Unexpected pleasure.

KATE: Captain Despard's men are just having a look round the yard. I explained, of course, that there was nobody — nothing

— there for them to find and they will be gone in a few minutes. Perhaps you had better go to mother in case she hears anything and is frightened.

DESPARD: Not an unfriendly visit, Alcock, don't take it unfriendly.

ALCOCK: I'll take it as I please.

KATE: Will you go, father? I'll look after Captain Despard.

DESPARD: Yes, Kitty's turning duty into pleasure.

ALCOCK: Come on, Kitty.

DESPARD: (*holding her arm*) No, no, cruel —

ALCOCK: (*suddenly exploding*) Let my daughter alone.

KATE: (*getting to* ALCOCK) Father!

ALCOCK: Do your duty, damn you, as quickly as you can, and clear out of my house.

DESPARD: Mind what you're saying, Alcock.

ALCOCK: Mind your own business.

DESPARD: You're all my business. You and your lovely village and Kitty —

ALCOCK: Leave my daughter.... (KATE *is trying to quiet him.*) Let me alone, Kitty.

KATE: Come to mother, father.

DESPARD: Yes, clear out of this, do you hear? Clear out, the two of you. (*He whips out his revolver.*)

ALCOCK: By God, if you threaten me —

KATE: Father, hush....

DESPARD: Upstairs with you. Hide. Under the bed.

ALCOCK: I see. You are drunk. Very pretty. Kate! (*He opens the door for her.*)

KATE: Not without you.

ALCOCK: I'm coming. (*To* DESPARD.) If you want us you will find us in the drawing-room, my wife, my daughter and myself. You know the way, you have been a welcome guest here — when your uniform was a different one.

(ALCOCK *and* KATE *go out.*)

DESPARD: Old fool! (*The light has been fading, the room is full of shadows. He gropes for his glass and knocks it over, it breaks.*) Damn! (*He drinks straight from the decanter, spilling the whiskey down his face. There is a sudden gust of wind, the casement behind him blows open, the curtain blows into the room. He starts violently and swings round to the window his revolver in his hand.*) Hands up! Who are you? Who are you, I say?

A WHISPER OUT OF THE DARKNESS: Ulick!

DESPARD: Ulick? Who are you? I warn you, don't come in through that window, don't, I say. Hands up or I fire. (*He fires rapidly in the direction of the window two or three shots. The glass splinters and falls. He blows a whistle.*) Taylor! Taylor! (*He fires again.*)

CURTAIN

SCENE III

An evening in February, 1923. The same scene as the previous one, but the room is somewhat changed, it is less emphatically a dining-room and more of a sitting-room. A comfortable armchair is above the fire, and in it MRS ALCOCK *is sitting knitting and reading, the room is lit by an oil lamp on the dining-room table, and there is a pair of candles on a little table beside* MRS ALCOCK. *Half a minute after the curtain rises* ANNIE *comes into the room, she has a large bundle of letters, newspapers, and postal packages in her hand.*

ANNIE: (*bringing them to* MRS ALCOCK) The post, ma'am.

MRS ALCOCK: Letters! Oh, what a surprise!

ANNIE: And the postman said Miss Doyle told him to tell you that there'd be likely be a post going out tomorrow about twelve o'clock.

MRS ALCOCK: Tomorrow? I see. I'll have a lot of letters to go. Will you tell the master that letters have come? He's in the library.

ANNIE: Yes, ma'am. (*She goes out.*)

(MRS ALCOCK *sorts the mail and starts to open her own letters.* ALCOCK *comes in, he is dressed in a dark lounge suit, he has a sheet of paper — an unfinished letter in his hand.*)

MRS ALCOCK: Letters, St. Leger. But only two from Kate.

ALCOCK: How is she?

MRS ALCOCK: I haven't had time to read them yet. Those are yours, they don't look very exciting, and there are all these "Times" and the "Lit. Sup." and "Punch" and "The Saturday Review" — plenty of reading anyhow.

ALCOCK: (*a little petulantly throwing the newspapers on the table*) I'll give up the "Times". Newspapers are bad enough taken in small daily doses, but when they arrive *en masse* they are completely indigestible, they're only waste of money.

MRS ALCOCK: Only a few lines from Kate... had a bit of a cold and very busy at the office... oh, she's changing her rooms going to a boarding-house just off Bloomsbury Square... Oh, imagine, St. Leger! Van O'Neill is going to be married Isn't that amazing?

ALCOCK: Well, why shouldn't he? Who's he marrying?

MRS ALCOCK: Kate doesn't know, Sissy just sent her a card asking her to go round to dinner and she'd tell her about Van who was engaged to be married.... That *is* exciting.... The next letter will tell me. (*She searches for it and opens it.*)

ALCOCK: (*opening and tearing up letters*) No, I do *not* want to lay down a hard tennis-court... *nor* install central heating... nor do I want to restock my cellar... stupid advertisers are, have they no imagination, do they never read the papers?... ah, a moneylender, he's more in the picture... (*But he tears it up.*)... your subscription... due.... Yes, I expect it is, don't they wish they may get it.... Your subscription.... What a post, I can't face it tonight.

MRS ALCOCK: (*having glanced through* KATE's *other letter*) This one is written earlier than the other, so we'll have to wait to hear about Van. It would be just like him to go and make a gránd match. Look at Flossie marrying that Bradford millionaire. (*She attacks other letters,* ALCOCK *bundles his torn papers into the fire.*)... Oh, Margaret's gone to Bournemouth, she likes the rooms and it's very mild she says. She'll stay there till Easter, then she's due at the Coddingtons, I must write to her tonight.... Did Annie tell you that there's a post out tomorrow, at twelve?

ALCOCK: No.

MRS ALCOCK: So if you have anything it must be ready by eleven. Have you finished your letter to Cosgrave?

ALCOCK: (*troubled, getting the sheet of paper he has carried in with him*) No. It doesn't satisfy me, I feel it's so inadequate. I'm sure he won't pay any attention to it — a letter from someone he's never seen, probably never heard of — in his place and with as much to do as he has, *I'd* pay no attention.

MRS ALCOCK: Well, by writing you've done all you can do.

ALCOCK: You talk as if I was writing just to satisfy myself, not really with the object of saving Nicholas. You know it's come back on us like a boomerang — all these letters I've written for years and years recommending idle wastrels as being sober, industrious and entirely trustworthy. Now when I write something that's true, and when it's a matter of life and death no attention will be paid to it. I really think I should go to Dublin and try to see the President myself.

MRS ALCOCK: What nonsense. In this weather. It's a terrible journey.

ALCOCK: I hate to leave you alone — if only Kitty wasn't in London. You wouldn't come with me?

MRS ALCOCK: It's so unnecessary.

ALCOCK: It's a matter of life and death, and Nicholas is such a sterling fine fellow.

MRS ALCOCK: Oh, they won't execute him. Condemning him to death is only to scare people. He'll be kept in prison for a couple of months and then he'll be made a cabinet minister. They're all in the same gang.

ALCOCK: My dear, it's not all bluff; they *have* executed people. There's no shutting our eyes to the fact that Nicholas is in very grave danger.

MRS ALCOCK: Well, he's got no one but himself to thank for the scrape he's in. You're not pretending you approve of what he's done?

ALCOCK: Of course not. But if I could make the President realise that he's not just disorderly, not the common kind of gun-man, that he's a man of very high principles and fine motives —

MRS ALCOCK: Oh, every murder no doubt committed from the highest motives!

ALCOCK: (*sighs, gives it up*) I'll think it over tonight, if I could be even sure of the post getting quickly through to Dublin, but the mail might be raided, the letters might never get through at all.

MRS ALCOCK: The letters are going all right now. Don't worry about it tonight anyway. Give me "Punch" and play me something.

ALCOCK: (*handing her "Punch"*) Here you are. (*He goes to a cottage piano.*) What shall I play?

MRS ALCOCK: Anything you like. (*He sits at the piano, worrying, he doesn't play.*)

MRS ALCOCK: (*discovering something in "Punch"*) Listen to this, St. Leger, this is rather good. "According to an evening paper Mr G.F. Preston, London Telephone Controller, who is retiring at the end of this month, has held the post for eleven years. We congratulate him in spite of our suspicions that this is the wrong number." Really, "Punch" is very witty.

ALCOCK: (*not listening*) Yes.

MRS ALCOCK: And listen to this: "A garden party on a gigantic scale is to be held at Los Angeles. We understand that tickets will be issued to admit 'bearer and one wife'." Isn't that amusing? (*She notices that he is paying no attention.*) Do play something, dear, take your mind off things.

ALCOCK: Yes. (*He plays for a moment or two.*) This beastly piano, it's out of tune too. (*He gets up.*) I can't play it. There must be a fire in the music-room tomorrow, the Steinway is getting damp.

MRS ALCOCK: Very well.

ALCOCK: This room is cold too.

MRS ALCOCK: You got perished sitting all the evening in that icy library. Sit near the fire and poke it up.

ALCOCK: Would you think it horrible of me to go to bed? I feel cold and cross. I'll only snap if I stay here.

MRS ALCOCK: Yes, do go to bed, you look wretched. I'll bring you a hot drink in bed.

ALCOCK: Ah, you needn't bother.

MRS ALCOCK: I'll bring it in a quarter of an hour. Take something to read, the "Saturday Review" — or take "Punch", I can read it tomorrow.

ALCOCK: No, thanks, too contemporary. I have "Tristram Shandy" upstairs. Sterne is pleasantly remote. Are you coming to bed soon?

MRS ALCOCK: Yes, I won't be very long after you. (KATE *has entered very quietly, she is in hat and coat.*)

ALCOCK: Really I feel inclined never to get up, just lie in bed till the summer and read the classics, and never, never look at a newspaper or hear any horrible "news".

KATE: No, you're not going to bed as early as you think.

ALCOCK: ⎫   Good gracious!
MRS ALCOCK: ⎰   Kate!

(KATE *flings herself round her father, and then on her mother.*)

ALCOCK: Kitty, is it possible?

KATE: Looks like it.

MRS ALCOCK: My dear! How? Why?

KATE: Sorry to take you by surprise like this —

ALCOCK: Oh, don't apologise.

KATE: But everything's so uncertain, I didn't know if I'd ever arrive.

MRS ALCOCK: How did you get here? You're starving, I'm sure. Ring for Annie.

KATE: They know, they're bringing tea. I came on Lordan's lorry from Cork; my, such a jolting, three bridges down, and we had to take to the fields and pay toll to every farmer. I walked up from the village lugging my suitcase. (*To her mother.*) You're looking blooming. (*Looking at her father.*) The boss is a little — a little wizened — I think that's the word.

ALCOCK: I'll get my bloom back now that you've come.

KATE: (*taking off her hat and coat and flinging herself into a chair*) My, it's good to be back. As the man said when he saw Rome — "You can 'ave Rome". Well, you can 'ave London. Never again, my dears, never again, except for a fortnight's holiday once a year.

MRS ALCOCK: Do you mean you've left for good — not just for a little holiday? But Mr Scholes — ?

KATE: I'm afraid you have me for good and all. Yesterday — or the day before — all this slow travelling has muddled my dates, I just felt I could bear it no longer. Columns in the paper about country houses going up in flames, Senators being kidnapped and all kinds of thrilling goings-on, and there I was secretarying for Scholes, dear siring and dear madaming and referring to theirs of the ult. and the inst. No, it was not to be borne. So I just up and told him I was going and swept out.

MRS ALCOCK: But surely you had to give him a month's notice?

KATE: Of course. That was what made him so cross. He didn't much mind my going — I'm a rotten secretary I expect — but he did mind my not giving him a month's notice. It hurt his sense of decency. Your countrymen are very queer, mother, the things that shock them — and the things that don't.

MRS ALCOCK: Well, a bargain is a bargain.

KATE: Of course it is, darling.

ALCOCK: Oh, damn Scholes. You're here, that's the great thing.

MRS ALCOCK: It's so disorderly, so — so Irish to run away like that.

KATE: I know it is, but I just felt "Oh, damn Scholes", and said it.

MRS ALCOCK: You didn't, Kate.

KATE: Practically; getting back here was all that mattered. I suppose he can have the law on me if he likes but he won't, he's too decent, he's got a nice tame English secretary by this time and is blessing his stars to be rid of me. But you're quite right, mother, in saying it was so Irish of me to cut and run, that's why I ran, because I felt myself going to pieces.

MRS ALCOCK: How, Kate?

KATE: Morally, mamma dear. You've no idea what it's like in London now, how an Irish girl feels, the things people say, the things the papers say, the "we-told-you-so-ness" of them all. Well you can take it in either of two ways, either you're a martyred émigré like Margaret de Burgh and are shown off and have people asked to meet you, and carry pictures of your castle *before* the fire and *after* the fire (so like an advertisement for a hair restorer or a baby food — why doesn't

Shell or Pratts take it up "Before using our No. 1 spirit the castle was like this — after — !"), and you dress very plainly and get asked out to very good luncheons and talk of being betrayed by England, thrown to the wolves, call yourself an outpost of the Empire and how you made a gallant last stand and, altogether, are more "I-told-you-so" than anyone else. (*She pauses for breath.*)

ALCOCK: Jealous! *You* had no photographs, we're still intact.

KATE: Exactly. I had no photographs. So I had to take it the other way, which means that I simply went livid green. I just damned people, I insulted the émigrés, I loathed their long, gloomy, Protestant faces, their whines and their appetite for luncheons; I insulted the English, I told them it was none of their business what we did with our own country, and anyway as we'd beaten them it would be more becoming if they kept their mouths shut. I made myself thoroughly objectionable to everyone and then I suddenly realised that I was behaving like any Irish girl in a tenth-rate novelette written by some horrible Colonial, that I was being "so Irish" as mother calls me. That shocked me profoundly, and I knew that for my soul's salvation the sooner I left the better, and I realised I'd better leave quick or maybe there'd be nothing to come back to. And here I am.

ALCOCK: We're not likely to be burned, I'm not a Senator.

MRS ALCOCK: Thank God.

KATE: Well, anyway I'm here, and now I'll be able to be myself again. I'll criticise and dislike Irish people — some of them — and be either a Free Stater or a Republican, I suppose I've got to be one or the other. In London, you know, I was just blatantly Irish, I wouldn't stand a word against De Valera *or* Cosgrave.... Oh, mother darling, I know I'm a disappointment to you coming back like this after all the trouble you took and the strings you pulled to get Scholes to take me and I know you wanted me to marry some nice quiet Englishman — but I've stood it for nearly a year and I couldn't bear it any longer and no nice Englishman wanted to marry me — not even a nasty one — I've had no followers, not one. I'm a failure, I'm back on your hands — for keeps.

MRS ALCOCK: It's lovely to have you.

ALCOCK: By Jove, it is. It's not been fun — this winter.

KATE: I suppose it hasn't. I suppose we've all been telling lies to each other for the last six months, you telling me everything was splendid and not to mind what the papers said, and I telling you that there was no place like London.... Well, we needn't pretend any more to each other. God, it's grand to be back to real things even if they're hideous things. In London — apart from the struggle to make a living — everything seems just sentimental play-acting. It's — it's fuzzy.

MRS ALCOCK: (*bitterly*) Sentimental? If you want sentiment in its essence you have it here.

KATE: Yes, I know. But you'll die for it. It's not fuzzy to die.

ALCOCK: Oh, Kate — no, I won't bother you with it tonight.

KATE: What is it? No, do tell me. I'm back for everything bad and good.

ALCOCK: It's Nicholas O'Connor — you remember Nicholas, Jer O'Connor's son?

KATE: Of course. Ulick thought so much of him, he got you to send him to the Model Farm. I thought you had put him in charge of the farms at Ballymacduff.

MRS ALCOCK: He left early in the summer. He went very Republican you know. I lost sight of him, apparently he was in the West fighting all the autumn. He's been captured and condemned to death.

KATE: Nicholas! Oh, father!

ALCOCK: Yes. I only heard today. A three days' old paper I saw.

KATE: But can't something be done? Nicholas was one in a thousand.

ALCOCK: I know. I've written a letter to Cosgrave — half written it, but it seems inadequate, I don't believe he'll pay much attention to it, he doesn't know me. I thought I ought to go to Dublin and see him but I didn't like leaving your mother.

KATE: Oh, go, I'm here now. Mother — imagine Nicholas — oh, it's too horrible.

ALCOCK: You've not come home to a picnic.

KATE: No. Forgive me for saying all those silly things, that was the end of the novelette, I'll try and be decent now. Yet I do like real things, if there has to be a battle I don't want it to be a sham fight.... How fond Ulick was of Nicholas. They used to fish together as boys, do you remember?

ALCOCK: Yes.

KATE: And they worked at Gaelic together in Ulick's holidays — but Ulick was better at Gaelic than Nick.

ALCOCK: I must save him, he was a decent fine fellow. Of course I don't approve of what he's done but — (*To* MRS ALCOCK.) My dear, you won't mind my going now?

MRS ALCOCK: No. It was wicked of me to try to stop your

going before. God knows I don't wish his death... there's been enough killing.... His mother.... (*She pulls herself together, she won't be "sentimental".*) Why don't they bring your tea, Kate?

KATE: No hurry. I'm not hungry, too excited. Oh, Sissy O'Neill saw me off. You'll not be surprised to hear that she "sent her love". The amount of love the O'Neills are always sending, I wonder they have any left.

MRS ALCOCK: And what's this about Van? I only got your letter tonight — five minutes before you came.

KATE: Oh, my dear, Van is making a splendid match.

MRS ALCOCK: There, St. Leger! Who is she?

KATE: American, the usual millions but not the usual American, lives in England altogether and likes to be thought English, has an English accent which Sissy speaks of as "magnificent". She's crazy about horses, Van was at Rathconnell's hunting — he *can* ride, poor Van — they met in the hunting field, he courted her from the back of a horse, he proposed to her from the back of a horse — the only place he'd have any courage — and they're to be married next month.

MRS ALCOCK: Well, if she admires the English accent what does she think of Van's?

KATE: She's obviously very much in love. But Van's has improved. You really wouldn't know any of the O'Neills, burning them out has done wonders for them. There's Flossie with her Bradford woollen man — countless thousands; Sissy in an office, her boss told me the other day she was "invaluable"; Gertie in Bond Street doing people's faces — Gertie who never washed her own! Maggie in a very comfortable little flat looking after her mother, and Helana in musical comedy. Can you beat it?

MRS ALCOCK: It's wonderful, it's unbelievable.

KATE: Compared to them I feel I'm a thorough failure, a returned empty. (*She looks round the room.*) But — I knew there was something odd and queer — why are you sitting here? What's that armchair doing and the table out of the small drawing-room, why the school-room piano?

MRS ALCOCK: Well, we haven't been using the drawing-room this winter.

KATE: Why not?

MRS ALCOCK: Oh, it doesn't seem worth while. Your father is out or in the library all day, we go to bed very early, no one ever calls — there's no one *to* call except the Browns, and they don't mind sitting in here —

ALCOCK: Don't mind her, Kitty; she's making decent, needless excuses. The truth is we're pretty nearly broke, and she's trying to run the house with only two servants, Annie and the cook. Every room less means a fire less.

KATE: I see.... You're eating next to nothing, of course; you always had the appetite of wrens, no wonder the boss looks pinched; it's about time I came home.

ALCOCK: Nonsense, we've plenty to eat.

MRS ALCOCK: But he would give up wine — even his glass of thin grog before going to bed.

KATE: I've saved ten pounds; I wish it was more, but it's awfully hard to save in London. We'll go on a burst, *pâté de foie gras* for you and champagne for the boss.

MRS ALCOCK: Darling!

KATE: I suppose no rents are coming in?

ALCOCK: Not a penny for three years.

KATE: Hm.... We are shrinking, aren't we? Do you remember the first winter of the war we shut up the north wing and did without two servants, the next winter we cut off the central heating, that meant never sitting in the hall, now the drawing-room's gone and the music-room, too, I suppose. Soon we'll be reduced to a single bed-sitting room.... Do you think it all minds it — feels it — the house itself, I mean — Ballydonal?

ALCOCK: In all the generations it's seen, it must have learnt patience.

KATE: Yes, I suppose an immense toleration for the animals who run about through its passages and rooms, and who pull down a bit here and build it up again fifty years later, and cover its walls with paper and then wash the paper all off, who tear out its vitals to put in hot water pipes and then let the pipes go cold. And feather beds are banished to lofts and wax candles give place to lamps, and they should have gone before this to make place for acetylene or electric light, and none of us live any longer or are any the happier, but we scratch and alter, scratch and alter, generation after generation.

ALCOCK: You're becoming quite lyric, Kitty.

KATE: Sorry. But you see when I was away from it I could see it in a way I never could before. When I lived here I couldn't see the house for the rooms.

MRS ALCOCK: They're awful, all those empty rooms on every side of us — above us all those garrets, below us cellars and empty cellars.

ALCOCK: Never mind, one of these days I'll sell it to the priests or the nuns.

MRS ALCOCK: I wish you would.

KATE: Is it true that Castle Bewley is to be a training college for South African missionaries?

ALCOCK: Quite true. And Carrigmore, of course, has dedicated it-self to the task of converting China . . . . One of these days Ireland will wake up and realise that all its best houses and much of its best land have passed into the hands of landlords who are entirely self-contained, who give no employment, who hold themselves aloof from the life of the community. A curious situation.

KATE: Well, the big houses have had their fling, drank claret deeply in their youth, gambled and horse-raced in their middle-age, so it's right they should be converted and turn pious in their old age. But I should think Castle Bewley would need not conversion but exorcism.

MRS ALCOCK: I hear Annie coming. Here's your supper at last. (*The door opens, three young men in trench coats and soft hats appear. The leader of them has a revolver.*)

LEADER: Mr Alcock, you have five minutes to leave the house. (*The* ALCOCKS *have risen, speechless.*)

ALCOCK: What do you want?

LEADER: You have five minutes to get out.

ALCOCK: You — you're going to —

LEADER: Blow it up and burn it. You have five minutes. Will you please leave as quickly as you can, you can take with you any-thing you like.

ALCOCK: (*bewildered*) Mary —

MRS ALCOCK: (*blazing with indignation, to the* LEADER) You dare? You dare? I don't expect you to have sense, that would be asking too much, but have you no decency? Do you know what house you're in, do you know who you're speaking to? Have you ever heard of Ballydonal House? Have you ever heard of Mr St. Leger Alcock?

LEADER: You have five minutes to leave.

MRS ALCOCK: Don't stand there prating of your five minutes. I'm English, thank God, if I'd my way I'd have been out of this house five years ago, five and twenty years ago.

ALCOCK: (*restraining her*) Mary, my dear —

MRS ALCOCK: (*shaking him off*) No, St. Leger . . . . (*To the* LEADER.) I don't know your face, are you a stranger here? If you are, before you destroy Ballydonal House go down to the village and ask the first person you meet what this house means, ask if anyone was ever turned away hungry from its door, ask them about Mr Alcock, what he's done for them, the years of his life he's spent on them, the money, the — the — oh, it's monstrous. What was he doing this very evening? Writing a letter to Cosgrave to try and save one of you — one of you who come now to —

ALCOCK: Stop, Mary. We're not begging off.

LEADER: I have my orders. Ye're to go and the sooner the better; I've other work to do tonight.

MRS ALCOCK: Nicholas O'Connor. He was writing to save his life, and now you —

LEADER: He's after the fair. Nick was executed yesterday.

MRS ALCOCK: Oh.

ALCOCK: Yesterday? Poor Nicholas!

MRS ALCOCK: Is that why we're to be burnt! It won't bring him back to life!

LEADER: I'm not here to argue.... (*To* ALCOCK.) Will you get the women out? They'd better get some coats or something, the night is dry but it's cold.

(ANNIE *appears at the door in coat and hat.*)

ANNIE: (*to* LEADER.) Me box and the cook's is in me room corded and all. Will you send the lads to fetch them down.

LEADER: (*shortly*) All right.

ANNIE: (*insolently taking out a cigarette*) Give me a light.

LEADER: A light?

ANNIE: (*with a grin*) You needn't tell me you've no matches. (*He gives her a box, she lights her cigarette.*) I suppose you'll give us a lift to the village.

LEADER: I will not. We're going the other way; I'll leave the boxes at the lodge.

ANNIE: You're not very civil.... (*To* MRS ALCOCK.) You owe me a fortnight's wages. You can send it to me, care of Miss Doyle. (*She goes.*)

MRS ALCOCK: She was packed and ready, she knew!

ALCOCK: Come, my dear. Come, Kate.

KATE: (*blazing*) No! they can blow me up here.

ALCOCK: Hush. No use talking like that. On with your coat. (*He helps her into her coat.*)

MRS ALCOCK: St. Leger! The birds!

ALCOCK: Oh.... (*To* LEADER.) It sounds quite ridiculous, but my wife has some canaries — two large cages — they're upstairs in the old nursery, if we could — ?

LEADER: (*to the men*) Let ye bring them down and hurry. Where are they?

KATE: No.

ALCOCK: I'll show the way myself.... See that your mother wraps up well. Now come.... (*He gets the women out, their heads are high; he turns at the door to the* LEADER.) It's up two flights, I'm afraid, and the cages are awkward things to carry — I'll just see that my wife has her warm coat. (*He disappears.*)

LEADER: (*to men*) When you have the birds and the servants' boxes out come back here. We'll put one mine here and another at the library door where Annie Daly showed us. I'll want two tins of petrol here and as many again in the hall, and.... (*he is continuing his orders when the curtain falls.*)

CURTAIN

SCENE IV

A corner of the garden. Two high stone walls form a right angle across which has been built a summerhouse — a roof supported by a couple of pillars. Below the stone walls are flower borders, empty now except for some withered stems of plants, on the walls some withered creepers and perhaps some evergreen ones, rose-trees gone a little wild. In the summerhouse and outside it on the path is a medley of furniture. It is just before sunrise, the morning after the previous scene, a cold light which grows brighter as the scene progresses. ATKINS, *collarless, dressed very hastily, and* MR BROWN, *also hastily dressed and very dirty, enter carrying between them a sofa.*

BROWN: (*dropping his end*) Just here, Atkins, we won't take it any further.

ATKINS: I'd like to get it into the summerhouse.

BROWN: There's not room. We'll get a cart later on and get all these things over to the rectory.

ATKINS: (*rather futilely dusting the sofa*) The murdering rascals. Will we bring the rest of the things, your reverence?

BROWN: I think they're as well on the gravel as they are here — now the summerhouse is full. For a wonder it doesn't look like rain. Michael will have an eye to them.

ATKINS: Oh, then, I know the sort of an eye Michael Dempsey will have to them, a covetous, thieving eye.

BROWN: Atkins!

ATKINS: Faith, Mary Dempsey will be living like a lady from this out, lolling back on her ladyship's cushions and drinking her tea out of her ladyship's cups.

BROWN: Nonsense. Michael is as honest as the day.

ATKINS: God help you, your reverence, 'tis little you know the class of people that's in this place. I was as innocent as yourself until I went to live beyond in the village. There's neither religion nor decency in the village, a low, thieving, murdering lot. Oh, my eyes were opened, I assure you. I learned things that surprised me, indeed and I did. Thanks be to God I come from the County Tipperary and never set

188

foot in County Cork till I took service with the poor master's father.

BROWN: (*sitting on the sofa and lighting a pipe*) I thought I remembered hearing that Tipperary had a reputation for wildness.

ATKINS: To be sure it has, but it's a decent kind of wildness; you wouldn't find a thing happening there like what happened here last night — burning Ballydonal House! God forgive me, I could curse like a tinker when I think of it. They're a low, mean, murdering crew, the people in this place, not a one of them would come up with me to lend a hand when the blaze of light on the window woke me this morning, but you'll see they'll be up in an hour's time, nosing around, picking up this thing and that, "saving them" moryah, "keeping them safe for Mr Alcock against the time he'll be wanting them". Do you know what I'd like to see this minute better than anything else in the world?

BROWN: What?

ATKINS: A regiment of English soldiers and my grandson in the middle of them marching into the village, horse, foot and artillery, and making smithereens of the dirty little houses is there and the dirty little people is living in them, and maybe then they'd know what it is to feel the way the poor mistress feels this minute with her lovely house destroyed on her and she without a roof to shelter her.

BROWN: No, no, you wouldn't wish them that. They're not responsible for what's happened.

ATKINS: Bedad, then, I'd make them responsible, and mark you me, it will come to that yet, and maybe quicker than any of us expect.

BROWN: Come to what?

ATKINS: People high up and low down screeching to the English to come back and protect them from themselves.

BROWN: I don't think that day will ever come.

ATKINS: Indeed and it will. God knows we need protection. How can we live in peace in a little country where everyone knows everyone else and every third man you meet is your second cousin? Sure 'tis well known that relations never agree and every man in Ireland is his own relation.
(*Enter* KATE.)

KATE: Here you are. I've been looking everywhere for you. Wouldn't you like a cup of tea? Michael kindled a fire in the coach-house and we've all been having tea.

BROWN: No, thanks, I'm having a pipe instead.

KATE: We've all been washing under the pump. I'm rather proud of the result.

BROWN: I've sent a message to the Goods asking them to send over a car to bring you all across to the rectory.

KATE: Oh, we could walk.

BROWN: The Goods may as well do that much for you.

ATKINS: Them Goods!

BROWN: You might have a look and see whether the car is there, Atkins. They won't know where to find us.

ATKINS: Very well, your reverence. (*He goes out.*)

BROWN: Poor old Atkins is in a state of tearing indignation. He takes it all as a personal insult to the family.

KATE: Yes.... What an amount of stuff you've got here!

BROWN: I gave up when the summerhouse was full, we'll get it all up to the rectory before night, there are plenty of empty houses in the yard.

KATE: (*looking into the summerhouse*) What a mixture!

BROWN: It is, rather.

KATE: My God, look! (*She pulls out a picture — Leighton's "Wedded".*) I saved that, Mr Brown, *I* saved it, a picture I've always hated and at any rate it's only a cheap reprint. I struggled through smoke and flame to save it and I never remembered till too late those fine Hones in the hall.

BROWN: How could you remember in all the excitement? I do wish I had known an hour earlier than I did.

KATE: Yes, if we'd had someone with a clear head — father was no use, once he found that there was no chance of saving the beloved Steinway, he just went numb. Mother, though you'd never have thought it, was the best of us, she kept her head and her sense, she made for the right things, made me get the miniatures and made father get at the safe and the papers.

BROWN: And Atkins?

KATE: Instinctively went for big pieces of furniture, things he'd known all his life, it meant that the nice Chippendale stuff was saved but also this hideous sofa. (*She sits on it.*) I suppose I'm a little hysterical but I can only feel everything — since the horror of the mine — as supremely ridiculous. If you could have seen us — but you can easily imagine it — literally risking our lives for the sake of certain bits of wood and china and glass. And we're supposed to be educated and intelligent and (as you'd remind me) we have immortal souls, but savages from darkest Africa couldn't have fought more desperately for some uncouth image of their god than we did for some piece of wood absurdly carved, for miniatures of our forebears, for Leighton's "Wedded". Pure fetish worship. Now that the excitement is over I realise what savages we were and what a nuisance this jetsam is going to be, so much better if everything had been burned. It's awful to think that we'll have to start again to live up to the Chippendale suite. Couldn't we — oh, don't you think we could — have a little private bonfire here of the contents of the summerhouse?

BROWN: The complications with the insurance people would be awful.

KATE: I suppose so. And anyway mother has the Chippendale in the coach-house. Joking apart, I'd like to have saved some of the books, a few of Ulick's for old sake's sake.

BROWN: Could you get nothing from the library?

KATE: Nothing. The explosion blocked the door and it went on fire at once. Oh, well, a lot of them were very dusty, and most of them I had never read, and God with amazing foresight has created Mr Andrew Carnegie.

BROWN: I'm glad that Ulick didn't live to see this, it would have broken his heart.

KATE: I wonder would it. We thought very much alike, Ulick and I, and do I look as if my heart was broken?

BROWN: I can't say you do.... I expect in your inmost soul you're glad to be quit of it all.

KATE: Glad? I feel — exalted! If only you knew what I feel and I'll tell you — but not now, here's father. Poor darling, he doesn't look exalted, we must get him to the rectory as soon as possible.

(*Enter* ALCOCK.)

ALCOCK: Your mother is wondering where you are.

KATE: I'll go to her. Is she still in the coach-house?

ALCOCK: Yes. I left her feeding the birds.

KATE: Right. I'll be back again. (*She goes.*)

BROWN: Sit down, St. Leger.

ALCOCK: (*sitting on the sofa*) I feel tired.

BROWN: Of course. Have a pipe.

ALCOCK: No, thanks. (*Feeling in his pocket.*) I don't believe I have a pipe.

BROWN: I have a second one — if you don't mind.

ALCOCK: I feel a pipe would make me sick — like a schoolboy. Silly, isn't it. But I'll try a cigarette.

BROWN: The Goods are sending a conveyance to bring you to

the rectory and after breakfast I shall pack you all off to bed.

ALCOCK: Yes.

BROWN: Kate is fine.

ALCOCK: Yes. I'm not and I'm not going to try to be fine. I feel as if nothing matters any more, as if everything was over.

BROWN: Ay.

ALCOCK: And that I'm just damned glad it's all over and that there's no reason to make an effort any more, no need to pretend ever again.

BROWN: To pretend what?

ALCOCK: That all this — all life here mattered — to me personally I mean, that I really cared what happened.

BROWN: You cared a lot, my dear man, you've been breaking your heart for four years.

ALCOCK: Because I hate cruelty and stupidity and waste, but not for any other reason. I'd have felt just the same if this had been Abyssinia.

BROWN: I doubt it.... And what happens now?

ALCOCK: I haven't an idea. I don't intend to have an idea.

BROWN: Kate — ?

ALCOCK: Exactly. Kate. I feel it's Kate's show. I leave it all to her and to my wife. My God, it's a relief to have it all over. I've felt for so many years like a bad actor cast for a part far too heroic for his talents, I haven't had technique enough for it, I haven't in any way been big enough for it, the audience has realised at last what I realised years ago, it's hissed me off the stage and sitting here in the wings wiping off my make-up I'm feeling devilishly relieved, almost happy, but at the same time I feel distinctly sick in the stomach.

BROWN: You want a nip of spirits — whiskey or brandy.

ALCOCK: Henry, I'm surprised at you!

BROWN: Oh, for your stomach's sake. There's some at the rectory. For years I've been preaching total abstinence and boasting that I'd never let a drop of the accursed stuff under my roof and I discovered the other day that all the time my wife was squirrelling a bottle of brandy — on the top of the wardrobe in my dressing-room of all places — keeping it for emergencies, she said. It's been there for twenty years. Aren't women the dickens?

ALCOCK: Excellent Alice! It was probably twenty years old to start with. It will be worth drinking. Do you think she'll consider me an emergency?

BROWN: Surely.

(*Enter* MRS ALCOCK *and* KATE.)

MRS ALCOCK: (*fussily*) Now, St. Leger, there's a message from the Goods to say they're sending a car, it will be here in five minutes. Are you ready to come?

ALCOCK: Quite.

MRS ALCOCK: We'll take the birds with us, they're all right, I fed them just now. Kate has arranged with Michael to have all the things brought over to the rectory and stored there for the present, of course we couldn't trust them here for an hour, and we'll order a motor to take us to Cork this afternoon.

BROWN: Oh, won't you stay at the rectory? We've plenty of room, you're all welcome as long as ever you like to stay.

MRS ALCOCK: I know it sounds rude but I'd rather go. They've burned us out, we've our pride still, I hope — at least I have — I know when I'm not wanted, I take the hint and go and I hope to goodness I never come back.

(BROWN *sighs.*)

Yes, I know it sounds horrible to you, dear Mr Brown, our best friend here, our oldest friend, but it's because you're such an old friend I can't pretend. But we'll only be parted from you for a little while. You must follow us, we'll get you some lovely quiet English parish with an ancient beautiful church and you'll be able to put flowers and a crucifix on the altar without your congregation thinking that you are heading straight for Rome.

BROWN: Dear Mrs Alcock!

MRS ALCOCK: I mean it. You can't pretend that you'd prefer the horrible bare barrack of a church you have here. St. Leger sits here as if he was dead, but I don't feel a bit dead, I'm an old woman, I suppose, but I feel as if life was just beginning for me. Even if we never get a penny of compensation for all this — and I suppose we'll get something — we can't be worse off than we've been here trying to support this white elephant of a house. We'll go to Bournemouth, my sister's there, we'll go to furnished lodgings. Oh, the peace of English furnished lodgings, the beautiful dull respectability of Bournemouth.

ALCOCK: Bournemouth after Ballydonal!

MRS ALCOCK: Don't get sentimental, St. Leger. Or do, if you like. Have a broken heart, it's quite a comfortable thing to have in a place like Bournemouth.

ALCOCK: What does Kate say?

KATE: It sounds a good plan.

MRS ALCOCK: Of course it's a good plan.

BROWN: You can leave my English parish out of it. I've been fighting with my Select Vestry for twenty years, they'd think they'd won if I left.

KATE: Oh, I meant for mother and the boss.

MRS ALCOCK: It's easy to run up to London from Bournemouth, Kate. You can go up for long weekends.

KATE: Don't bother about me. I'm not in that picture.

MRS ALCOCK: Where are you then?

KATE: Here. Right here.

MRS ALCOCK: Rubbish.

KATE: We'll get to Cork this evening, we sleep there and go on to England tomorrow or the next day. We go to Bournemouth, I find you really nice, stuffy, respectable lodgings, I hire a good piano, I stay with you till the Vicar calls on you — that launches you into society — and then I'm coming back.

MRS ALCOCK: My dear! Nonsense.

KATE: (*low, almost singing it*) I'm coming back, I'm coming back, I'm coming back.

MRS ALCOCK: Where to?

KATE: Atkins' pantry, I think. Did you notice how wonderfully Providence almost completely spared it? I want three pieces of corrugated iron to make a roof and a few little odds and ends — Mr Brown must get them for me. (BROWN *laughs*.)

MRS ALCOCK: Oh, I see it's a joke.

KATE: No, it isn't. The corrugated iron part is but the rest isn't. As we are planning our futures I may as well say what I have to say now as later. I am coming back to live here at Ballydonal.

ALCOCK: Is this bravado or mere obstinacy?

MRS ALCOCK: As I said before, I have my pride, I know when I'm not wanted.

KATE: I have my pride too. Until last night I thought we were not wanted, that's what sickened me, that's what drove me to work in London, I saw everything sweeping past us and leaving us behind, high and dry like some old wreck, useless and forgotten, I couldn't bear that — my beastly conceit, I suppose.

MRS ALCOCK: And after last night do you feel you're wanted?

KATE: I can't flatter myself that we're wanted, but we're not forgotten — ignored.

MRS ALCOCK: I could have put up with being forgotten, there are some ways of being remembered —

KATE: I know. "Say it with petrol!" But still, even to have it said that way, to have it said any way —

BROWN: By Jove, I see. Last night showed you that you still mattered.

KATE: More than ever we mattered before. When those men came in I was furiously angry, I'd have shot them if I had a gun, but deep down in me there was something exulting, something saying, "This is real".

ALCOCK: Your passion for reality, Kitty!

KATE: I mean it was sincere. I've seen time after time father having interviews with people like those young men about one thing or another, but they were never quite real interviews, father wasn't real or they weren't real, but last night! — Did you notice they kept their hats on?

MRS ALCOCK: I've no doubt they did.

KATE: I don't think they meant to be rude, it was just typical of their attitude towards us, they sort of kept on their hats in their minds. We were equals — except that they had revolvers and we hadn't. It was — it was grand.

MRS ALCOCK: Well, if it pleases you to know that you're hated, to know that there's no gratitude in the country for all your father has done, you have ample reason for rejoicing. I suppose Annie's falseness and insolence was a great pleasure to you too.

KATE: No, Annie was hateful. But they didn't like her falseness, you could feel they didn't.... It's not quite that they hate us, it's fear. They're afraid of us.

ALCOCK: "They", "us"! Do you remember, Kate, the evening after Maggie Leahy was shot?

KATE: Yes. But now I don't want to give up the "they" and "us", I glory in it. I was wrong, we were all wrong, in trying to find a common platform, in pretending we weren't different from every Pat and Mick in the village. Do you remember that gray filly we had long ago that I christened "Pearl" and Michael always called it "Perr'l" and so we all called it "Perr'l" not to seem to criticise Michael's pronunciation? That's a trifling example, but it's the sort of democratic snobbishness we went in for. We were ashamed of everything, ashamed of our birth, ashamed of our good education, ashamed of our religion, ashamed that we dined in the evenings and that we dressed for dinner, and, after all, our shame didn't save us or we wouldn't be sitting here on the remnants of our furniture.

ALCOCK: And what can save you now, it's too late?

KATE: If it was too late they wouldn't have bothered to burn us; *they* don't think it's too late so why should we? They're afraid of us still.

MRS ALCOCK: (*with a bitter laugh*) We do look formidable, don't we?

KATE: We are formidable if we care to make ourselves so, if we give up our poor attempt to pretend we're not different. We must glory in our difference, be as proud of it as they are of theirs.

BROWN: But why?

KATE: Why? What do you mean?

BROWN: Why "must" you glory?

KATE: Why, because we're what we are. Ireland is not more theirs than ours.

BROWN: Or ours than theirs.

KATE: Exactly. But do let's leave them to see their own point of view. We've spent so much time sympathetically seeing theirs that we've lost sight of our own. Ah, Mr Brown, you've been as bad as any.

BROWN: As bad?

KATE: How many converts have you made during the twenty years you've been rector of Ballydonal?

BROWN: Converts? I'm not ministering among the heathen.

KATE: Shouldn't you feel, as a Protestant parson, that Roman Catholics are next thing to heathens? If you don't feel like that why are you a parson?

BROWN: (*smiling*) Do you want me to turn to souperism?

KATE: Why not? You used to rail at the Irish country gentleman and say that he was putting up no fight. What sort of a fight have you put up? If you really believed in your Protestantism you wouldn't hesitate at a trifle like souperism.

BROWN: You'll never get me to stoop to that.

KATE: Oh, well, religion's not my business and I'm too fond of you to quarrel with you but you'll have to go, all you amiable Protestant parsons, and make room for parsons who believe in their religion enough to fight for souls with every weapon that God has put into their hands. If they don't come, Protestantism itself goes.

ALCOCK: It's going now.

KATE: Because the Mr Browns are letting it slip through their fingers just as you'd let Ballydonal slip through yours.

ALCOCK: It seems to me it's been snatched.

KATE: Pooh! What's a house? Bricks and stones. Aren't there plenty of both in the world. We'll build it up again.

MRS ALCOCK: Nonsense. Never. Not for me.

KATE: I'll build it for myself. I'll build it with my own hands if

I'm put to it. I believe in Ballydonal, it's my life, it's my faith, it's my country.

ALCOCK: My dear, don't. Don't waste your life here. If you were a man, if you were Ulick, I wouldn't say a word to stop you, but a single woman! —

KATE: I must marry if I can. That's another thing Mr Brown must look out for me; three pieces of corrugated iron and a husband, please, Mr Brown.

BROWN: I wish I could get you the husband as easily as the other. What sort of husband do you want?

KATE: Well, I ought to marry someone like Van O'Neill but I'd like to marry wildly, out of all reason, I'd . . . like to marry a — (*She stops.*)

MRS ALCOCK: Well Kate, who?

KATE: No, it's a dream, it's quite impossible. But I should like to marry a Republican Catholic curate.

MRS ALCOCK: Kate!

KATE: I've always adored them.

(ATKINS *comes in.*)

ATKINS: The Goods' car is here now, sir.

MRS ALCOCK: Thank goodness, it puts an end to this ridiculous conversation. St. Leger, wake up, come along.

ALCOCK: (*getting up slowly*) Yes, I suppose so.

MRS ALCOCK: Take my arm.

ALCOCK: My dear, you should take mine.

MRS ALCOCK: I don't need it. Come.

ALCOCK: (*as he goes out*) Bournemouth after Ballydonal!

MRS ALCOCK: Ssh! (*They go out.*)

BROWN: I believe you mean it, Kate; I see it in your eye.

KATE: Every word of it. Go after them, I have a word to say to Atkins.

(MR BROWN *goes out.*)

We're going to Cork this afternoon, Atkins, and then to England. The master will send you your money as usual. Here's something to go on with. (*She hands him a pound note.*)

ATKINS: You're going away, miss? Ah, sure, it had to be.

KATE: But in a few weeks, in a month or two, I'm coming back.

ATKINS: You're what, miss?

KATE: Coming back to live here for good.

ATKINS: Thank God for that.

KATE: You can tell it in the village. (*She goes out.*)

ATKINS: (*looking after her*) God bless Miss Kate. (*He looks at the furniture.*) The murdering ruffians!

(*He is lifting a chair into the summerhouse, he drops it and starts back in terror.*) Miss Kate, Miss Kate, Miss Kate!

KATE: (*coming back quickly*) What is it, Atkins? What's the matter?

ATKINS: (*babbling*) I seen him there — in the summerhouse — as clear as the day — Master Ulick —

KATE: Ulick? Go away, Atkins, go away. (*She pushes him out. She turns to the summerhouse and speaks softly.*) Ulick! Are you there?... (*Her face lights up.*) Oh, my dear, you've come to me again, after all these years.... And you're smiling, so I'm right, it's what you'd have done.... (*A pause, she seems to listen to someone talking.*) Yes.... Yes.... So — kiss me, my dear.... (*She raises her face as if she were being kissed, she closes her eyes.*)

CURTAIN

DRAMA AT INISH

A play in three acts

For Dolly

ACT I. A private sitting-room in the Seaview Hotel, Inish. A July
    morning.
ACT II. The same, early evening, ten days later.
ACT III. The same, a week later, morning.

CHARACTERS

JOHN TWOHIG, proprietor of the Seaview Hotel, Inish.
ANNIE TWOHIG, his wife
LIZZIE, his sister
EDDIE TWOHIG, his son
PETER HURLEY, the local T.D.
CHRISTINE LAMBERT
HECTOR DE LA MARE, an actor
CONSTANCE CONSTANTIA, an actress, his wife
HELENA, a servant
MICHAEL, the boots
JOHN HEGARTY, a reporter
TOM MOONEY, a Civic Guard
WILLIAM SLATTERY, P.S.I.

The first production of "Drama at Inish" took place in the Abbey on the 6th February, 1933. The cast was as follows:

John Twohig	W. O'GORMAN
Annie Twohig	ANN CLERY
Lizzie	CHRISTINE HAYDEN
Eddie Twohig	JOSEPH LINNANE
Peter Hurley	ERIC GORMAN
Christine Lambert	GLADYS MAHER
Hector de la Mare	PAUL FARRELL
Constance Constantia	ELIZABETH POTTER
Helena	NORA O'MAHONY
Michael	REX MACKEY
John Hegarty	FRED JOHNSON
Tom Mooney	J. WINTER
William Slattery	DON BARRY

The Play was produced by the Author. It was subsequently done in the Ambassador's Theatre, London, and in New York, under the title "Is Life Worth Living?"

ACT I

*Inish is a small seaside town in Ireland of not much importance
save for the three summer months when it is a point of attraction
for people seeking sea breezes and a holiday. It has boarding
houses but only one hotel of any size — the Seaview Hotel — owned
by* MR JOHN TWOHIG, *who is the most important man in the
town, chairman of most of its committees and a genial despot. We
are looking at a private sitting-room in the hotel. A bright, comfortable, unpretentious room, well-worn furniture, perhaps a
piano, certainly a sideboard ornamented by a fern or an aspidistra.
There is a syphon of soda water on the sideboard, half a dozen
glasses, a decanter of port. No fire burns in the grate, for it is a
fine summer morning and sunshine is streaming through the
window. There is a small table in the middle of the room and a
larger table against the wall. This table is littered with letters
and bills, and the confusion is being made worse by a middle-
aged woman,* MISS LIZZIE TWOHIG, *who is distractedly hunting
through the papers. She is a pleasant-looking woman, well dressed
but obviously a spinster. After a little ineffectual hunting she
goes to the door, opens it and calls:*

LIZZIE: Helena! Helena! (HELENA *appears: a neat little servant
just over twenty.*)

HELENA: You called, ma'am — miss, I mean?

LIZZIE: I should think I did call; I've been calling you for the
last hour. Where at all have you been?

HELENA: I was getting the hins out into the back yard.

LIZZIE: Why couldn't Michael have done that?

HELENA: Sure Michael's gone to meet the train.

LIZZIE: It can't be that late. (*She looks at her watch.*) My
gracious, it's gone half eleven; the train will be in any minute.

HELENA: It's in already, miss; I heard it puffing and I in the
yard.

LIZZIE: (*in a great fuss*) Well now, Helena, we must keep clear
cool heads. There's quite a crowd of people arriving on that
train, but there's no need for us to get into a fuss; quite the
contrary, quite the contrary. 'Twould be a queer thing if we

201

weren't able to deal in a quiet business-like way with half a dozen or ten guests.

HELENA: (*coolly*) Yes, miss, to be sure.

LIZZIE: If ye'd only come the first time I called you —

HELENA: Sure I was with the hins, miss.

LIZZIE: I know, I know. Where's Master Eddie?

HELENA: Gone to the train, miss.

LIZZIE: Why so?

HELENA: I don't know, miss. He put on his new suit after breakfast, and I heard him telling his pappy he was going to meet the train.

LIZZIE: Oh, to be sure, to be sure. Miss Lambert's amongst the arrivals. Which brings us back to business, Helena. She'd better have number twelve.

HELENA: She don't like that room, miss; 'tis too noisy. 'Tis number tin she always has.

LIZZIE: Very well. Ten for her. Then there's Mr Cronin and Mr Hunt —

HELENA: The min about the land?

LIZZIE: (*with dignity*) The gentlemen from the Land Commission. Let them have twelve and thirteen.

HELENA: Neither of them will look at thirteen. Them Commissioners are very suspicious.

LIZZIE: Dear, dear, what a bother. Well, give them eleven and twelve.

HELENA: The master said no one was to go into eleven till he'd have the bed repaired.

LIZZIE: Well, we'll give them nine and ten.

HELENA: Sure you've put Miss Lambert into tin.

LIZZIE: (*growing more and more distracted*) Good gracious me, what'll we do at all, at all?

HELENA: 'Tis easy enough, miss. What's wrong with fifteen? To be sure it's a double bed, but Mr Hunt would be glad of it. Sixteen stone if he's an ounce and —

LIZZIE: No. I'm keeping that room for Mr de la Mare and Miss Constantia.

HELENA: (*shocked*) Mr — and Miss Constantia! Glory, miss!

LIZZIE: It's quite all right, Helena. Actresses they are — I mean she's an actress and so is he — I mean he's an actor and so is — well, anyhow, they're man and wife these years and years. O'Hara or some name like that I believe they are really.

HELENA: I see, miss.

LIZZIE: Where were we at all? Miss Lambert in number twelve —

HELENA: Let you leave it to me, miss, I'll straighten it out. (*She gabbles off.*) Mr Hunt number twelve, Miss Lambert tin, Mr Cronin fourteen, and the play-actors in fifteen.

LIZZIE: I believe there are one or two others coming, but I've lost the bit of paper.

HELENA: It doesn't matter, miss; sure there's lashings of rooms.

LIZZIE: That's a good girl, that's a good girl. But mind, no fuss or excitement, be cool and business-like. I suppose the master's gone to the train too?

HELENA: Yis, miss. And the mistress is in her bedroom trying on some dresses came from Dublin by the first post.

LIZZIE: More dresses? And what about the one she got for the races only ten days ago?

HELENA: I know, miss. Stacks of them she has, but she said she'd be out at the theatre every night nearly for the next month —

LIZZIE: Oh yes, of course; I forgot. Ah, here's the first arrival.

(*For the door opens and admits* MISS CHRISTINE LAMBERT *and* EDDIE TWOHIG. CHRISTINE *is a capable-looking, handsome young woman of twenty-five:* EDDIE *a nice but rather soft young man a year or two younger.*) Well, Miss Lambert, it's welcome you are. How are you at all, at all?

CHRISTINE: (*letting herself be kissed*) Good morning, Miss Twohig, how are you? You're looking splendid.

LIZZIE: I can't complain, thank God.

CHRISTINE: And how are you, Helena?

HELENA: Very well, miss.

LIZZIE: It's been a grand summer so far, hasn't it?

CHRISTINE: Yes, indeed, but Dublin has been stifling. I was glad to get out of it.

LIZZIE: I'm sure you were. Ah, well, the sea breezes will soon bring the colour back to your cheeks — not indeed that you're looking pale, but nowadays there's no telling the natural bloom from the false.

CHRISTINE: Oh, Miss Twohig!

LIZZIE: Only my little joke, dear. You mustn't mind me. Sure when you're young you might as well be dead as not be in the fashion. Don't I remember. Helena, run and make Miss Lambert a cup of tea.

CHRISTINE: Please don't bother.

LIZZIE: No bother at all. I always have one myself about this hour to shorten the morning. Hurry, Helena.

HELENA: Yes, miss. (*She goes out.*)

CHRISTINE: I had breakfast on the train.

LIZZIE: Sure that's hours ago. What you should have is a cup of tea and a nice little nap and then you'll be in smart shape for your lunch.

CHRISTINE: Indeed, no. I must make an appearance at the factory before lunch and let the secretary know I've arrived.

LIZZIE: Ah, let the factory wait. How long will you be staying?

CHRISTINE: Three or four weeks, I suppose. It always takes that long to get through the factory's accounts.

LIZZIE: That's grand news for Eddie. How well he found out the train you were coming on!

EDDIE: (*blushing*) Ah, go on, Aunt.

CHRISTINE: I wouldn't believe it was Inish station if Eddie wasn't waiting on the platform for me.

LIZZIE: Indeed, but he's the faithful boy. I can tell you, Miss Lambert, there's girls breaking their hearts in Inish for Eddie, but not a look will he look at one of them. No, his heart's stuck away up in Dublin.

CHRISTINE: Now Eddie, there's a reputation you're getting.

EDDIE: Ah, go on, Christine.

LIZZIE: While Helena is wetting the tea I'll just slip upstairs and see is your room all right. Poor Helena — willing enough, but no system. We're putting you into number — number — which number at all is it?

CHRISTINE: I'm generally in ten.

LIZZIE: That's it. Ten, of course. "Helena," says I, "ten Miss Lambert's accustomed to have and ten she must get." Well, I'll be back in a few minutes. I'm leaving you in careful hands. (*She goes out.*)

CHRISTINE: It's nice to be back again, Eddie.

EDDIE: Is it? Do you really mean that?

CHRISTINE: Of course I do. And it was very nice of you to meet me at the station, and that's a nice suit you've got on. In fact everything's very nice.

EDDIE: I got it last week for you — I mean, against your coming.

CHRISTINE: That's great extravagance. Didn't you get one before you came up to Dublin for the Spring Show?

EDDIE: I did.

CHRISTINE: (*Teasing*) I don't believe your Aunt Lizzie is right at all. I believe you've fallen for that pretty Miss MacCarthy — or would it be for the little Mulcahy girl — Bubbles Mulcahy?

EDDIE: You know that's not true. I — I'd like to ask you something, Christine.

CHRISTINE: Same old question, Eddie?

EDDIE: Yes.

CHRISTINE: Isn't it a bit soon? I'm not here an hour yet.

EDDIE: I can't help it. Have you — have you changed your mind at all?

CHRISTINE: No, Eddie, not at all. You're a dear nice boy and I'm very fond of you, but I don't want to marry you.

EDDIE: I see. (*He is depressed for a few seconds but quickly cheers up.*) Well, maybe you'll change your mind. What about a round of golf this afternoon?

CHRISTINE: Imposs. You forget I'm down here to work. After tea, maybe; it's light till nine these evenings.

EDDIE: I'm taking you to the theatre tonight.

CHRISTINE: The theatre? The Pavilion? Oh, Eddie I'm sick of those comic troupes; I don't even get a good laugh out of them. They're very stupid and vulgar.

EDDIE: They're not comics, just you wait and see. We're running a first-class repertory company this summer.

CHRISTINE: You're what?

EDDIE: Intellectual sort of plays, *you* know.

CHRISTINE: You're joking.

EDDIE: Not at all. You know how Inish has been going down the last two summers, people going more and more to Shangarry Strand just because the bathing was better, and then the troupe that was here last summer was the limit — too vulgar altogether, real low.

CHRISTINE: The Comicalities? Wasn't that what they called themselves?

EDDIE: Yes. Anyhow the Monsignor got a lot of complaints about them, so he and Pappy and Peter Hurley the T.D. put their heads together and decided something must be done to improve the tone of the place, and the De La Mare Repertory Company is opening their season tonight.

CHRISTINE: For goodness' sake! I don't think I ever heard of them.

EDDIE: Oh they're very high-class, I believe; do nothing but serious stuff; Russian plays and all that sort of thing, just what you like. I've a pair of season tickets, so we'll go every night.

CHRISTINE: I'll go tonight certainly to sample them. What's the play?

EDDIE: I forget. There's a handbill in the bar. I know Wednesday night is "A Doll's House" — I remember that because it's such a funny name; and either Thursday or Friday there's "The Powers of Darkness" — isn't there a play called that?

CHRISTINE: Yes. But Inish will never support that sort of stuff.

EDDIE: We'll give it a try, anyway. Didn't you see Pappy at the station?

CHRISTINE: Yes, in the distance, in the middle of a lot of queer-looking people.

EDDIE: That's them. I mean that's the Repertory Company. The two principals — Mr de la Mare and Constance Constantia — are stopping here. We're putting them up free because, of course, Pappy owns the Pavilion. I suppose they'll be along in a few minutes; they had a deal of baggage to look after.

CHRISTINE: Well, I think this is most exciting. I'm sure they'll be more comic than the Comicalities, anyway.

EDDIE: I was dead keen for them to come.

CHRISTINE: Why, Eddie?

EDDIE: I feel very ignorant along with you, Christine. You get books in Dublin and go to plays and things, and I don't get a bit here. I thought these plays would improve my mind, like.

CHRISTINE: You've a very nice mind, Eddie — leave it alone.

EDDIE: Ah, no; I'm only a kind of a country lout. You're right to keep on refusing to marry me. But maybe by the end of the summer —

CHRISTINE: Now, now; no more of that. (HELENA *puts her head in, all excitement.*)

HELENA: The play-actors are coming, miss. Michael has a truck of luggage — such boxes you never seen, and you're in number tin, miss, in case Miss Twohig makes any mistake.

CHRISTINE: All right, Helena.

HELENA: And I'll be a bit delayed with your tea. (*She goes.*)

CHRISTINE: Eddie, I'm feeling quite excited; aren't you?

EDDIE: No.

CHRISTINE: Have you no imagination? Suppose that in another moment that door opens and a ravishing young actress comes in and —

EDDIE: Ssh! (*For the door is opening and admits, first, big genial* JOHN TWOHIG; *he ushers in* CONSTANCE CONSTANTIA *and* HECTOR DE LA MARE. *Goodness knows what age* CONSTANCE *is; her dyed dark-red hair may make her look older than she is instead of younger, as she hopes. Although it is summer she is wearing a heavy fur coat. Her handbag is an exaggeration. She moves with beautiful grace — but knows she does. She has played so many parts that her face has little character of its own; just now it is made up a little too tragically for a bright summer morning.* HECTOR *is very black in the hair, very black in the clothes, very pale in the face.*)

JOHN: Come in, come in. This is the sitting-room I was telling you about, Miss Constantia. It's our private room, but you're welcome to use it.

CONSTANCE: Ah, what a charming room! Isn't it divine, Hector?

JOHN: Oh, Miss Lambert, how are you? You got here before us. This is Miss Constance Constantia and Mr Hector de la Mare.

CONSTANCE: How do you do? (*Mutual shaking of hands between the three.*)

JOHN: Miss Lambert comes from Dublin; she's with that big firm of accountants in O'Connell Street and she comes down to audit the accounts of our factory twice a year and see we don't make off with the money. She's quite an old friend of ours and that boy of mine is breaking his heart over her.

EDDIE: (*blushing, as usual*) Ah, go on, Pappy.

JOHN: Come and shake hands with Miss Constantia, Eddie. Where's your manners?

EDDIE: (*shaking hands*) I'm pleased to meet you.

CONSTANCE: Charmed. (*He shakes hands with* HECTOR.)

JOHN: Has Eddie been telling you, Miss Lambert, about the plays?

CHRISTINE: Yes, indeed. I think it's a splendid idea. I'm awfully interested.

HECTOR: An experiment, Miss Lambert, an experiment. A seaside audience — to me, I confess, an unknown quantity.

CONSTANCE: You remember, dear, that week in Southsea three years ago?

HECTOR: I had forgotten. We played —?

CONSTANCE: To miserable audiences of ignorant people.

HECTOR: Did we? But I meant, what play?

CONSTANCE: "The Lyons Mail".

HECTOR: Ah, I never quite do myself justice in melodrama. That tour was a mistake — financially and artistically — yes, a financial and artistic mistake.

JOHN: That was a pity, then. But won't you all sit down? There's a comfortable chair, Miss Constance — Miss Constantia, I mean.

CONSTANCE: Thank you. (*They all sit.*)

HECTOR: Yes, Miss Lambert, I now confine myself entirely — with the co-operation of Miss Constantia — to psychological and introspective drama. The great plays of Russia, an Ibsen or two, a Strindberg — I think very little of the French.

JOHN: The Monsignor was dead against French plays.

HECTOR: He was perfectly right. The French theatre is superficial; no feeling for the psyche; of the flesh, fleshy.

JOHN: Tch, tch, tch.

HECTOR: The English theatre —

JOHN: We thought, things being the way they are, it was safer to keep off English plays this summer.

HECTOR: You lose but little. Of course there is Shakespeare. (*A reverential little murmur of "Of course" runs round the room.*)

CONSTANCE: My Lady Macbeth — do you remember, Hector, in Dundee?

HECTOR: Perfectly, darling. A most marvellous performance, Miss Lambert.

CHRISTINE: I love "Macbeth". The last Lady Macbeth I saw was Mrs Patrick Campbell's.

CONSTANCE: (*with gentle pity*) Ah, poor Mrs Pat. Did you like her?

CHRISTINE: Immensely.

CONSTANCE: Really? (LIZZIE *and* ANNIE — MRS TWOHIG — *come in.* ANNIE *matches her husband, large and genial. Her clothes are a little too smart for that hour in the morning.*)

JOHN: Here's my wife. Annie, this is Miss Constantia.

ANNIE: How are you, Miss Constantia?

CONSTANCE: How do you do?

JOHN: And my sister, Miss Twohig. (*Mutual greetings.*) Mr de la Mare, my wife, my sister. (*Mutual greetings.*) My sister helps me to run the hotel and the shop; it gives my wife more time to be thinking of dresses and fal-lals.

ANNIE: Get away with you, John. Oh, Miss Lambert, dear, I never saw you. How are you?

CHRISTINE: (*kissing her*) Splendid, Mrs Twohig.

ANNIE: You're looking very smart. That's a dotey little suit you're wearing; where did you get it?

JOHN: (*to the others*) What did I tell you? Clothes all the time.

ANNIE: Wisha, don't mind John. He'd be the last to want me to go around like an old ragbag. Won't you all sit down?

CHRISTINE: I'll just slip up to my room and wash my hands. I'll be down again to have my cup of tea with Miss Twohig. (*She goes to the door.*)

EDDIE: Will I carry your case up?

CHRISTINE: No, Michael will have taken it up, I'm sure. Stay where you are. (*She goes out.*)

ANNIE: I think we might all have a little tea.

JOHN: (*going to the sideboard*) I have something here that will do Mr de la Mare better than tea after his long journey. What about a drop of whiskey, sir?

HECTOR: I rarely touch anything in the daytime, not till after the show, except in the most exceptional circumstances.

JOHN: Well, glory be to goodness, could any day be more exceptional than today — high-class plays in Inish? Come, now, I'll take no denial.

HECTOR: Well, if I must, I must.

LIZZIE: I warn you, Mr de la Mare, my brother will find some excuse to make every day and every hour of every day exceptional. Helena fills that decanter every morning, and many's the evening we have to send down to the bar for a fresh bottle.

JOHN: Ah, what matter, woman dear. A little drop for you, Miss Constantia?

ANNIE: Nonsense. A nice creamy cup of tea is what Miss Constantia would like. Don't I know?

JOHN: Can't you let her speak for herself?

CONSTANCE: I confess I am partial, occasionally, to a small whiskey and soda.

JOHN: That's the spirit. These women of mine think of nothing but tea, tea, tea all the day long. Bring along the siphon, Eddie.

EDDIE: I have it here, Pappy.

LIZZIE: I hope we'll be able to make you comfortable here, Miss Constantia. If everything's not to your liking you must just come to me. Helena — the servant — is as willing as can be, but flighty; no head on her at all.

CONSTANCE: I am sure we shall be most comfortable.

LIZZIE: This place is quite a home from home — that's what a traveller wrote in our book one day; very clever and terse, don't you think?

CONSTANCE: Oh, quite.

JOHN: (*having mixed and handed the drinks*) Now, Miss Constantia and Mr de la Mare, here's to your very successful season.

HECTOR: And here is to you, sir, and to Inish. May our visit be profitable to the town — spiritually, I mean.

CONSTANCE: I should like to associate myself with Mr de la Mare's remarks.

JOHN: Faith, I hope it will be profitable in every way. Them Comicalities last year had me on the brink of ruin.

ANNIE: Indeed they were very low.

HECTOR: I hope, Mr Twohig, you will not set too much store by material profits. Often, alas, plays of this kind draw very small audiences and make very little money.

JOHN: And why do you go in for them so, if it's not a rude question?

HECTOR: Because, Mr Twohig, they may revolutionise some person's soul.

ANNIE: Ah, sure, we've had enough of revolutions.

HECTOR: I mean that some young man in the audience may see himself there on the stage, in all his lust, in all his selfishness, in all the cruelty of his youth — a young man such as your son. (*He suddenly swings on* EDDIE *who shrinks away.*)

LIZZIE: Is it poor Eddie? There never was a more innocent boy.

HECTOR: I meant nothing personal. (*And now it is* JOHN *who inspires him.*) Or some middle-aged man, in all outward appearances respectable, will see himself stripped naked, the sham cloak of virtue torn from his shoulders, and he will stand exposed as the rotten sham he is. (*And now it is* LIZZIE'*s and* ANNIE'*s turn.*) Women will see themselves vain, shallow, empty-headed, scheming for power, scheming for husbands, scheming for lovers.

ANNIE: Heaven defend us!

LIZZIE: (*awed*) 'Tis like a mission.

HECTOR: It *is* a mission, Miss Twohig, a tremendous mission where the pulpit is the stage and the great dramatists preach the sermons. I am myself a convert.

JOHN: Do you mean you used to be a Protestant?

HECTOR: I am not speaking in the strictly religious sense. It happened more than twenty years ago. I was a very young man — in Cork. There used to come to the Opera House once or twice a year a company headed by Octavia Kenmore and her husband in a repertory of Ibsen plays. They played to wretchedly small audiences, and I went every night — to the gallery, for I was very poor. I saw every rotten sham in Cork exposed on that stage. I could translate every play in terms of the South Mall or Montenotte or Sunday's Well. I saw myself on the stage — young puppy that I was —

ANNIE: Ah now, Mr de la Mare, I am sure you were never that.

HECTOR: I was. But those plays changed the current of my life.

JOHN: And did they change Cork?

HECTOR: They did not. We played there two summers ago; the same miserable little audiences of cynical people, the same corruption, public and private.

JOHN: Ah well, here in Inish we don't think much of Cork. But indeed you'll find us quiet, decent people. I don't think there's much here to expose at all. Is there, Annie?

ANNIE: Sorra a thing. 'Tis too quiet we are: not that I want

murders or big crimes or anything of that sort — God forbid —
but we're often blue-mouldy for a bit of innocent scandal. We
women can't live without that, you know. Amn't I right, Miss
Constantia?

CONSTANCE: "To speak no scandal, no, nor listen to it." Ever my
motto, Mrs Twohig, ever my motto.

LIZZIE: And a very nice one too, my dear.

ANNIE: "Always merry and bright." That was someone's motto,
wasn't it?

HECTOR: That, I believe, is an excerpt from some vulgar musical
comedy. (PETER HURLEY *comes in; an insignificant little
mouse of a man.*)

JOHN: Ah, here's me bold Peter. Mr de la Mare, I want to intro-
duce our local T.D., Mr Peter Hurley.

PETER: How are you?

HECTOR: (*shaking his hand very formally*) I am honoured to meet
you, Mr Hurley.

JOHN: And this is Miss Constantia.

PETER: How are you, miss? 'Morning, Annie: 'morning, Lizzie.

ANNIE: ⎱ Good morning, Peter.
LIZZIE: ⎰

JOHN: What about a drop of whiskey, Peter?

PETER: Ah, no, thank you, John.

JOHN: You could chance it, the Dáil's not sitting now.

PETER: Things being the way they are, we might be summoned
any minute.

HECTOR: And may I ask, Mr Hurley, which party you represent?

JOHN: (*who is getting* PETER's *whiskey*) Oh, Peter's a sound
Government man. Aren't you, Peter? Always on the spot when
your vote is wanted. He's not much of a speechifier, Mr de la
Mare, but he's a sound party man. Did you speak in the Dáil at
all yet, Peter? I don't believe you did.

PETER: I riz twice one day but someone else riz quicker.

HECTOR: They also serve, Mr Hurley, "they also serve who only
stand and wait".

PETER: Thank you, sir.

JOHN: Never mind, Peter, my son, you'll come out strong one
of these days. There's a whiskey for you — I won't take "no".

PETER: Thank you, John. Here's to us all.

CONSTANCE: (*finishing hers and getting up*) Perhaps we should be
going to the hall, Hector.

HECTOR: I'm afraid Murphy won't have the scene set for another
hour.

LIZZIE: And it will be nearly time for your dinner then.

CONSTANCE: And I must rest all the afternoon or I shall be an utter rag.

HECTOR: I'll go down to the hall after dinner and see that everything is all right.

CONSTANCE: Oh, it's not that — it's that scene, the end of the fourth act — I'm so nervous about it.

HECTOR: You're word perfect, darling.

CONSTANCE: Yes, I have it here, (*touching her forehead*) but have I got it here? (*touching her heart*) Have I, Hector, have I?

HECTOR: I know what you mean. It doesn't vibrate.

CONSTANCE: Or the vibrations are wrong. I don't know, Hector, I don't know! (*She is working herself up very effectively.*)

HECTOR: When the moment comes, *it* will come, right and true.

CONSTANCE: Oh, will it, will it?

HECTOR: It will. Take my hands. (*She takes them. They are standing looking into each other's eyes. He clenches her hands in his.*) IT WILL.

CONSTANCE: (*faintly*) Thank you, Hector, thank you.

HECTOR: But to make assurance doubly sure, if the company will excuse us we'll retire to our room and go over the scene there.

JOHN: Certainly, certainly.

LIZZIE: What is it you want to do?

HECTOR: Just to run over a short scene that is in the play tonight. We can do it in our room.

LIZZIE: With actions?

HECTOR: With, as you say, actions. Of course, without props.

ANNIE: Props?

HECTOR: Properties. The correct furniture, the samovar, the little empty cradle.

LIZZIE: Well, indeed, I've seen that room since all your boxes went up, and between them and the big double bed there's not room, as they say, to swing a cat. Besides, Helena hasn't the room tidied up yet.

HECTOR: Dear, dear.

JOHN: What's the matter with this room? It's a big airy room, and you're welcome to every bit of it. Sure when the Temperance Society was putting on "The Coiner" last winter, 'tis here they used to hold their practices.

HECTOR: But so inconvenient for you all.

JOHN: Not at all; we can go down to the bar, and I'm sure my wife will want to be showing Lizzie all the grand dresses she got from Dublin this morning. Come on, all of you.

CONSTANCE: It seems so cruel to disturb you.

JOHN: Not another word. Come along. (*There is a general move to the door.*)

EDDIE: (*low to his father*) Pappy.

JOHN: Well, son?

EDDIE: Ask them could I stay.

JOHN: Stay? Nonsense.

EDDIE: Ask them, Pappy.

HECTOR: What is that?

JOHN: A bit of nonsense of Eddie's. He wants to stay and hear you.

HECTOR: No, no, my boy. Wait for the real thing tonight.

CONSTANCE: (*dramatically*) Hector, a moment. He must stay. They must all stay. I must have an audience. Even three or four people will make all the difference to me — tell me if I vibrate or if I do not vibrate. (*She swoops on* ANNIE.) Mrs Twohig, I implore you, lend me your ears — and your heart. You are a mother. *I* am a mother in this play — an erring one, I admit, but still a mother. I entreat you, stay and hear me.

ANNIE: (*kindly*) To be sure I'll stay if that's the way you feel about it. And Lizzie too, I'm sure.

LIZZIE: I'll wait. Sure me tea is due any minute.

CONSTANCE: Thank you, oh, thank you. Hector, set the stage.

(*He considers the room for an instant and decides to have the stage on the side of the room facing the door. He instructs* EDDIE *to move the chairs and the table from the middle of the room. While this is going on —*)

PETER: (*to* JOHN) I have to be off. I've to see the Monsignor.

JOHN: Right-o, Peter. You'll be at the Pavilion tonight?

PETER: I will, to be sure. (PETER *goes out.*)

HECTOR: Will you all sit over here, this side?

(*He gets them seated in a little row facing the stage.* CONSTANCE *has taken off her coat and hat and has seized a coloured shawl which had been draping a chair or a sofa and has put it over her head.* HECTOR *gets back into his overcoat and hat and turns up the collar of the coat.*)

I needn't explain the whole play to you; this is the scene which closes the fourth act. The scene is a poor kitchen in Russia; there is a large Russian stove, a samovar, of course — on this table (*placing the aspidistra on the table*) —

JOHN: A what?

HECTOR: A samovar. Of course you know what that is.

ANNIE: (*digging* JOHN *in the ribs*) Of course.

HECTOR: Miss Constantia's name is Elina; she is a poor servant girl whom I have betrayed earlier in the play. My name is Michael —

JOHN: Have they a name like that in Russia? I thought Michael was a good Irish name.

HECTOR: It is a very common name in Russia.

JOHN: And do they ever shorten it to Mick?

HECTOR: No. Well, she hasn't seen Michael for several years, and in the meantime she has had a baby.

LIZZIE: The creature!

HECTOR: This is the scene of their meeting. Perhaps Master Eddie would hold the book. (*He gives it to him.*) The bottom of that page, and don't prompt unless we really dry.

EDDIE: (*bewildered*) Dry?

HECTOR: Fluff. (*Which is just as bewildering.*)

CONSTANCE: (*sitting in a chair with her foot rocking an imaginary cradle*) I am rocking a cradle, an empty cradle.

ANNIE: In heaven's name, for what?

HECTOR: Ssh! Ready, Constance?

CONSTANCE: Yes. (*She starts to croon a Russian cradle song:*)

"Bala, bala balaika,
Bala, bala, bala mo."

HECTOR: (*coming in stamping his feet and shaking the snow off his coat*) I am looking for Serge Ilyvitch. I am told he lives here.

CONSTANCE: (*not looking at him*) No one of that name lives here.

HECTOR: But Petro Petrovitch told me — Elina! You?

CONSTANCE: (*looking at him now*) You! Michael!

HECTOR: Yes, it is Michael.

CONSTANCE: (*rising slowly*) Why have you come back, back into my life?

HECTOR: I did not know you were here. You ran away from old Alex.

CONSTANCE: He beat me.

HECTOR: Where did you go?

CONSTANCE: To Moscow, to Niji, to Tobolsk, to — anywhere. (*She sits down again and starts rocking and crooning.* HELENA *comes in with a small tray and two cups of tea on it. She stands unnoticed in the background listening.*)

HECTOR: Why are you rocking a cradle, Elina?

CONSTANCE: Can you ask that, Michael?

HECTOR: (*peering at the imaginary cradle*) But it is empty.

CONSTANCE: Indeed it is empty.

HECTOR: Why is it empty?

CONSTANCE: My baby is dead, *our* baby is dead, Michael. (*She rises slowly.*)

HECTOR: (*slowly covering his face with his hands*) Our baby? I do not understand.

CONSTANCE: You do understand — betrayer. (*With a great cry.*) Michael, Michael, give me back my baby!

HECTOR: Elina —
(HELENA *lets the tray fall with a crash. Everyone swings round in surprise.*)

ANNIE:
LIZZIE: } Helena!
JOHN:
EDDIE:

HELENA: (*echoing* CONSTANCE) Michael, Michael, give me back my baby!

LIZZIE: You're crazed, Helena.

HELENA: Michael! Michael!

ANNIE: (*rushing to her*) 'Tis only play-acting, child.

JOHN: Come now, my girl —
(*The door opens and* MICHAEL, *the boots, appears, a good-looking, honest young fellow.*)

MICHAEL: You were calling?

HELENA: (*rushing to him and flinging her arms round his neck*) Michael, Michael, our baby!

MICHAEL: (*trying to disengage himself*) Here, hould on —

HELENA: The baby, the baby!

MICHAEL: (*backing out of the room*) What baby?

HELENA: (*going out with him still clinging to him*) Our baby, Michael, Michael.
(*They disappear; the words "Michael" and "Baby" fade away in the distance.*)

JOHN: Thunder and turf! Annie, what's the meaning of all this?

ANNIE: Ah, don't bother me. (ANNIE *goes out quickly.*)

HECTOR: A highly-strung temperament, no doubt.

LIZZIE: (*picking up pieces of cups*) And the lovely tea gone.

EDDIE: What was she saying, Pappy?

JOHN: I know no more than yourself. Just nonsense.
(CHRISTINE *comes in.*)

CHRISTINE: Is anything the matter? I heard shouting. Oh, is that my tea?

LIZZIE: That's your tea, Miss Lambert, I'm sorry to say.

EDDIE: It got spilled, Christine.

CHRISTINE: Yes, Eddie; I gathered that it had got spilled.

JOHN: It slipped out of Helena's hand.

CHRISTINE: I see. (*She senses that everyone is a little awkward and busy with their own thoughts, and is silent.*) I think I'll go down to the factory.

EDDIE: Will I come with you?

CHRISTINE: No. Stay here. I'll be back in an hour.

(ANNIE *comes in.*)

I'm going out for an hour, Mrs Twohig. I won't be late for dinner.

ANNIE: (*half listening*) Yes, dear. Eddie, I'd like you to go and have a walk on the strand for yourself.

EDDIE: Why, Mammy?

ANNIE: There's no why. Off with you.

EDDIE: Yes, Mammy.

CHRISTINE: See me to the factory first, Eddie.

EDDIE: Right-o. (CHRISTINE *and* EDDIE *go out.*)

HECTOR: I apologise, Mrs Twohig, if anything we did or said has caused a reverberation —

ANNIE: I sent her to her room, but not before she shouted it out in the bar and three men heard her.

JOHN: But in heaven's name what's it all about?

ANNIE: You may as well know; it will be all over the town in an hour. Two years ago — do you remember when I sent Helena to Dublin to have her eyes tested?

LIZZIE: She stayed there four months with your sister, didn't she?

ANNIE: It wasn't her eyes; she had got into a little trouble here and I wasn't going to desert her, a nice little girl like that with no one belonging to her.... Well, the baby died.

JOHN: Heavens above! I knew nothing of this.

ANNIE: Of course you didn't, nor Lizzie, nor one of you.

JOHN: But — Michael — ?

ANNIE: It was Michael the boots.

JOHN: Michael that's here now?

ANNIE: Of course not. The Michael we had two years ago — don't we call every boots Michael to save trouble, none of them ever staying more than a few months? It was that Michael that hopped off to America with your new suit — d'you remember?

LIZZIE: But she said Michael here.

ANNIE: I know. The playacting turned her head for the moment. It's most unfortunate. God forgive you, Miss Constantia. I'd better go and see after her.

LIZZIE: I'll come with you, Annie. (ANNIE *and* LIZZIE *go out.*)

JOHN: Well, well. Imagine her keeping that from me all this time. Aren't women the dickens? And Helena such a nice little girl. I'd better go to the bar and see what's after happening.

(JOHN *goes out.* HECTOR *is about to follow but* CONSTANCE *who has remained rather apart from all this, a little wrapt, stops him.*)

CONSTANCE: Hector!

HECTOR: Yes, dear?

CONSTANCE: I am not afraid for tonight. My vibrations were right.

(*He takes her in his arms and kisses her reverently.*)

CURTAIN

ACT II

SCENE I

The same scene, ten days later. Late afternoon with no sunlight, in fact raining heavily. HECTOR *is seated at the writing table doing the accounts.* CONSTANCE *comes in in a mackintosh and hat.*

HECTOR: Are you going already? Isn't it very early?

CONSTANCE: I know, but I have some mending to do. I tore my dress at the matinee and I must mend it before the show.

HECTOR: If things continue as they are going you'll be able to have a dresser next week. Imagine that!

CONSTANCE: Imagine! I haven't had a dresser for years.

HECTOR: I've just told Murphy to reserve another row of seats for tonight and till further notice.

CONSTANCE: Isn't it marvellous?

HECTOR: It just bears out what I have always said: give people the right stuff, well put on and intelligently acted, and they will support it. I hear there weren't a hundred people in the picture-house last night.

CONSTANCE: Splendid! Oh, those pictures, how I hate them.

HECTOR: The first three days of this week are fourteen pounds two and threepence better than the first three days last week; we're a clear twenty pounds to the good already; we'll be over forty by the end of the week.

CONSTANCE: We'll be able to settle O'Byrne's account; he's so odious, threatening us with writs.

HECTOR: And we can settle with Kelly and Shea and that hotel in Clonmel.

CONSTANCE: Would there be enough for me to send Mother a little? Poor darling, she's so hard up.

HECTOR: Of course. Let's send her five pounds. That'll be a nice surprise for her. Oh — and I was thinking of Uncle Bill.

CONSTANCE: What about him?

HECTOR: I thought he might join us. He's a good old character actor.

CONSTANCE: Darling, he's very old, and he does get so very drunk.

HECTOR: I know. But he ought to have a share in our success. After all, he taught me my first stage lessons.

CONSTANCE: Then let's just send him some money.

HECTOR: All right. I will. But you must spend something on yourself, darling.

CONSTANCE: Oh, I want nothing but a few dresses. And what will my boy get for himself?

HECTOR: I was wondering if I could pick up a car cheap — a small one, of course. I believe it would pay for itself very quickly; it would save so much in the way of railway fares.

CONSTANCE: Of course, it would. That's a splendid idea. Oh — and there's May, we forgot May.

HECTOR: So we did. She must get something, of course.

CONSTANCE: Of course. Something really substantial.

HECTOR: We won't have anything left at the end of the week if we're not careful.

CONSTANCE: The bills can all wait; they must. I always think family comes first, don't you?

HECTOR: Undoubtedly. After all, it is we who are making the money, and we have a right to spend it any way we like.

CONSTANCE: Of course. (*She shivers.*)

HECTOR: Cold, darling?

CONSTANCE: A little. The weather is depressing, isn't it? If we we weren't doing such good business I'd be in the blues.

HECTOR: Strange how the weather broke the day after we opened. Not a gleam of sun since. However, it all helps business.

CONSTANCE: I was wondering whether we couldn't run a children's matinee next week, "Midsummer-Nights Dream", or something like that. I could be Titania.

HECTOR: That's an idea. I could play Bottom. (LIZZIE *comes in extricating herself from a wet mackintosh.*)

LIZZIE: Oh, Miss Constantia, what an afternoon! I'm dripping. Wouldn't you like a cup of tea?

CONSTANCE: We've had ours, thanks, and I'm just off to the Pavilion.

LIZZIE: I hope you had a good audience this afternoon. I wasn't able to go, unfortunately, the hotel takes so much of my time.

CONSTANCE: We had a very good audience.

LIZZIE: I'm glad. What is on tonight?

CONSTANCE: "The Powers of Darkness" again.

LIZZIE: Oh yes, that's where they murder the baby in the cellar. I thought that was a very good one.

HECTOR: An extraordinarily powerful play.

LIZZIE: Yes, indeed. Talking of babies and all that reminds me that the business about Michael and Helena just goes from bad to worse. Annie had a terrible time this afternoon with Michael's mother.

HECTOR: I'm sorry to hear that. What happened?

LIZZIE: It seems the mother drove over from Shangarry Strand in an ass and cart and she gave Annie all sorts; said that her boy's character had been taken away and that the town had no right to be saying — as they *are* saying — that there's nothing for poor Michael to do but marry Helena. She blames it all on Annie for calling Michael out of his name — his real name, it seems, is Aloysius — blaming Annie, mind you, who is the best friend the poor girl ever had!

CONSTANCE: That seems very unfair. Ah, it's what always happens; the woman pays, to the uttermost farthing.

LIZZIE: (*sighing deeply*) Yes, indeed, it's a troublesome world.

HECTOR: I'm sure you can't have many troubles, Miss Twohig, with your nice home here and your brother and sister-in-law so fond of you and the interest of looking after the hotel.

LIZZIE: (*sighing more deeply*) I don't seem to take any interest in the hotel any more. I don't know what's come to me. Anyway, it's not the same as having a real home of my own.

CONSTANCE: (*with soft sympathy*) Of course it's not. I know.
Oh, to have a little house!
To own the hearth and stool and all!
The heaped-up sods upon the fire,
The pile of turf against the wall.

To have a clock with weights and chains,
And pendulum swinging up and down!
A dresser filled with shining delph,
Speckled and white and blue and brown.

LIZZIE: Exactly, dear. Ah, it takes a woman to understand a woman — if you'll excuse me, Mr de la Mare. I lay awake all last night thinking of that play by — I never get the name right — it's like a cold in the head.

HECTOR: A cold in the head? I confess —

CONSTANCE: I know who she means, darling. Tchekov, isn't it, Miss Twohig?

LIZZIE: That's it, dear. Tchekov. Do you remember the woman in it? She had her chance and threw it away, and there she was drifting into middle age, alone and neglected, just like myself.

CONSTANCE: You threw away your chance, Miss Twohig?

LIZZIE: I did, dear, I did. If I hadn't been a foolish girl, I'd now be a T.D.'s wife.

HECTOR: No!

LIZZIE: A fact, Mr de la Mare.

CONSTANCE: Which T.D.?

HECTOR: Hush, Constance. We have no right to probe into an old sorrow.

LIZZIE: It's such an old story that I can talk of it now. Yes, indeed, I might this minute be Mrs Peter Hurley, T.D.

HECTOR: Dear, dear!

LIZZIE: And my picture in the papers and asked to parties in Dublin and all. And if I cared to, I could dress better than Annie — I've kept my figure better than she did — but what is the use of dressing grand? Sure fine clothes are a poor consolation for a broken heart.

HECTOR: Very true.

CONSTANCE: Why did you throw him over?

LIZZIE: I didn't throw him over, Miss Constantia. Peter Hurley behaved shameful. We were never exactly engaged — thank God, I never gave him the chance to jilt me — but he behaved shameful all the same. He played with my affections, and in the end without so much as by your leave or with your leave took himself off and married a small publican's daughter from the County Clare.

HECTOR: Too bad, too bad. Well, you must remember that "Sorrow's crown of sorrows is remembering happier days". You must be brave, Miss Towhig, and live for the next generation; teach them to see clearer, think straighter, be more fearless.

LIZZIE: (*with a sniff*) I must, I suppose. (ANNIE *comes in and sinks into a chair.*)

ANNIE: I'm jaded.

CONSTANCE: Indeed you look worn out, Mrs Twohig.

ANNIE: Such a day! I never thought I'd live to be called the things that woman called me this afternoon.

HECTOR: Did Mr Twohig not deal firmly with her?

ANNIE: I never set eyes on John since dinner-time.

LIZZIE: He spent the whole afternoon in the bar.

ANNIE: Did he?

LIZZIE: You'll have to speak to John, Annie; 'tis terrible the way he's drinking.

ANNIE: Ah, not at all.

LIZZIE: Though he's my own brother, I'll have to say it. You're married to a man who's on the high road to becoming a drunkard.

ANNIE: You've no right to say things like that, Lizzie, about your own brother. I hope I see John's faults as clearly as the next, but he is not, never was, and never will be a drunkard.

LIZZIE: (with her usual sigh) Well, I only hope you're right.

ANNIE: Everything seems going astray lately, the weather and all.

HECTOR: Except the Pavilion, Mrs Twohig; don't forget the Pavilion. Though you don't patronise us often, I'm sorry to say.

ANNIE: I don't know why, but I couldn't bring myself to go after the second night. They made such a terrible show-up of things. I remember Lizzie here saying the day you came — you were telling us the sort of plays they were — " 'Tis like a mission." And I suppose it is. Maybe I'm stupid and flighty, but I don't hold with those plays at all — of course, it's only here I'd say such a thing; I'd never breathe a word outside for your sakes and John having the Pavilion. And sure you couldn't wear nice clothes going to that class of play; the best you could do would be a sort of half mourning.

LIZZIE: I couldn't live without those plays. I was mad that I couldn't get to the matinée this afternoon. (MICHAEL puts his head in the door.)

ANNIE: Am I wanted, Michael?

MICHAEL: You're not, ma'am, but did you hear the terrible thing that's after happening Jim Clancy?

ANNIE: No, what is it?

MICHAEL: Threw himself off the end of the pier.

ANNIE: For pity's sake!

LIZZIE: Dear, dear, dear! (Everyone rises in concern.)

ANNIE: Was he drowned dead?

MICHAEL: No, ma'am. Bruised. The tide was out.

ANNIE: Thank God.

HECTOR: What was the reason for it?

MICHAEL: No one knows, sir. He kem out of the Pavilion — he'd been watching the play — and he went to the end of the pier and stood there for a bit and then lepped over. The Fehily boys were watching him; 'tis they pulled him out.

CONSTANCE: Only bruised?

MICHAEL: Yes, ma'am; 'tis one of them congested piers, and when the tide is out there's only a sup of water. He must be out of his senses to think he could drown there. Now if he'd gone to the white rocks there'd be some chance for him.

ANNIE: Well, indeed, I'm glad he didn't.

MICHAEL: Well, he's roaring on the bed in the mother's place and saying it's there he will go the next time he has a free minute.

The doctor's with him; he says he's sort of melancholy. (JOHN's *voice is heard calling "Michael"*.) There's the boss calling for me. (MICHAEL *goes out*.)

LIZZIE: Ah, it's a sad, sad world.

ANNIE: (*sitting down again*) Everything seems going astray.

HECTOR: Yet it is interesting to find a temperament like that in Inish. We Irish, we're very like the Russians really.

CONSTANCE: Quiet on the surface but with such hidden depths of feeling — like Miss Twohig here.

ANNIE: Is it Lizzie?

HECTOR: Yes. Your sister-in-law has allowed us to know a little of her tragedy.

ANNIE: Her tragedy? What under heaven are you talking about? (JOHN *bursts in. He has some papers in his hand*.)

JOHN: (*to* ANNIE) Do you see these?

ANNIE: I do, to be sure.

JOHN: Do you know what they are?

ANNIE: They look like bills.

JOHN: Then they look like what they are — bills, bills, bills. This one from Kelletts, this one from Arnotts, these two from shops in Grafton Street I never heard the names of before. Woman, dear, do you want to ruin me?

ANNIE: I do not.

LIZZIE: You've been drinking, John.

JOHN: I have not, and if I had itself wouldn't I have good reason to try and drown my troubles? Where in heaven's name am I to get money to pay all these?

ANNIE: There can't be so much in them after all.

JOHN: Not so much? Look here — nineteen pounds and eleven pence. And here — ten pounds nineteen and sixpence, and here —

LIZZIE: It's not very nice to be saying these things before Miss Constantia and Mr de la Mare.

JOHN: Ah, keep out of this, you.

CONSTANCE: As a matter of fact I'm just going.

HECTOR: So am I.

JOHN: I don't want either of you to go. What I've got to say can be heard by the whole world. I've tried to rear Eddie well and respectable and leave a nice business behind for him, and here's my wife stabbing me in the back all the time, buying a mountain of clothes, hats, ribbons and the like to flaunt around the town.

CONSTANCE: I'm sure Mrs Twohig becomes them well and does you credit. I think you should be proud of her.

LIZZIE: Indeed he should, Miss Constantia.

JOHN: (to ANNIE) You say nothing?

ANNIE: No, but I'm thinking a lot.

JOHN: Slowly my eyes are being opened, and I begin to see what a fool I've been all these years, just making a home for you, making a nest for you, making — a — a — a —

LIZZIE: Making a doll's house for her.

JOHN: Exactly. A doll's house. You took the words out of my mouth.

HECTOR: (aside to CONSTANCE) You know, dear, it is the curious converse of Nora Helmer's case.

JOHN: But it has got to stop. If it doesn't, one or the other of us leaves this house.

LIZZIE: John, you wouldn't dream of such a thing.

JOHN: Why wouldn't I? I've my own life to lead, haven't I? I'm not just a blank chequebook, am I? (PETER HURLEY comes in.)

PETER: I dropped in, John, to say I have to go to Dublin by the evening train. The Dáil meets tomorrow.

JOHN: Well, isn't that a pity. You can't be with me to the play tonight?

PETER: No, John, worse luck. Though indeed I think it's a shame the way I'm taking Annie's seat every night.

ANNIE: You're welcome to it, Peter.

PETER: Thank you, Annie. You've been out, Lizzie? (She looks stonily in front of her.) I was asking had you been out?

LIZZIE: I think, Mr Hurley, in the future the less conversation you and I have together the better.

PETER: Lizzie! Why so?

LIZZIE: I needn't say.

ANNIE: What ails you, Lizzie?

LIZZIE: Please ask me no questions, Annie; I've said my say.

JOHN: Sure you can't leave it like that and Peter such an old friend of yours.

LIZZIE: (with a sniff) Old friends, indeed!

JOHN: Well, isn't he? Didn't you play together as childer?

LIZZIE: Maybe that's what I'm thinking of, and thinking, too, of the way he treated me when I wasn't a child any longer.

PETER: How I treated you?

LIZZIE: Yes, but we'll say no more about it. You can leave me with my thoughts.

PETER: What does she mean, John?

JOHN: I don't know, Peter. What's the matter, Lizzie girl?
(But LIZZIE won't answer.)

HECTOR: Miss Twohig is, no doubt, thinking of the rather heartless way you behaved long ago.

PETER: Heartless?

HECTOR: Yes, heartless. When you abandoned her — for another.

PETER: I never did anything of the kind. There never was anything between us except maybe a bit of innocent skylarking now and again.

LIZZIE: Oh, Peter!

CONSTANCE: It may have seemed only skylarking to you, Mr. Hurley, but it broke Miss Twohig's heart.

ANNIE: Did it, Lizzie? I never heard a word of this.

JOHN: Nor I. Such codology was never known. Don't be making an old eejut of yourself, Lizzie.

LIZZIE: (*rising with dignity*) I am sorry I intruded my personal tragedy on you all; I apologise. And now, John, your "old eejut" of a sister will take herself away. (*And she goes out.*)

JOHN: Well, can you beat that?

ANNIE: Ah, don't mind her. Did you hear about Jim Clancy?

JOHN: Of course I did. Everyone's talking of it. I'm sorry for the poor boy, and I'm sorry for ourselves too, for there'll be one less in the audience every night, Mr de la Mare. Jim never missed a performance once.

HECTOR: I see. A real enthusiast.

PETER: But, John, I'm uneasy about Lizzie. It's not in my mind that I've anything to blame myself about, and anyway it was all twenty and more years ago, and we've been the best of friends all along, and she's been a good friend to my wife too.

JOHN: Don't give it a thought, Peter. Some little fancy that came to her. Maybe the weather's accountable for it; I don't feel at all myself this evening.

PETER: I see. Well, I'm off.

JOHN: Will you be staying in Dublin over the weekend?

PETER: Not at all. I'll be home for Saturday. I wouldn't miss the play that night for anything. Good night to you all.

EVERYONE: Good night. (PETER *goes out.*)

CONSTANCE: I must go too. Hector, are you ready to come?

HECTOR: Yes, I may as well go. (*He goes to the door.*) You'll be at the play tonight, Mr Twohig?

JOHN: Of course.

CONSTANCE: (*at the door*) And Mrs Twohig?

ANNIE: No, thank you, I'll stay at home and read a magazine I've just bought.

CONSTANCE: Indeed. What magazine is that?

ANNIE: (*a little grimly*) "Comic Cuts."

CONSTANCE: Indeed!

(*They make a dignified exit not certain whether to be offended or not.*)

JOHN: Did you mean that for a slap at them, Annie?

ANNIE: They can take it any way they like.

JOHN: You don't care much about them, I think.

ANNIE: Oh, I suppose they're all right.

JOHN: (*trying to make it up*) Annie; I spoke too sharply to you a while ago and I'm sorry.

ANNIE: You have a right to be. You disgraced me before the whole room.

JOHN: Still, those bills — they were a bit of a slap in the face, coming all by the one post.

ANNIE: I'll see that you're not troubled with any more. I'll never get another dress in Dublin as long as I live; old Peg Murnane can run me up some old skirt and blouse if ever I want a new one — once a year maybe. And I suppose I can sell what I have to some secondhand place and get a few pounds for them, and I'll hand every penny I get to you.

JOHN: Now, now, I don't want you to do anything of the sort. All I'm asking for is a little moderation.

ANNIE: I'm not going to have my own husband telling me I "flaunt" around the town.

JOHN: I shouldn't have said that; I don't know what came to me.

ANNIE: I think I know.

JOHN: The drink? Maybe I had one too many this afternoon.

ANNIE: I wasn't thinking of the drink at all.

JOHN: (*getting frightened*) Maybe it's getting a hold of me, like in that play where the man went raving mad and threw a lamp at his wife.

ANNIE: I'd like to see you attempt to throw so much as a spoon at me.

JOHN: And there was that other play — ah, but sure it was vodka they were drinking, not decent Irish.

ANNIE: You take those plays too seriously; sure what are they, only a way of passing an evening?

JOHN: Maybe I do, but they're powerful all the same. Anyway, those same plays are doing well by us. I hear Shangarry Strand is a wash out — of course the bad weather has killed the bathing — but even so we have them bet. The people who have taken houses for the month are fit to be tied because they went there instead of here, and they're having to run two extra buses across here each evening to bring them to the Pavilion. I believe the circus there is empty, and the manager of the Royal Hotel is trying Shakespeare readings in the lounge, but even that won't keep people from dropping over here. We're on the crest of the wave.

(EDDIE *comes in; he looks years older; he probably has gone into horn-rimmed glasses. He sits down at the writing table. His parents observe him, and after a pause —*)
Well, Eddie, son, how's tricks?

EDDIE: (*Deep in a book — he has brought two in with him*) Oh, all right. (*Pause.*)

ANNIE: Did you get a swim today?

EDDIE: No.

JOHN: Too wet, I suppose. (*Silence.*) D'je hear about Jim Clancy?

EDDIE: Yes. (*Silence.*)

JOHN: Are you coming to the play tonight?

EDDIE: Of course. (*Silence.*)

JOHN: What's the old book?

EDDIE: Just a play.

JOHN: What's it called?

EDDIE: "The Dance of Death."

JOHN: Oh. (*Silence; but* ANNIE *tries to make things pleasanter.*)

ANNIE: When I was Eddie's age I always liked plays with a bit of dancing in them. (*Silence.*)

JOHN: And what's the other book?

EDDIE: (*with a murderous look at him*) It's called "Fathers and Children" and it's not a play; it's a novel by Turgenev, and it's about the way the old misunderstand the young and how damnable everything is.

JOHN: I see. (*There is a dreadful silence.* JOHN *gets up quickly.*) I'm going to get my tea. Are you coming, Annie?

ANNIE: I'll stay for a bit with Eddie. (JOHN *goes out.*) What's (JOHN *goes out.*)
What's wrong, Eddie?

EDDIE: (*still sullen*) Nothing.

ANNIE: I don't like you being rude to Pappy.

EDDIE: I wasn't rude.

(ANNIE *sighs: gives it up.* CHRISTINE *comes in and* ANNIE *rises with relief.*)

ANNIE: Oh, Miss Lambert, dear, I know you're famished for your tea. It should have been ready half an hour ago, but I can't do anything with Helena these days. I'll go and hurry her up.

(*She goes out.* CHRISTINE *sits down rather wearily.*)

EDDIE: Tired, Christine?

CHRISTINE: Just a bit. The accounts seemed specially tangled today, and then the weather — doesn't it give you the hump?

EDDIE: No, it doesn't. I like it like this. When you think of the terrible things that go on in the world every day — every day, Christine — it seems as if the sun had no right to shine at all.

CHRISTINE: That's a dreadful thing to say, Eddie.

EDDIE: Isn't it the truth?

CHRISTINE: No, I'm sure it's not. I think there are lots of lovely things in the world. Little children, and flowers, and the sea and — and oh, all sorts of things.

EDDIE: But the children seem to suffer the worst of all, and the flowers die, and the sea wrecks ships, and —

CHRISTINE: Oh, come off it, Eddie.

EDDIE: What do you mean?

CHRISTINE: You'll be giving me the blues next. What's the matter? You're looking so solemn the last few days.

EDDIE: (*very solemn*) Perhaps I'm beginning to realise what life means.

CHRISTINE: If you know that, you'll know a lot, Eddie — more than the wisest man ever knew.

EDDIE: I think one learns through suffering.

CHRISTINE: (*involuntarily*) Good Lord! Excuse me, Eddie.... Tell me, are you ever going to go to work?

EDDIE: I do work.

CHRISTINE: Not what I call work.

EDDIE: Do you want me to go away somewhere; get a job?

CHRISTINE: Maybe.

EDDIE: Why should I? I have this place to walk into some day, I help Pappy in the business, I do quite a lot of work.

CHRISTINE: That seems — soft.

EDDIE: I'd like to improve people — or rather help them to improve themselves.

CHRISTINE: But have you no ambition for yourself?

EDDIE: There was one time I had.

CHRISTINE: When was that?

EDDIE: You know very well.

CHRISTINE: Oh!

EDDIE: You killed it stone dead when you turned me down time after time.

CHRISTINE: I want to live my own life, free and independent, or else marry a husband I can respect — someone who is doing big important work, not a — a —

EDDIE: — son of a country hotelkeeper with a grocery business and a bar at the back of the shop? Go on, say it.

CHRISTINE: You've said it.

EDDIE: Thank you. I can see your point, Christine. You'd never have liked to be my doll, my plaything.

CHRISTINE: No, Eddie, I wouldn't.

EDDIE: You are quite right. But I, too, Christine, have my life, my destiny to work out, my —

CHRISTINE: Oh, Eddie, come off it. Can't you be friendly and nice the way you used to be? Why, we were as jolly as possible the day I arrived last week. Don't you remember?

EDDIE: Maybe I didn't realise —

CHRISTINE: Well, stop realising. Be nice, Eddie.

EDDIE: You've not been so nice to me.

CHRISTINE: I'll try to be.

EDDIE: Well, here it is for the last time. Will you marry me?

CHRISTINE: (*wearily*) Oh, forget it, Eddie.

EDDIE: (*with real passion*) Never, never, as long as I live. Christine, will you marry me?

CHRISTINE: No.

EDDIE: (*with dignity*) Thank you. I am sorry I bothered you. I won't do it again.

CHRISTINE: (*trying a little to flirt with him*) I rather liked being bothered, you know.

EDDIE: Did you? That shows how little you understood.

(LIZZIE *comes in, in excitement.*)

LIZZIE: Miss Lambert, you're a woman of the world; what's a suicide pact?

CHRISTINE: Good heavens! Surely you weren't thinking — what are you talking about?

LIZZIE: Tom Mooney of the Gardaí has been telling me — it's all over the town — a young couple at Shangarry Strand turned the gas on and left a bit of a note, posted it to the girl's mother in fact, saying 'twas a suicide pact; but sure it was a penny-in-the-slot meter and it gev out, and I suppose the young couple thought better of it, or maybe they had no change in the house; anyway, they're alive and little the worse of it.

CHRISTINE: What a wonderful escape. Who were they?

(ANNIE *comes in.*)

LIZZIE: The young fellow had a job shifting scenery with Mr de la Mare and the wife sold chocolates in the theatre. They'd come and go by the bus every day to Shangarry. The man was dismissed last Saturday because he'd be all night with his eyes and ears glued to some crack in the scenery listening to the plays and never doing a tap of work; but he came back every night this week, and the girl used to smuggle him into the back of the pit. It must be on the head of losing his job that he tried to destroy himself.

ANNIE: There's some queer madness in the air. Everyone's behaving strange and different.

EDDIE: (*with sincere passion*) Why should you think them mad? Mightn't what they were going to do be the most sensible thing in the world? To kiss — and die!

ANNIE: Eddie, that's wicked, shameful talk. Where's your religion — and your common sense?

EDDIE: Oh, common sense be hanged! Is life worth living?

LIZZIE: I don't hold with suicides, Annie; I never did. But in a way, Eddie's right. There are times when we all feel that life is not worth living.

ANNIE: I never felt that way, thank God. Did you, Miss Lambert?

CHRISTINE: Eddie has just got a bad touch of growing pains, Mrs Twohig. I wouldn't take him too seriously.

EDDIE: That's right; throw my youth in my face!

CHRISTINE: I didn't mean to do anything of the kind, Eddie.

EDDIE: You've always treated me as a child and Mammy has too. Well, I'd have you know I'm no longer a child.

ANNIE: (*soothing*) Of course you're not, son.

EDDIE: (*rising*) And I'd have you know that I've just asked Christine for the last time if she'll marry me, and she's said "no", so that's finished — for ever. And let you and Pappy stop making jokes about me and her, or I'll — well, I'll do something anyway that will make you sorry. (*He bangs out of the room.*)

ANNIE: Wisha, the poor boy! (*She looks appealingly at* CHRISTINE.) Miss Lambert, dear?

CHRISTINE: I'm afraid it's no use, Mrs Twohig. I'm very fond of Eddie, but that's as far as it goes.

LIZZIE: Poor Eddie! I know what he's going through, I know.

ANNIE: (*sharply*) Lizzie, don't be a fool.

LIZZIE: (*with a little tragic laugh*) Ah, that's what they'll call us, Eddie — fools, fools!

ANNIE: Glory be to goodness, I think you're astray in the head too. Come on, Miss Lambert, dear, till I get you your tea. (ANNIE *and* CHRISTINE *go out. A thunder shower must be coming up, for since* CHRISTINE *'s entrance the room has grown very perceptibly darker.* LIZZIE *sits in the shadows happily sighing to herself.*)

LIZZIE: Poor Eddie and poor me! Ah, Peter, Peter!

CURTAIN

SCENE II

The scene is the same as before. The table is laid for supper for two. The standing lamp at the desk is lit. The time is about eleven o'clock at night. CONSTANCE *comes in, followed by* HECTOR. CONSTANCE *goes to the fireplace, throws her wrap on the armchair and then lights the brackets at the fireplace.* HECTOR *is at the table.*

HECTOR: Cold beef again.

CONSTANCE: Any pickles?

HECTOR: Only onions.

CONSTANCE: How odious.

HECTOR: (*pouring himself a whiskey*) I have quite made up my mind; that scene at the end of the third act must go.

CONSTANCE: My scene with Petro Petrovitch?

HECTOR: Yes. It is unnecessary; the act ceases with my exit. The rest is sheer padding.

CONSTANCE: (*nastily*) Strange how the audience responds to the "padding" — and your exit never gets a hand.

HECTOR: Because you deliberately kill it by making that move.

CONSTANCE: I have to move then. I shall continue to make that move and I shall continue to play that scene. Hector, if you cut that scene, I shall refuse to play.

LIZZIE: (*enters*) Oh, here you are. I'm trying to get your supper right for you.

HECTOR: Where's Helena? (*He pronounces the name in a classical manner.*)

LIZZIE: Helena is incapable with the toothache. Eddie's been out of the house since six — he hasn't been at the play — Annie's gone to bed in tears and John stumped up to his room the minute he got back from the Pavilion. The whole house is on my shoulders.

231

CONSTANCE: Poor Miss Twohig.

HECTOR: (*looking at the table*) Dear, dear. Well, you seem to have got together a very appetising little supper, Miss Twohig.

LIZZIE: I hope everything will be to your liking.

CONSTANCE: (*sitting*) I'm too tired to eat anything.

HECTOR: You must keep up your strength, darling.

CONSTANCE: I suppose I must. (*She drinks.*) Pass me the onions, Hector.

HECTOR: (*passing the onions*) Darling! A little bread?

LIZZIE: What sort was the audience tonight?

HECTOR: Deplorable. I don't think there were thirty people in the hall. The whole town was looking at the fire.

CONSTANCE: (*bitterly*) Imagine people looking at an ordinary little fire when they might have been watching a masterpiece.

LIZZIE: I'll have to admit I slipped out to have a look at the fire myself.

HECTOR: And remember, darling, it was not quite an ordinary fire. I am told that Mr Maloney is suspected of having set fire to his shop himself, and is likely to be arrested on the charge of incendiarism.

LIZZIE: Poor Tim Maloney! As honest a man as ever breathed.

HECTOR: Of course it's only a suspicion. But ah, Miss Twohig, what depths and what depths there are in people's characters.

LIZZIE: I know, I know. There's my tragedy —

HECTOR: Exactly. Is there any cheese?

LIZZIE: I'm sorry to say we're run out of cheese.

HECTOR: No matter. Will you eat nothing yourself?

LIZZIE: Ah, no thanks. Anything I took at this hour of night would prey on my stomach. It amazes me to see Miss Constantia able to eat so heartily.

CONSTANCE: (*her mouth full*) I've taken the merest mouthful.

LIZZIE: You're welcome to everything, dear. Well, I must leave you for a few minutes. I must see is everything locked up downstairs. As I told you, the entire house is on my shoulders tonight. (*She starts to go, meeting* MICHAEL *in the door.*) What is it, Michael?

MICHAEL: Nothing, miss.

LIZZIE: Sure it must be something.

MICHAEL: 'Tis a kind of message I have for Mr de la Mare.

LIZZIE: Well, out with it. (MICHAEL *hesitates.*)

HECTOR: What is it, my boy?

MICHAEL: 'Tis sort of private.

LIZZIE: Oh, more troubles and mysteries! What's the world

coming to when the boots as good as tells me to leave the room? I'm bothered out of my life! (*She leaves the room angrily.*)

CONSTANCE: And what is the message, Michael?

MICHAEL: 'Tisn't exactly a message, ma'am.

HECTOR: No?

MICHAEL: But I couldn't say what I have to say before the ould one.

HECTOR: The old one?

MICHAEL: Ould Lizzie Twohig.

CONSTANCE: Not a respectful way to talk of your master's sister.

MICHAEL: Ah, what matter? I was wondering, sir — At school I was always grand at recitations —

HECTOR: Yes.

MICHAEL: I want to be an actor, sir.

CONSTANCE: Michael!

HECTOR: An actor! You?

MICHAEL: Yes, sir.

HECTOR: No, no, my poor boy. Any profession save that.

MICHAEL: Why so?

HECTOR: I think if I had my life to live again I'd rather be the boots in the Seaview Hotel than Hector de la Mare.

CONSTANCE: Hector!

MICHAEL: Is it you, the boots?

HECTOR: Yes.

MICHAEL: You don't know what you're talking about. Do you know the kind of life I lead? Up every morning at half-six; cleaning knives, cleaning boots, knocking up commercial travellers out of their beds — powerful sleepers every one of them; rousing Helena to get their breakfast; carting their grips to the early train; snatching a bite of breakfast myself, God knows when; feeding the hins and the brood sow; doing a bit of odd gardening; meeting every train that comes and goes; serving in the shop; carrying coals and whiskey up here; never seeing my own bed till midnight or later — ah, get along with you, sir.

HECTOR: Even so, it would be better than —

MICHAEL: Now, if I was the like of you, I'd be travelling the length and breath of Ireland, maybe England, maybe the whole wide world itself. I'd be speaking grand speeches and wearing fine clothes. I'd be having people frozen cold in their seats with the terror I'd put on them — the way you stiffened myself out the other night. Or I'd have them rocking themselves sick with the laughing — not indeed that you are much of a comic, Mr de la Mare. I'd be leaving a name after me that would be remembered through the land. I'd not just be "Michael the Boots at the Seaview" — and even the same Michael not being my christened name at all.

CONSTANCE: (*touched*) I shall always call you Aloysius in the future, Michael.

MICHAEL: Thank you, ma'am.

HECTOR: You'd like to give up your nice place here and your kind master and mistress to drag from one small town to another, playing in small halls and dirty little theatres, staying in frowsy lodgings; with no home, no permanent abiding-place; seeing yourself getting older and shabbier every year —

CONSTANCE: Hector, what are you saying?

HECTOR: (*almost hysterically seeing himself for a moment as he really is*) It's true, Constance, it's true; you know it is. Saying to myself, "Shall I ever get a chance? Must it always be the smalls of England and Ireland for me? Oh, my God, to play — even for one night — a great tragic part in a great theatre, thousands hanging on every word I uttered — "

MICHAEL: (*fired*) That's it, sir, that's it. I know, sir. But if you'd only hear me recite.

HECTOR: No. No!

MICHAEL: Please, sir.

CONSTANCE: Let him, dear. It can do no harm.

HECTOR: Very well. Proceed.

MICHAEL: What'll I do? A comic or a serious?

HECTOR: I should prefer something serious.

MICHAEL: (*after thinking a little*) Well, I learned this after I left school. It wasn't in the reading-book, but I took a fancy to it. I'm told it was written by a man who walked off one day and was never heard of again. 'Tis called "Ballyvourney", which is a place in the mountains of County Cork and a great place for the Gaelic. (*He recites the poem with a serious, simple intensity:*)

"He came from Ballyvourney and we called him 'Ballyvourney',
The sweetest name in Erin that we know,
And they tell me he has taken now the last, the last long journey,
And it's young he is, it's young he is so very far to go.
Before our eyes, just like a flower, we saw his life unfolding,
As day by day he grew in bloom in early manhood's grace:
Ah, Death, to pluck the flower and to snatch from our beholding

The head of rippled gold and the happy morning face."
Sure that's a sad ould poem. Maybe you'd like this better. (*He
rattles off, half-singing, half reciting:*)

> "While going the road to sweet Athy,
>   Hurroo — Hurroo —
> While going the road to sweet Athy,
>   Hurroo — Hurroo —
> While going the road to sweet Athy,
>   A stick in my hand and a drop in my eye,
>   A doleful damsel I heard cry,
>   "Och, Johnny, I hardly knew ye.
> With drums and guns and guns and drums
>   The enemy nearly slew ye,
> My darling dear, you look so queer,
>   Och, Johnny, I hardly knew ye."

LIZZIE: (*who has come in at the last part of the verse*) In the
name of goodness, what are you doing, Michael?

MICHAEL: (*abashed*) Nothing, miss.

LIZZIE: Nothing? Nonsense. Off to bed with you. You were
shocking late getting up this morning.

MICHAEL: Yes, miss. Good night to you all.

CONSTANCE: }
HECTOR: } Good night. (MICHAEL *exits.*)

LIZZIE: You shouldn't let him be bothering you with his capers,
Miss Constantia.

CONSTANCE: I like Aloysius.

LIZZIE: Aloy — who? Oh, Michael, you mean?

HECTOR: You may have something of a genius there, Miss Twohig.

LIZZIE: Ah, nonsense. No genius ever could come out of a back-
ward place like Shangarry Strand — or Inish itself, for that
matter.

HECTOR: "It bloweth where it listeth —" (*Rising.*) Well, well, I
think I shall retire. I have had a very pleasant supper, Miss
Twohig, and for that, many thanks. Are you for bed, Constance.

CONSTANCE: (*Rising*) Yes, indeed, I'm worn out. Good night,
Miss Twohig.

LIZZIE: Good night, dear.

HECTOR: Good night, Miss Twohig. (*The two go out.* LIZZIE *does
a little tidying up at the table and switches off the lights at
the fireplace.* EDDIE *enters. He looks more gloomy and dis-
traught than ever.*)

LIZZIE: Oh, Eddie, darling, you're back, I was worried about you
the whole evening. Where were you?

EDDIE: Just walking and walking and walking.

LIZZIE: I know. You wanted to be alone with your thoughts.

EDDIE: Yes. It's foolish of me, I suppose.

LIZZIE: (*sits*) Foolish? That's what they call us, Eddie, foolish. 'Tis little they understand.

EDDIE: I'll take my books and go to bed.

LIZZIE: Before you go let you sit down for a minute. I want to talk to you.

EDDIE: What is it? (*sitting*)

LIZZIE: Ah, no — sit here — at my feet.

EDDIE: (*sitting at her feet*) We're like the aunt and the nephew in that play on Monday night.

LIZZIE: Aren't we? Eddie, I'd like to tell you the story of my life.

EDDIE: And I'd like to tell you about myself, Aunt Lizzie.

LIZZIE: You see, Peter and I knew each other from the time we were little children.

EDDIE: I was grown up when I first met Christine.

LIZZIE: We lived next door to each other, and we saw one another every day of our young lives.

EDDIE: I'd never see Christine only twice a year, unless I chanced to go to Dublin.

LIZZIE: He had an elder brother that everyone was struck on but I could see nothing in him. It was Peter for me always.

EDDIE: When I first met Christine, Aunt Lizzie, it was like — like —

LIZZIE: (*with a touch of impatience*) Wait till I tell you about Peter.

EDDIE: It was like sunshine in a dark cellar. (*They now speak together paying no attention to what the other is saying. Entirely engrossed in making pretty, untrue pictures for themselves.*)

LIZZIE: He was a year or two older than I was, a bright curly-headed boy. There was another boy — Jack Murnane — terribly gone on me, but Peter beat him one day, and after that he kept away from me. He'd bring me flowers and sweets, and he called me his little sweetheart. And as we grew older he learned to love me with a man's love, and one day he wanted to buy me a ring, and I wouldn't let him. He was afraid of his mother, and I think it was she who drove Peter from me —

EDDIE: It was only two years ago, and it seems to me as if I had never lived until she came to Inish. I'd never cared about a girl in my life, only Katie Walsh and one or two others, and that was only to pass the time. I loved her from the minute I set eyes on her, but I was always a bit afraid of her. I was like a dog: she could whistle and I'd come to her. I've always kept a handkerchief she dropped one time; it's in the press in my room and sometimes I sleep with it under my pillow. I've never kissed her. I wouldn't dare....

(*Somewhere about here the* CURTAIN *mercifully falls.*)

ACT III

Scene: The same, a week later. Morning; dull, raining slightly.
LIZZIE *comes in, ushering* MR HEGARTY, *a young man.*

LIZZIE: Will you come in here, Mr —— , Mr ——

HEGARTY: Hegarty, John Hegarty.

LIZZIE: Oh, yes, you told me, of course. Will you sit down Mr Hegarty? I'm afraid my brother is out and my sister-in-law too; they went out after breakfast and I haven't seen them since.

HEGARTY: That doesn't matter at all, Miss Twohig. I am sure you can give me all the information I want.

LIZZIE: Well, of course I can tell you about the hotel, seeing that I more or less run it. I can let you have a very nice room from about —

HEGARTY: No, no. I'm afraid I'm not staying. I just want a little information.

LIZZIE: Information?

HEGARTY: I always think that in these little country towns there's no place like the hotel for gathering news. The hotel is the hub of the town, so to speak.

LIZZIE: Maybe.

HEGARTY: (*suddenly and dramatically*) Miss Twohig, why has Inish suddenly put itself on the map of Ireland?

LIZZIE: Sure it was always there — on big maps, anyway.

HEGARTY: Why has Inish suddenly become news? Not yet front-page news, but front-page news maybe tomorrow.

LIZZIE: Front-page? Oh, you're from a newspaper?

HEGARTY: I thought I had explained that. I'm not from any particular paper, I'm free lance. It's part of my business to read all the Irish papers every day, and during the last two weeks one word has caught my eye again and again. Inish! Attempted suicide at Inish. Boy breaks open till in Inish. Respectable butcher called McClusky beats up his wife at Inish. Young couple attempt suicide pact, couple employed at Inish. Now I happen to know Inish. My sister and I spent a month here two summers ago, for our sins. It was very expensive and it was deadly dull.

LIZZIE: Where did you stay?

238

HEGARTY: Not here. You were even more expensive. But that's not the point. The point is that during that month nothing happened. There wasn't even a decent dog-fight, and now all these things happen — in ten days. An outbreak of this kind doesn't come by chance. I've been putting two and two together — I believe I'm the first journalist in Ireland to put this particular two and two together, and I'm here this morning to try and find out what they make.

LIZZIE: I don't understand all you say, but sure there was nothing at the back of that boy breaking into McGarry's till except that he wanted money to go to the theatre. McGarry let him off, and Mr de la Mare gave him a season ticket, and there's been no more about it.

HEGARTY: Yes, I hardly expected there was anything in that particular incident, but I've been all round the town this morning — I came from Dublin by the early train — I've been into shops and pubs, and I notice the strangest kind of attitude in the people. Everyone seems suspicious, watching everyone else, expecting something strange to happen. If you mention anyone to anyone else, you're met with a kind of veiled suggestion that they are not what they seem to be; that they have a shady past and are likely to have a blacker future. I hasten to add that no one has had a word to say against you, Miss Twohig.

LIZZIE: Did you mention my name?

HEGARTY: I don't think I did.

LIZZIE: Well, let you try mentioning it and see what happens. You're right, Mr Hegarty; this town is full of gossipers and slanderers, and I could tell you things about some of them that would make your hair stand on end.

HEGARTY: But they weren't like this two years ago. They just seemed nice, ordinary people, a little on the dull side. Come, Miss Twohig, there's something at the back of it all. What is it?

LIZZIE: Indeed, I couldn't tell you — unless it would be the weather. Rain every day for a fortnight.

HEGARTY: If rain were accountable for crime, all Ireland would have murdered itself long ago. No, no, it can't be the weather.

LIZZIE: Maybe it's politics. Them and the weather are about the only things we think of outside our own business.

HEGARTY: Yes, I hadn't thought of politics. It might be a curious result of recent legislation. Perhaps your local T.D. could help to elucidate this point.

LIZZIE: Is it Peter Hurley?

HEGARTY: Yes.

LIZZIE: You'd do well not to go near Peter Hurley; he's the deceiver if ever there was one.

HEGARTY: In what way?

LIZZIE: I'd rather not say; it's a personal matter. But be deceitful in one way and you'll be deceitful in every way. Isn't that right, Mr Hegarty?

HEGARTY: I suppose so.

LIZZIE: Anyway, you can't see him today because he's away in Dublin at the Dáil.

HEGARTY: Oh, yes, of course. They were having a very important all-night sitting last night.

LIZZIE: (*laughing*) Imagine poor old Ireland depending on the votes of men like Peter Hurley. I have to laugh.

HEGARTY: The division was likely to be very close, I believe.

LIZZIE: Oh, they can depend on Peter. Peter'll vote the way he is told to vote. The creature hasn't the courage of a mouse. (HECTOR *and* CONSTANCE *come in. They look rather gloomy.*) Oh, come in, come in; this is a young gentleman from a newspaper — Mr de la Mare and Miss Constantia — Mr Hegarty. (*Mutual greetings. Everyone sits down.*)

HECTOR: You wanted to interview me?

HEGARTY: Well — er — I'm not sure.

HECTOR: Or perhaps it was Miss Constantia you wanted to talk to?

CONSTANCE: No, please, Hector; you know how I hate publicity and all my pictures are at the theatre.

HECTOR: There are times, darling, when one must sacrifice oneself to the great hungry public.

HEGARTY: I am just looking for general information.

HECTOR: Well, we opened our season here nearly three weeks ago, and we have had the most — I won't say astonishing, because I have always believed that the public at heart — *au fond*, as the French say — is quite sound and wants the best. Fine plays, well presented, mind you, and with suitable *décor*. I admit that our *décor* is not at present all it might be. You can understand, Mr Hegarty, how the exigencies of continual touring —

HEGARTY: (*light breaking on him*) Oh, you're actors?

HECTOR: (*with exaggerated humility*) Well, I hope we are actors. Are we, Constance, my love?

LIZZIE: The De la Mare Repertory Company, Mr Hegarty. (*To* HECTOR.) Mr Hegarty is from Dublin, and he's maybe a bit out of touch with things, you must forgive him.

HECTOR: I quite understand and there is nothing to forgive. We have not played Dublin for years. When were we there last, darling?

CONSTANCE: I really can't remember.

HEGARTY: What theatre did you play in?

HECTOR: One of the big ones, of course; I can't remember which.

HEGARTY: And you're doing well here?

HECTOR: We have been doing extraordinarily well — up to this week. Miss Twohig, can you explain the curious falling off in the audiences this week?

LIZZIE: I can not. And I don't know why everyone this morning is asking me to explain everything.

HECTOR: I'm sure the repertory was varied enough — some new plays and some old favourites, but no one comes — at least only a handful. Things seem to be happening in the town all the time, and everybody is so busy talking about what has just happened or waiting for the next thing to happen to have any inclination or time to come to the Pavilion.

HEGARTY: Ah, so you've noticed it too?

HECTOR: Noticed what?

HEGARTY: The accumulation of incidents of a mildly criminal nature.

HECTOR: Oh, there have been many strange things which have not got into the papers.

HEGARTY: It's extraordinarily interesting.

CONSTANCE: It's extraordinarily distressing, Mr Hegarty, when as a consequence we play to empty houses.

HECTOR: Never mind, dearest. We've learned to take the rough with the smooth.

CONSTANCE: We have. " 'Tis not in mortals to command success, but we'll do more, Sempronius, we'll deserve it."

HECTOR: (chiming in) "We'll deserve it."

HEGARTY: Bravo!

LIZZIE: I wish you could see some of their plays, Mr Hegarty. They're gorgeous — though sometimes it's a bit hard to get to sleep after them. That one, Mr de la Mare, where you throw the lamp at Miss Constantia and are then put in a strait-waistcoat — that was a very good one, but of course my favourite is where the baby is murdered in the cellar.

HECTOR: Perhaps you will come to the theatre tonight, Mr Hegarty? Any representative of the press is, of course, more than welcome.

HEGARTY: I am afraid I have to get back to Dublin.

HECTOR: Well, shall you be here for a little time?

HEGARTY: I think so. At any rate I'll be knocking around the town until the afternoon train.

HECTOR: I see.... I thought, Constance, we might stroll to the Pavilion and look for letters, and if we chanced to come on any photographs, Mr Hegarty might like to have them. Just as a little souvenir, Mr Hegarty; just as a little souvenir.

HEGARTY: Thank you very much.

HECTOR: (*rising*) We won't be more than a few minutes. The Pavilion is just round the corner. Will you come, Constance?

CONSTANCE: (*rising*) Yes, I should like a walk. I want to feel the sea-spray beating on my face.

LIZZIE: I'm afraid it's quite calm this morning, dear. The sun was trying to come out a little while ago.

CONSTANCE: What matter? I shall at least get a breath of ozone.

HECTOR: Shall I reserve your seat as usual, Miss Twohig?

LIZZIE: (*sadly*) No, I can't come tonight.

HECTOR: You've missed every night this week. Fie, fie!

LIZZIE: No one is sorrier than myself. But I don't like the way Eddie is going on at all and I want to keep an eye on him.

HECTOR: Dear, dear!

CONSTANCE: What's the matter with Eddie, Miss Twohig?

LIZZIE: Haven't you noticed him yourself? So dark and shut up in himself. And, worse than that, he's broken his pledge.

CONSTANCE: Oh, Miss Twohig!

LIZZIE: Yes, dear, never took a drop in his life till now. I feel quite frightened.

HECTOR: Where is he?

LIZZIE: I don't know. He's not around the house. I'm sorry, Mr de la Mare, but I must stay at home tonight.

HECTOR: That's quite all right, Miss Twohig, quite all right. Constance, let us go. (*They go out.*)

HEGARTY: (*very keen*) Who is "Eddie", Miss Twohig?

LIZZIE: My brother's only child.

HEGARTY: And he's behaving queerly?

LIZZIE: He is indeed.

HEGARTY: I'd like to speak to him.

LIZZIE: He's out, as you heard me say; but indeed you'll get nothing from him. I'm the only one he speaks to — whenever he does speak — I'm the only one knows what's preying on his mind.

HEGARTY: And what is that?

LIZZIE: The old story, Mr Hegarty, the old, old story — love's young dream, as Thomas Moore said long ago... Are you married, Mr Hegarty?

HEGARTY: (*rather taken aback*) Why — yes.

LIZZIE: And happy?

HEGARTY: Very happy.

LIZZIE: (*disappointed, but making the best of it*) Ah, you're one of the few lucky ones so. (*A tap at the door.*) Come in. (*Enter* SLATTERY *furtive and poorly dressed.*) Oh, good morning, Mr Slattery.

SLATTERY: Good morning, Miss Twohig.

LIZZIE: My brother is out, but can I do anything for you?

SLATTERY: You're just the one that can. (*From under his coat he produces a large tin.*) D'ye see that?

LIZZIE: I do.

SLATTERY: 'Tis a grand weed killer you sold to Mick Tobin a few years back. I want one the like of it, and they told me below in the shop it's you had the key of all the poisons.

LIZZIE: (*taking tin and looking at it*) So I have... "Kill-em-Quick" — ah, Mr Slattery, isn't it a pity, we're not allowed to stock that any longer; 'twas too poisonous altogether.

SLATTERY: (*very dejected*) Is that so? Well, have you anything in the nature of rat poison?

LIZZIE: I have, to be sure.

SLATTERY: Can I buy some?

LIZZIE: Lashin's of it. Wait till I get me keys.

HEGARTY: Just a minute; Mr Slattery — pardon my butting in — but what do you want the weed killer for?

SLATTERY: For me weeds.

LIZZIE: Of course.

HEGARTY: And, failing the weed killer, you want rat poison?

SLATTERY: For me rats.

LIZZIE: Of course.

HEGARTY: I see.... (*He takes up the tin and examines it thoughtfully.*) I imagine, Mr Slattery, that you are very unhappily married. (SLATTERY *gapes.*)

LIZZIE: Sure the poor man's not married at all.

HEGARTY: (*taken aback*) Oh!

LIZZIE: He lives with an old termagant of an aunt who is rotten with money and won't let him have more than sixpence a week in his pocket — pardon me saying so, Mr Slattery.

SLATTERY: It's no more than the truth.

HEGARTY: But you'll come into all her money when she dies?

SLATTERY: I suppose I will.

HEGARTY: Hm. Very interesting.

LIZZIE: I'll have me keys in a minute.

SLATTERY: (*trying to take back the tin*) Maybe I won't mind today. I'll get a few penn'orth of sweets instead.

LIZZIE: No trouble at all.

HEGARTY: (*holding on to the tin*) I think I'll keep this.

SLATTERY: (*snatching it from him*) You will not. (*Very rapidly and noiselessly he leaves the room.*)

LIZZIE: (*turning; she hadn't seen him go*) I can't find — oh! he's gone! Isn't that very queer now?

HEGARTY: Very queer, Miss Twohig. I think I've put that two and two together anyhow. This may be a case for the police.

LIZZIE: The police? (*And immediately the door opens and* MOONEY, *a Civic Guard, appears.*) Oh! heaven protect us!

MOONEY: 'Morning, Miss Twohig. Is your brother about?

LIZZIE: He's not.

MOONEY: Or the mistress?

LIZZIE: She's out too. Why do you want them? Can I do anything for you?

MOONEY: Well — I wanted to prepare them like.

LIZZIE: Prepare them?

MOONEY: Break the news, as you might say.

LIZZIE: Merciful heavens, what's happened?

MOONEY: It's Master Eddie.

LIZZIE: Eddie! Eddie! He's dead?

MOONEY: No, no, miss. But he's terrible wet.

LIZZIE: Wet?

MOONEY: Yes, miss. He was in the sea.

LIZZIE: Bathing?

MOONEY: No, miss. In his clothes.

LIZZIE: Is he after falling in? Poor little Eddie!

MOONEY: No one knows rightly how he got into the sea, miss.

LIZZIE: And who rescued him?

MOONEY: He rescued himself, miss. It seems he got out of the sea at the White Rocks. Maybe he fell in, or maybe he — no matter. Anyway, he walked out of the sea himself, and then he hid among the rocks because he was ashamed-like to walk through the town dripping wet; but a lad came on him and brought him back, and he's having a sup of whiskey at Breen's, so I thought I'd just come ahead and give you all the bend.

LIZZIE: I'm sure it's very kind of you, Tom. Oh! I wish Annie was here, or Helena — I haven't seen her all the morning either. I'd better get a cup of tea for him, anyway.

MOONEY: Don't bother about the tea, miss. Put him to bed the minute he comes in.

LIZZIE: Yes, that's a good idea.

MOONEY: And have a couple of hot water bottles ready.

LIZZIE: Yes.

MOONEY: And give him two aspirins.

LIZZIE: Two? Yes.

MOONEY: And tell the master I'll be back in a little while as soon as Master Eddie is dried off. I'm afraid there'll be a few questions I'll have to put to him.

LIZZIE: (*fussing about the room*) What an upset it all is — poor Eddie — aspirin and hot-water bottles — where are my keys? Tom, do you see my keys anywhere?

MOONEY: (*starting to look*) What class of keys?

LIZZIE: Oh, just a bunch of keys. Oh, Eddie, Eddie! Mr Hegarty, for goodness' sake have a look round for a bunch of keys. (*They all start looking.*) The kettle's sure to be off the boil — 'twould be bound to happen. If Helena was here itself —

MOONEY: I have them here, miss, here on the writing table.

LIZZIE: (*taking them*) Thank you, Tom. I won't be two minutes now. (*She goes out.*)

HEGARTY: Is there any statement you'd like to make?

MOONEY: About what?

HEGARTY: Master Eddie.

MOONEY: Who the devil are you?

HEGARTY: I write for the papers, and —

MOONEY: Ah! go to blazes.

HEGARTY: There is nothing you want to say?

MOONEY: There is not.

HEGARTY: I see. It's a pity. It might have got your name before the public.

MOONEY: I don't want my name before the public. I want to live quiet. Here, out with you.

HEGARTY: Before I go I have a statement to make in connection with poisons.

MOONEY: I won't hear it. I'm bothered out of my life with people coming to me with statements about attempted murders and suicides and God knows what. I'll hear no more of them. (CHRISTINE *comes in, in evident distress.*)

CHRISTINE: Is Eddie —? Oh! I beg your pardon.

MOONEY: That's all right, Miss Lambert. (*To* HEGARTY) Out of this, you.

HEGARTY: But really —

MOONEY: No more talk. (*He pushes him out.*) Master Eddie's as right as rain and will be here in a minute.

CHRISTINE: They told me at the factory he was drowned.

MOONEY: Wisha, bad luck to them for story-tellers.

CHRISTINE: Then in the street they said he had only got a ducking.

MOONEY: Let you sit down. You're all of a tremble.

CHRISTINE: Thank you, Mr Mooney.

MOONEY: (*moving to the door*) I'll see that they send Eddie home; he should get out of his wet clothes and not be drinking at Breen's. (*He hesitates: he comes back to her.*) Miss Lambert, if you'll excuse the intrusion, we've all a great respect for John Twohig and the family and I'd be sorry anything to happen Eddie.

CHRISTINE: Happen Eddie? But he's safe, isn't he?

MOONEY: He is in one way, and he isn't in another. It'll be my business, I'm afraid, to find out what brought him into the water today, and, begging your pardon, it'll be a little bit your business too.

CHRISTINE: (*getting up indignantly*) I had nothing to do with it. What do you mean? What are you accusing me of?

MOONEY: (*soothingly*) Now, there's no use flying out at me. I'm too old, and I'm married; that makes me patient. Everyone in town knows you and Master Eddie. Everyone likes the two of you; and that's a sweet little place John has outside the town.

CHRISTINE: I don't know it.

MOONEY: 'Tis well you know it. The last time you were down here, didn't I see you and Eddie walking the land? Good land and a smart, tidy little garden all going to waste because John's too busy to live out there. A doaty little house — a woman living out there would be crowned. However, I won't go into all that. I'll just hint that, under certain circumstances (*Voice of* EDDIE, *off*), I might overlook any charges I might have to bring against the young gentleman in question. I think I hear him coming. (*He goes to the door and looks out.*) Come in here, Eddie, for a minute before you go to your room. There's someone wants to see you.

EDDIE: (*heard off*) Who is it?

MOONEY: 'Tis Miss Lambert.

EDDIE: (*heard off*) No, no, I can't come in.

MOONEY: (*going outside the door*) In with you and no nonsense.

(*There is a bit of a scuffle outside and* MOONEY *shoots in* EDDIE. EDDIE *looks very woebegone; he has no hat and his hair is tousled and wet. Someone has lent him an overcoat, old and too big for him. Below it are seen two wet flannel-trousered legs.*) Here he is for you, Miss Lambert.

CHRISTINE: (*rushing to him*) Eddie, darling!

MOONEY: Exactly. (*He goes softly out.*)

CHRISTINE: My darling, what happened to you?

EDDIE: (*rather stiffly*) Let me go, Christine. I'm not — I want to change, I'm dripping.

CHRISTINE: I know, darling. But what happened?

EDDIE: Oh, nothing.

CHRISTINE: Nothing? Nonsense. What did you do?

EDDIE: (*glibly*) Well, I was on a rock and I got giddy and fell into the sea.

CHRISTINE: That may be a good enough story to tell round the town but it's not good enough for me. (*Softly*) Won't you tell me, Eddie?

EDDIE: (*sniffing*) I was so miserable, Christine.

CHRISTINE: I know, darling.

EDDIE: It didn't seem worth going on with.

CHRISTINE: I know.

EDDIE: And there seemed no hope things would ever come right.

CHRISTINE: I know.

EDDIE: So — so I tried to make an end of it all.

CHRISTINE: My poor darling.

EDDIE: I'm no good at living, Christine.

CHRISTINE: Hush, hush.

EDDIE: But if I'm no good at living, I'm as bad at dying. For the minute I felt the cold of the water I wanted to get out of it quick and go on living and unfortunately I'm an awfully strong swimmer so — so I just swam ashore and — and that's all.

CHRISTINE: Darling!

EDDIE: Wasn't I the fool to try and destroy myself by drowning? I should have tried any other way but that.

CHRISTINE: Darling! . . . Eddie, do you know I've called you "darling" about a dozen times in the last two minutes?

EDDIE: (*quite dumb*) Have you, Christine?

CHRISTINE: Yes, darling.

EDDIE: Well?

CHRISTINE: Oh, you donkey!

EDDIE: You don't mean —? Oh, Christine!

CHRISTINE: (*in his arms*) Of course I mean. If you'd been drowned,

Eddie, I'd have been the next off that rock, and I can't swim. (ANNIE *appears. She is in outdoor clothes. She takes in the situation at a glance.*)

ANNIE: (*a little stern*) Hm! Upstairs with you, Eddie, and get out of your wet things.

EDDIE: Yes, Mammy. But Christine says she'll —

ANNIE: I think I know quite well what Christine says, but off with you. Do you want to get your death of cold?

EDDIE: No, Mammy. Very well, Mammy. I won't be five minutes changing, Christine.

ANNIE: You'll have a hot bath and you'll go to bed. Your Aunt Lizzie has everything ready for you.

EDDIE: Very well, Mammy. But I'm not going to bed. (*He dashes out.*)

ANNIE: (*softening*) I had to hunt him, Miss Lambert. I don't want him down on our hands with pneumonia.

CHRISTINE: Do you mind, Mrs Twohig?

ANNIE: Mind?

CHRISTINE: Eddie and me —?

ANNIE: Sure my dear, it's what I've been wanting ever since I set eyes on you. Eddie's foolish in some ways and a bit young, but he's as good as gold and I know you'll make a fine man of him.

CHRISTINE: Eddie's splendid, Mrs Twohig, splendid.

ANNIE: We'll talk it all out by and by. I've a lot of things on my mind this morning. You'll stay, won't you? It's not worth going back to the factory before dinner.

CHRISTINE: Yes, I'll stay. I'll just run upstairs and tidy myself. I rushed out of the factory without so much as a hat — and I think I've been crying.

ANNIE: Well, off with you. (CHRISTINE *goes out.* ANNIE *goes to the door and calls.*) Helena! Helena! Bad luck to that girl; there's no getting any good out of her these days. (*She goes out. There is a little pause.* JOHN *comes in, pushing* PETER *in front of him.* JOHN *looks very stern;* PETER *very frightened and small.* JOHN *locks the door.*)

JOHN: Tell it to me again. I want to know are me ears mad or what.

PETER: (*in a tiny voice*) Well, 'twas an all-night sitting, as you know, and the late Minister for Agriculture made a terrible powerful speech and —

JOHN: To hell with the late Minister for Agriculture. Why did you listen to him?

PETER: I couldn't sort of help it. He made a terrible powerful speech and —

JOHN: And you let yourself be swayed by a bit of mob oratory?

PETER: It was not mob oratory, John, it was not. It was facts and figures and —

JOHN: Facts and figures! What the hell business have you with facts and figures? Your business is to vote with the Government.

PETER: I know. But —

JOHN: But?

PETER: It was that play, "An Enemy of the People" — do you remember it, John? I couldn't get it out of my head.

JOHN: Oh, those bloody plays!

PETER: Do you remember when the doctor in the play said that nobody should act so that he'd have to spit in his own face? I felt I sort of had to tell the truth, and the only way I could tell the truth — I'm no speechifier — was by my vote.

JOHN: So you voted against the Government?

PETER: I did.

JOHN: And defeated the bill?

PETER: Yes.

JOHN: And now the Government has to go to the country?

PETER: I suppose so.

JOHN: Suppose so? Don't you know? And don't you know that this place is disgraced for ever in the eyes of the world? Why, thunder and turf, man, what's going to become of public life at all if members of Parliament start being swayed this way and that by speeches and arguments, facts and figures, moryah? There's an end to all stability in public affairs; nobody will know where they stand; no party will know from day to day whether it has a majority or not; it's chaos, man, pure chaos.

PETER: I know, I know. I'll never do it again.

JOHN: You'll never have the chance to do it again, me bucko. Do you think you're going to be a candidate at the next election?

PETER: I suppose I won't.

JOHN: I know you won't.

PETER: It was that play — "An Enemy of the People".

JOHN: "An Enemy of the People." Faith, that's you; that's your name from this out.

PETER: I nearly cried in the car coming down — I got a lift as far as Shangarry Strand and I kem on by bus. I'm afraid to face the wife, though she herself was mad about that same play.

JOHN: Ah, don't talk to me about those plays, they have been the ruination of this place. However, thanks to Annie, I have already made up my mind how to deal with them. (*He goes to the door and unlocks it.*) You'd better be off home, Peter, and get over it. We'll be friends again one of these days, but for the next week for God's sake keep out of my sight.

PETER: (*meekly*) Very well, John. (*He goes out.*)

JOHN: (*calling from the door*) Annie! Annie!

ANNIE: (*heard off*) Yes, John.

JOHN: Come here. (ANNIE *comes in.*) It's even worse than you thought.

ANNIE: What is?

JOHN: That play business. Peter Hurley's put out the Government on the head of some blasted play.

ANNIE: In heaven's name! That's awful, John.

JOHN: 'Tis a national tragedy — and to think that we're to blame for it all. Are they upstairs? Fetch them down. The sooner the whole thing is settled the better.

ANNIE: I think they're just after coming in from the Pavilion. I'll get them.

JOHN: Do so. And, Annie, come back yourself. You'll be a great help in case they turn nasty.

ANNIE: Very well. There's one thing, John. Eddie had a little accident this morning; he got a wetting. Say nothing to him about it, and if you hear any gossip in the town pay no heed to it.

JOHN: What do you mean? What's all this about?

ANNIE: Nothing at all. Pay no heed to anything but what I tell you. All's turned out for the best, and Eddie's going to marry Miss Lambert.

JOHN: The devil he is! Well, I'm delighted. Me bold Eddie!

ANNIE: I knew you would be. I'll go call Mr de la Mare. (*She goes out.* JOHN *sits at the writing table, takes out a cheque book and writes a cheque.* HECTOR *and* CONSTANCE *come in.* HECTOR *has a large envelope in his hand.* ANNIE *follows them.*)

HECTOR: You wanted to see us, Mr Twohig?

JOHN: I did. Will you sit down? (*The three sit.* JOHN *stands.*) It's a bit hard for me to say what I have to say. Maybe I'd better begin by giving you this. (*He hands him the cheque.*)

HECTOR: (*looking at it*) Fifty pounds? What is this for?

JOHN: Maybe you don't remember that it was in our agreement that the contract at the Pavilion could be terminated on either side without notice on payment of fifty pounds?

HECTOR: Oh.... But — I do not understand. I admit that the audiences this week have been a disappointment, a sore disappointment, but I am confident that they will improve as the week goes on.

CONSTANCE: Miss Joyce bought three seats while we were there just now.

JOHN: It's got nothing to do with the audiences.

HECTOR: You can't have any complaint about the acting, I'm sure.

JOHN: I've nothing against the acting — 'tis very good.

ANNIE: Too good.

HECTOR: Or the conduct of the company?

JOHN: No. Decent people, every one of them.

HECTOR: Then, I repeat, I do not understand.

JOHN: Well, it's this way. Queer things have started to happen here, things that never happened in fifty years, and it was Annie who put her finger on the root of the trouble.

CONSTANCE: What sort of things do you refer to, Mr Twohig?

JOHN: You know very well, Miss Constantia. Nasty things that were getting Inish into the paper.

CONSTANCE: And what have we to do with such things?

JOHN: Annie, maybe you could explain better than I can.

ANNIE: In a word, it's all you and your plays, Mr de la Mare; and mind, I'm not saying a word against you personally or Miss Constantia either, but maybe they're too good for the like of us or we're too simple for them. I remember saying the morning you came — God forgive me — that we were blue-mouldy here for want of a good scandal or two; well, it seems there were lots of scandalous things going on in the town that no one knew anything of except the parties concerned. We were all more or less happy and comfortable, good tempered and jolly — until these plays began to put ideas into our heads. We got suspicious of our neighbours and of our own families. The young people got asking themselves "Is life worth living?" If I've heard that question asked once in the last week I've heard it asked a dozen times. My own boy asked it of me! Sure never before did we think of asking ourselves such a ridiculous question.

HECTOR: It is far from ridiculous, Mrs Twohig. *Is* it worth living? I often wonder.

ANNIE: Ah, don't talk nonsense, man. Of course it is.

CONSTANCE: You have faith, Mrs Twohig.

ANNIE: I have my religion, Miss Constantia. Did you ever see a big stone in a field, Mr de la Mare?

HECTOR: Of course I did.

ANNIE: You might be sitting by it, idle-like, some sunny afternoon,

251

and then for no reason at all you'd turn it over. And what would you see? Worms. Little beetles that'd run this way and that, horrible little creepies that'd make your stomach turn, and you'd put the stone back as quick as you could, or you'd run away.

HECTOR: I see, I see! A splendid simile, Mrs Twohig. We have lifted the stone, we have exposed Inish. Constance, it's wonderful. We have a mission here, a great duty.

JOHN: Oh no, sir, you haven't. Your duty is to get yourself and your traps out of the hall as quick as you can. Annie and myself saw the Monsignor early this morning and he agrees with the course I'm taking.

ANNIE: He agrees that there must be a stop put to people going into suicide pacts on the head of "Is life worth living?"

CONSTANCE: What nonsense. It shows great moral courage.

ANNIE: Whining and running away? A thing we never did before in Ireland.

HECTOR: You know you really can't turn us out like this at a moment's notice.

JOHN: The agreement says I can, and things is so desperate that I have to stick by that agreement even if it seems a bit hard on you. Do you know that we'd have a murder on our consciences only by the good luck that McCluskey the butcher is such a bad shot with a hatchet?

CONSTANCE: I don't believe that had anything to do with our plays.

JOHN: And Tommy McCluskey in the front row every night? Of course, we all knew he fought now and again with Julia, but the night he threw the hatchet was the night he came home after seeing Mr de la Mare throw the lamp at you.

HECTOR: But there are quite a number of seats booked for tonight, Mr Twohig. Are you going to disappoint those people?

JOHN: (*with a confident smile*) They'll get their money's worth.

HECTOR: In what way?

JOHN: I was on the 'phone this morning to Shangarry Strand. I'm having the circus over.

HECTOR: (*really pained*) A circus!

JOHN: It's on the road now. It will be in the town any minute.

CONSTANCE: (*outraged*) This is an insult, a deliberate insult.

JOHN: It's nothing of the kind.

CONSTANCE: You are a narrow, bigoted man; you are afraid of the truth, and your wife is worse; she is an ignorant provincial. She has only seen our work twice —

ANNIE: Twice was enough.

CONSTANCE: We were giving you great art. I have played here as I have never played before. Mr de la Mare has given himself — all of himself — night after night to an audience of — clodhoppers. And now, when we stir something in these clods, waken them to some spark of life, you say they must go to sleep again, and you rock them to sleep with a circus! It's an insult to them and to us.

ANNIE: I don't know what you mean by awakening them to life, Miss Constantia. It seems to me you were awakening them to kill each other or themselves, and to say mean, slanderous things of each other and —

JOHN: And to put out the Government. Oh! when I think of that Peter Hurley —

ANNIE: The long and the short of it is, you were doing no good here and you must be gone.

HECTOR: You really mean this?

JOHN: I do.

HECTOR: I can only say that I am sorry. I think you are mistaken — tragically mistaken — in your attitude, but you have treated us fairly all along and I am not going to stoop to a sordid quarrel. (*He puts the cheque in his pocket.*) My wife has said some things she should not have said, but I know that you'll forgive her.

ANNIE: Of course. Sure, dear, I'm sorry for you.

CONSTANCE: (*sitting down and crying a little*) We were so happy here; you were all so kind to us, I thought we were fixed for the whole summer. I'm so tired of dragging from place to place.

ANNIE: (*going to her with lovely sympathy*) I know, dear, I know. But you mustn't think of going away, not until you've settled where you can go. This is your home for as long as you care to stay. Isn't that so, John?

JOHN: To be sure it is. I'll take it badly if you go away in a huff.

CONSTANCE: (*sniffing*) Thank you, Mrs Twohig.

ANNIE: Ah, sure, call me Annie.

HECTOR: I appreciate your attitude Mrs Twohig, and I am very grateful for your offer of hospitality. We shall probably avail ourselves of it for a few days. I think it will be only for a few days, because our success here has had reverberations elsewhere and I have at least two very good offers in my pocket.

JOHN: I'm more than delighted to hear that.

HECTOR: Let us go to the Pavilion, darling, and start to pack.

CONSTANCE: (*rising*) Very well. (*As they reach the door* CONSTANCE *whispers something to* HECTOR.)

HECTOR: Oh, yes .... Mrs Twohig, if that young newspaper man comes back you might give him this envelope; it contains some photographs he particularly asked for.

ANNIE: (*taking the envelope*) Certainly.

HECTOR: (*to* JOHN) And keep a couple of seats for us tonight, please; it's twenty years since I've seen a circus. (*They go out.*)

JOHN: Well, that's over. They took it very nicely.

ANNIE: They did, the creatures.

JOHN: (*crossing to the sideboard*) I think I deserve a little drink after that.

ANNIE: You do, to be sure.

JOHN: You ought to make a cup of tea for yourself.

ANNIE: I'll have a glass of port instead.

JOHN: (*astonished*) Annie, what's come to you?

ANNIE: I don't know, but I feel so light in the heart, as if a big cloud was gone.

JOHN: Faith, you're welcome to a bucket of port, but here's a wineglassfull to begin with. (*As he is pouring it out,* HELENA *comes in. She is in outdoor clothes.*)

ANNIE: Helena, where were you? I was looking everywhere for you.

HELENA: I know, ma'am. I was at the chapel, ma'am.

ANNIE: And what were you doing at the chapel this hour of the morning?

HELENA: I was getting married, ma'am.

ANNIE: Merciful heaven! Who to?

HELENA: Michael, of course. Who else?

ANNIE: Oh, my poor girl, is this what has come of all that nasty talk? Why didn't you tell me? I'd have told you not to mind a thing they said and not to tie yourself up for life with a man who's no more to you than the next.

HELENA: It's not that way at all, ma'am. Michael and me have been promised to each other for the last two months, only I could never bring myself to tell him about — you know what. I was delighted it slipped out of me that morning. Anyway, to stop tongues wagging, we thought we might as well be married at once.

JOHN: Well, thunder and turf! That's one good thing the plays did, anyhow. Where's Michael?

HELENA: Outside the door, listening. (*Raising her voice.*) You can come in, Michael, they're not mad at all. (MICHAEL *comes in a little sheepish.*)

JOHN: Oh, there's the bold bridegroom. Hold up your head, Michael. Here, put the hand there and I wish you the best of luck.

MICHAEL: Thank you, sir.

ANNIE: And I wish you the same, and the best of luck to you, Helena, and years of happiness.

HELENA: Thank you, ma'am, you've always been the good friend to me. (LIZZIE *hurries in.*)

LIZZIE: A band, John, a band!

ANNIE: Where?

LIZZIE: Coming up the street, I think. I heard it from the upper window.

JOHN: (*coolly*) Did you ever hear of a circus without a band?

LIZZIE:
HELENA: } A circus?
MICHAEL:

JOHN: In the Pavilion tonight, and free seats for all the town. (*Music is heard.*)

LIZZIE: Glory!

MICHAEL: I hear the band myself. Come out to the door, Helena. (*He and* HELENA *rush out.*)

LIZZIE: And look, there's the sun bursting out.

ANNIE: My heart's lepping with joy.

(*It is quite true; the room is flooded with sunshine.* CHRISTINE *and* EDDIE *rush in and make for the window.* EDDIE *is dressed in his nicest suit.*)

EDDIE: A band, Pappy, a band!

CHRISTINE: Eddie, am I mad or do I see a clown?

LIZZIE: (*crowding to the window*) A clown? Clowns are my joy.

EDDIE: (*with a shout*) Two clowns!

CHRISTINE: (*topping him*) Three!

LIZZIE: And a doaty little girl in spangles on a piebald pony. John, what's the meaning of it all?

JOHN: We've put back the old stone, Lizzie, thank God.

LIZZIE: I don't know what you mean. Anyhow, it sounds grand. (*The music has swelled nearer. The band is playing "Stars and Stripes For Ever",* EDDIE *and* CHRISTINE *can't resist it. They must do a little dance together in the background.* LIZZIE, *staring out the window, is softly clapping her hands and smiling.* JOHN *and* ANNIE *are near the front.*)

JOHN: Annie, get on the telephone to Dublin.

ANNIE: Why so?

JOHN: Get on to the best shop in the city. I think I owe you a new dress.

255

ANNIE: Maybe you do.... Have you got six coppers? (*He fingers for them. The music fills the room. The* CURTAIN *falls.*)

THE END

CHURCH STREET

A play in one act

For
Norreys Davidson

Human Will and Human Fate:
What is little, what is great?
Howsoe'er the answer be,
Let me sing of what I know.

William Allingham

CHARACTERS

JOSEPH RIORDAN, Manager of the National Bank, Knock
KATE RIORDAN, his wife
HUGH, their eldest son
JACK, their other son
MOLLIE, Jack's wife
AUNT MOLL, Joseph Riordan's aunt
MRS DE LACY
MISS PETTIGREW, her sister
SALLIE LONG
JIM DALY
HONOR BEWLEY
DOCTOR SMITH
NURSE SMITH
A CLERGYMAN

The first production of "Church Street" took place on May 21st, 1934, in the Abbey Theatre, Dublin with the following cast:

Joseph Riordan	BARRY FITZGERALD
Kate Riordan	MAUREEN DELANY
Hugh	ARTHUR SHIELDS
Jack	JOSEPH O'NEILL
Mollie	JENNIFER DAVIDSON
Aunt Moll	EILEEN CROWE
Mrs de Lacy	CHRISTINE HAYDEN
Miss Pettigrew	MAY CRAIG
Sally Long	SHELAH RICHARDS
Jim Daly	F.J. McCORMICK
Honor Bewley	ANN CLERY
The Evoked Hugh	DENIS O'DEA
Doctor Smith	MICHAEL J. DOLAN
Nurse Smith	FROLIE MULHERN
A Clergyman	P.J. CAROLAN

The Play was produced by the Author.

The play begins and ends in MRS RIORDAN's *drawing-room,*
but, on occasion, passes to MISS PETTIGREW's *house or* HONOR
BEWLEY's *bedroom, or to a doctor's waiting-room near Paddington,*
or to JIM DALY's *lodging-house in Dublin, or to a graveyard. The*
period of the play varies from one evening to a few months.

The scene is the drawing-room in the National Bank, Knock.
Comfortably furnished, not overcrowded, an upright piano, a
largish table in the middle of the room. Dark wallpaper. A fire-
place on the audience's right, a door in the middle of the wall
left (leading to the dining-room), another door in the back wall
towards the right. When the play begins MRS RIORDAN *is poking*
the fire, which is already blazing brightly; she is a pleasant-looking,
middle-aged woman. At the table in the centre facing the audience
but hidden from them by a "Manchester Guardian" which she
is reading sits AUNT MOLL. *It is evening, and the room is brightly*
lit by electric light. If a window has to be shown, it is heavily
curtained. The door at the right opens and HUGH *comes in.*
He is about twenty-eight years old, dressed carelessly, grey flannel
bags, a pullover, an old tweed jacket. His mother is quite grandly
dressed as if for an evening party. HUGH *has a tired, discontented*
look.

MRS RIORDAN: Oh, Hugh darling, there you are. Did you have a
nice rest?

HUGH: No. Never slept a wink.

MRS RIORDAN: Now, isn't that too bad? But you can get to bed
early.

HUGH: What a hope! With all these awful people coming?

MRS RIORDAN: They won't stay late. You've forgotten what early
hours we keep in Knock — not like your London. They'll all
be gone by ten o'clock — half-past ten at the latest.

HUGH: I wish to goodness you hadn't asked them at all.

MRS RIORDAN: Darling, they're all dying to see you, and it was
the only evening I could have them this week.

HUGH: (*with a little sneer*) Has Knock suddenly become so gay?

MRS RIORDAN: Well, I don't know how it is but there seems to be something almost every night — there's badminton in the Town Hall every Wednesday, and there's the bridge club and of course the pictures; they change them twice a week, so that's two nights gone and —

HUGH: And a little party at the Moore's or the Daly's, *I* know.

MRS RIORDAN: Anyway I had to seize this evening, you're such a fly-away: why last time you were here — four years ago — you only stayed three days, do you remember?

HUGH: I remember.

MRS RIORDAN: Having them tonight does mean your father giving up his game of bridge at the Munster and Leinster Bank; he was a little touchy about it, but I said he must be here.

HUGH: He needn't have given it up.

MRS RIORDAN: Maybe not. For this time you'll stay weeks and weeks, won't you? But I can never trust you. Some theatre will be wanting to put on one of your plays and off you'll fly.

HUGH: Put on one of my plays? That *is* likely, after their last experience with me.

MRS RIORDAN: I wouldn't mind that for a minute. You can't be a success all the time.

HUGH: *All* the time!

MRS RIORDAN: I know, darling, you haven't been properly appreciated yet, but you will be. All great writers have had to struggle just as you have. (*He contemptuously shrugs his shoulders.*) Have you unpacked your bags?

HUGH: No.

MRS RIORDAN: You've very little time to change. They'll be here any minute.

HUGH: I'm not changing. If they don't like me as I am, they can just lump me.

MRS RIORDAN: Oh .... Of course they'll like you no matter how you're dressed; but Honor's coming, and Jack's wife; she's so nice and rather smart, and I'd like the first time she sees you — I'd have your things unpacked in a jiffy. I'm sure you've a very smart London suit upstairs.

HUGH: No, don't bother.

MRS RIORDAN: (*starting to go*) No bother at all. I should have unpacked you the minute you arrived.

HUGH: (*stopping her*) Please don't, Mother. It's not worth while.

MRS RIORDAN: Not worth while?

HUGH: No. The fact is I'm — I'm not staying.

MRS RIORDAN: Not staying?

HUGH: Well, just till tomorrow morning.

MRS RIORDAN: (*sitting down, almost crying*) But why? You've only just come. Is it a new play?

HUGH: No.

MRS RIORDAN: Then what is it? Oh, Hugh, I've been looking forward to your coming for so long.

HUGH: I know. Darling, I've a better idea. You'll come back to London with me.

MRS RIORDAN: But — but —

HUGH: Don't you remember, two years ago, the swell time we had?

MRS RIORDAN: I couldn't go now. Jack's going to have a baby — I mean his wife is, I must be here. What's happened? What have we done?

HUGH: Nothing. At least *you*'ve done nothing. But the place!

MRS RIORDAN: The place? The town?

HUGH: Yes, Knock. Kay, en, o, cee, kay. My God, as I walked up from the station I could feel it closing in on me with every letter of its dull name. Its drabness, its lifelessness, dullness, dead.

MRS RIORDAN: Of course, I suppose, after London —

HUGH: I said to myself in London, after the crashing failure of my play, "Oh, to get home again, to have some peace, to collect one's thoughts, to find a new subject, to find inspiration!" What a fool I was. I had forgotten my Knock. I realised in my five minutes' walk from the station that this place is as dead as a door-nail.

MRS RIORDAN: You're just tired, Hugh, you're imagining things —

HUGH: I am not. I couldn't imagine anything in connection with Knock.

(*The newspaper is suddenly slapped down, and we see* AUNT MOLL. *She is a little old woman, over seventy, plainly but not eccentrically dressed.*)

AUNT MOLL: That's the truest word you've spoken yet, Hugh me boy. You've no imagination.

HUGH: (*good-temperedly*) I forgot you were there, Aunt Moll.

AUNT MOLL: Oh, everyone forgets Aunt Moll, but I'm here most of the time.

MRS RIORDAN: Well, indeed, we don't forget you. What a thing to say.

AUNT MOLL: With all the grand goings on tonight there'll be little thought for Aunt Moll. All I asked for was me usual glass of milk and me two Marie biscuits, but could I get them? Oh, dear me, no. Jellies and trifles galore, but no glass of plain milk for poor old Aunt Moll.

MRS RIORDAN: I'll see you get them.

AUNT MOLL: You needn't trouble then. I made Maggie leave them on the sideboard for me. If you want a thing done, do it yourself.

HUGH: Or rather, get Maggie to do it for you.

AUNT MOLL: Humph!

MRS RIORDAN: (*laughing*) As if you didn't rule the house.

AUNT MOLL: Humph!

HUGH: And so I've no imagination? That's a funny accusation to bring against a writer of stories and plays.

AUNT MOLL: You have not. Not an ounce of it. Walking up from the station and finding Church Street dead, moyah!

HUGH: Yes, dead. Dead as mutton.

MRS RIORDAN: It's early-closing day — no, it isn't.

AUNT MOLL: And would you say the same thing of Station Street and Main Street?

HUGH: Deader.

AUNT MOLL: You're a fool.

MRS RIORDAN: Aunt Moll!

HUGH: Oh, let her fire away, Mother.

AUNT MOLL: I'm sorry, Kate, but a fool is what he is. I tell you, me boy, there's comedy and tragedy trailing their skirts through the mud of Church Street if you'd only the eyes to see them. But, oh no, not at all! You must needs write about high London society, nightclubs, cocktail parties, things you know as much about as — as me boot. And what good does it do you? I don't suppose you've earned a hundred pounds in the seven years you've been in London.

HUGH: I got money down for my last play.

AUNT MOLL: And it ran a week.

HUGH: Anyway, it's not altogether a question of what one earns —

AUNT MOLL: Faith, I think it is. The proof of the pudding is the currants in it.

MRS RIORDAN: It is not, Aunt Moll. Neither Joseph nor I grudge the little bit of money it costs to keep Hugh in London. We all know he's a steady boy, doesn't gamble or drink. What we spend on him is money invested and well invested. Even if he doesn't make a fortune for himself there's the books he writes and the plays —

AUNT MOLL: Not many people seem to want to see them — or read them.

MRS RIORDAN: That's a very unkind thing to say.

HUGH: I don't mind what you say, Aunt Moll, but mother does. So give it a rest.

AUNT MOLL: I don't want to be unkind, Kate; you know I'm fond of the child, I know he has talent. That's why it drives me near crazy to hear him saying a stupid thing like that. Church Street dead! Ha, ha!

HUGH: I wish you'd show me where it's alive.

AUNT MOLL: And I could too. I could tell you —
(*A noise of voices and laughter outside.*)

MRS RIORDAN: Goodness gracious, can this be them? (*She looks at her watch.*) It is, it's half-seven.

(*The door at the back opens and admits* JACK, MOLLIE, MISS PETTIGREW, MRS DE LACY, SALLIE LONG, JIM DALY *and* HONOR BEWLEY. JACK (HUGH's *brother*) *is an ordinary, stocky, cheerful young man. His wife* MOLLIE *is a pretty ordinary young woman, rather swaggering in the fact that she is going to have a baby at the first legitimate moment.* MISS PETTIGREW *is quite old and dressed almost fantastically in a semi-evening dress of thirty years ago; her sister,* MRS DE LACY, *is a little older, but very quietly and decently dressed in black.* SALLIE LONG *is a charming girl of twenty-two or twenty-three.* JIM DALY *is an odd, clever-looking fellow of twenty-six or twenty-seven.* HONOR BEWLEY *is about the same age, dressed in a simple black dress. All come in awkwardly, in a bunch, and having got in don't quite know what to do with themselves. The scene which follows must be so well produced that it gives the impression of not having been produced at all. People must move when they should not, mask each other, speak through each other's speeches — and yet every speech must be heard — the audience should say to each other, "What bad acting, what rotten production".*)

JACK: The whole bunch of us met on the doorstep, Mother. Hello, Hugh, back again; fine to see you.

HUGH: (*shaking hands*) How are you, Jack?

JACK: Meet your new sister-in-law. Come here, Mollie. Where at all have you got to?

MOLLIE: (*extricating herself from the little crowd*) Here I am. How do you do, Hugh? I suppose I can call you that.

HUGH: Of course. I'm delighted to meet you at last.

MOLLIE: Yes, you were a swine not to come over to give Jack away.

HUGH: I had a play —
(*His sentence is drowned by* MRS RIORDAN's *greetings.*)

MRS RIORDAN: How are you, Mrs de Lacy? You're looking frozen. Come near the fire. Oh, and what a pretty dress, Sarah.

(*This to* MISS PETTIGREW.)

MISS PETTIGREW: Such an old rag.

MRS RIORDAN: I don't believe it. It looks the latest thing.

JACK: (*to* HUGH) Well, you'll have to come over for the christening — or stay over for it. Won't he, Mollie?

HUGH: Christening?

JACK: You're to be godfather. We fixed that, didn't we, Mollie, and if it's a boy we're going to call it Hugh, after the genius of the family.

MOLLIE: And if it's a girl — Moll —

JACK: After the demon of the family.

MRS RIORDAN: Jack, please! Hugh, you haven't forgotten Miss Pettigrew?

HUGH: (*shaking hands*) Of course not.

MISS PETTIGREW: (*simpering*) Indeed, I don't know why you should remember — Such an old woman now. Years and years. And this is my sister — Lucy!

MRS DE LACY: (*approaching*) You wanted me, Sarah?

MISS PETTIGREW: This is Hugh. My sister, Mrs de Lacy.

HUGH: How do you do? (MRS DE LACY *bows.*)

MISS PETTIGREW: I don't think you've seen her since she was a child — no, I mean since you were a teeny, weeny child with the loveliest curls I ever saw. She married into Carlow, you know, and then the beet came and her husband died and —

MRS DE LACY: I'm sure, Sarah, Mr Hugh doesn't want to hear all that. You were in your pram when I saw you last. You *have* grown.

HUGH: Yes, I suppose I have.

MRS DE LACY: I remember you distinctly, but I do *not* remember any curls. My recollection is that you were entirely bald.

MISS PETTIGREW: Oh, not bald, Lucy. Fluff. Down.

MRS DE LACY: Bald.

HUGH: Probably.

MRS RIORDAN: (*bringing* SALLIE *forward*) And here is Miss Long. She's a newcomer, the rector's daughter.

HUGH: How do you do?

SALLIE: How do you do?

MISS PETTIGREW: Such a nice man, Hugh, only been in the town for a year. Came from somewhere near Lismore, didn't he, Sallie?

SALLIE: Yes, Miss Pettigrew.

MRS DE LACY: On our honeymoon my husband and I *did* the valley of the Blackwater.

SALLIE: Really?

HUGH: Charming.

MISS PETTIGREW: I've always heard that Lismore Castle — (*Their conversation is lost for a moment; it is presumably about scenery and the Duke of Devonshire. Above the other conversation* AUNT MOLL's *voice is heard; she is talking to* JIM DALY.)

AUNT MOLL: No, James Daly, there is no use in your trying to ram down my throat the fact that you are a medical student in your last year — almost a doctor. I do not approve of inoculation. I stand where I have always stood, right beside Mr George Bernard Shaw.

JIM: Lucky George! But the statistics —

AUNT MOLL: Prove nothing. Or anything you want them to prove. Don't talk to me of your statistics. Come·up to my room.

JIM: No, really!

HONOR: You ought to. Aunt Moll's room is a treasure-house.

MRS RIORDAN: Come here, Jim. You and Hugh used to be great chums before you went to the National.

JIM: (*going to* HUGH *and shaking hands*) Hallo, old man.

HUGH: Hallo, Jim. Nice to see you again.

JIM: I read about you in the papers from time to time. You're quite a person in literary London, aren't you? Makes me feel cocky to think that we were both at Rockwell together.

HUGH: Cocky? Rot. I'm a bloody failure. It's you that are getting the gold medals.

MRS RIORDAN: Now you've met everyone, I think. Oh no, there's Honor hiding in the background. You don't need any introduction to *her*.

HUGH: No indeed. (*He crosses to meet her and shakes hands with her. There is a forced brightness and cordiality in his manner.*) How are you, Honor?

HONOR: (*quite friendly and composed*) How do you do, Hugh? It's nice for your mother to have you back.

HUGH: Oh yes.

HONOR: I was reading about your play. It was such a shame it wasn't more successful, it sounded so interesting. Of course I don't know anything about those sort of people but — (*The rest of the conversation fades because* AUNT MOLL *tops it; she is talking to* MOLLIE.)

AUNT MOLL: I hope you take a good rest every afternoon. That's a very important thing. *I* know.

JACK: (*laughing*) How could you know, Aunt Moll?

AUNT MOLL: I do. And another thing — James Daly, come here. Although I thoroughly disapprove of your views on inoculation and vivisection I think that you and I could tell this young woman that if she wants — no, don't run away — (*She pursues her to a corner of the room and captures her.*)

HUGH: (*to* HONOR) I was so sorry to hear of your bereavement. I meant to have written, but you know how it is.

HONOR: Poor father. He suffered so much. It was what is called a "blessed release".

HUGH: (*always speaking with a little restraint*) You have your nice house still? You're going to stay on there?

HONOR: It's being auctioned next week.

HUGH: Oh, I say! You don't mean that — that he left you — ?

HONOR: He left me plenty of money and that lovely old house.

HUGH: Then — then why?

(*Before she can answer* MISS PETTIGREW *is at* HUGH's *elbow.*)

MISS PETTIGREW: We hear you've had a play on the boards in London and that it was a tremendous success.

HUGH: It ran a week *and* two matinées.

MISS PETTIGREW: Isn't that magnificent? The one the Temperance Society put on at the Town Hall only ran two nights, though it was very good, I believe. Of course I couldn't go, my sister still being in mourning; only two years since Bob, my brother-in-law, died; a moving clot they said it was, very sad for all concerned. Of course I know that nowadays people go out of mourning faster than they go into it, but we're old-fashioned people, my sister and I, and —

MRS DE LACY: Sarah!

MISS PETTIGREW: Am I talking too much, Lucy?

MRS DE LACY: You are.

MISS PETTIGREW: I always was a bit of a rattle-tongue.

MRS DE LACY: You were.

MISS PETTIGREW: You're always so grim with me, Lucy.

HONOR: You've the kindest tongue and the kindest heart in the town, Miss Pettigrew.

MISS PETTIGREW: Have I, dear? Thank you. And you've the prettiest face.

MRS RIORDAN: (*taking the floor*) I think we should go into tea at once and not wait for Mr Riordan.

HONOR: Where is he, Mrs Riordan?

MRS RIORDAN: He's playing golf.

JACK: Playing in the Captain's prize; he's bound to be late.

AUNT MOLL: The Captain's prize! We all know what that means.

SALLIE: Daddie's playing too.

AUNT MOLL: Oh, your father's all right. Band of Hope. But that nineteenth hole — !

JIM: You know everything, Miss Riordan.

AUNT MOLL: I don't play golf, thank God, but I'm not a fool. (*To* MOLLIE.) I hear you've made Jack give up his golf?

MOLLIE: Yes, he gardens instead.

AUNT MOLL: Splendid. That bending. So good for the liver.

MOLLIE: And he's taken up his singing again.

JACK: I really only married her because I thought she might be able to play my accompaniments.

MOLLIE: Quite so, my dear.

AUNT MOLL: Jack had the makings of a good voice. (*She turns to him with perhaps the first touch of softness she has shown.*) Will you sing to me tonight, me dear? Nothing very old and nothing very new, just something seventyish or eightyish — like meself.

JACK: (*taking a small pile of songs from the piano where he has laid them down when he came in*) I don't know if there's anything here you'd like. There are piles of others in the press.

AUNT MOLL: (*turning them over*) "Bois Epais" — too smug and dreary. "The Erl-King" — you haven't guts enough to sing that properly. "So we'll go no more a-roving." Where did you get that?

JACK: It's an old song now, but still quite well known and a fine song. The music is by Maude Valerie White.

AUNT MOLL: I don't know it. I only know the poem, the most heartbreaking he ever wrote.

JACK: Who wrote? I never looked at the author of the words.

AUNT MOLL: Of course you didn't. He was called George Gordon Byron.

JACK: Oh — Byron? Did I learn him at school?

AUNT MOLL: It doesn't matter — for all the good it seems to have done you. How does it go? Hum it to me.

JACK: (*He sings very softly into her ear, so that it doesn't disturb the conversation in the room.*)

> "So, we'll go no more a-roving
> So late into the night,
> Though the heart —"

(MR RIORDAN *comes in. Middle-aged, genial. Plus-fours.*)

RIORDAN: Hallo, everyone.

MRS RIORDAN: We were just giving you up, Joseph.

(*She rings a bell.*)

RIORDAN: I'm not so late. Playing in the Captain's prize, you know. I tied for second place. That damned parson won — Oh, beg pardon, Miss Long, didn't see you, but you know that your father and I are the best of friends; damned decent fellow. Hallo, Hugh. Sorry couldn't get to the station to meet you, but Captain's prize, you know, couldn't be missed. How's London and all that? Gaiety girls, ha-ha! Ah, Mrs de Lacy, I've a little letter for you downstairs in the office — don't let me let you go without giving it to you; and there's your sister looking as pretty as a picture — you should have been my little mascot today, waved success to me from the pavilion; and Honor — you look half a nun already, bless you, my dear; and there's my old witch of an aunt with her broomstick parked in the landing — and Jim — your father wasn't out this afternoon, scratched at the last minute.

JIM: He's not feeling too fit — a touch of flu.

(RIORDAN *is only a little tipsy, and everyone on his journey round the room has met him very kindly and more than half way.*)

MRS RIORDAN: I've rung for tea.

RIORDAN: Good. I'm as hungry as a hunter.

AUNT MOLL: (*ominously*) Not *thirsty*, I expect.

RIORDAN: No, not thirst — yes, *very* thirsty.

AUNT MOLL: Humph!

MRS RIORDAN: Well, by the time we're sitting down Maggie will have the tea and coffee up, so come along everyone. It's the simplest sort of cold supper — (*Babbling other courteous words she shoos them to the door on the left.* HUGH *hangs back and* AUNT MOLL *doesn't move.*) Hugh, aren't you coming?

HUGH: Give me just a minute to finish this cigarette.

MRS RIORDAN: Well, don't be long.

MISS PETTIGREW: (*as she goes out*) You're our lion tonight, you know.

AUNT MOLL: Send me in me milk and biscuits, Kate. I couldn't bear to go in there and see you all gulping blancmange.

MRS RIORDAN: Very well, Aunt Moll.

(*They all go into the next room except* HUGH *and* AUNT MOLL.)

AUNT MOLL: She'll forget, oh, she'll forget, she never remembers anything for more than five seconds. Oh well, Aunt Moll has the use of her own legs still, thank God; she can fetch her own milk and biscuits. A kind, feckless woman, that's what Kate is. She wouldn't even quench some of the lights. All that Shannon business has just led to extravagance and waste. Shannon scheme — oh, "scheme" is the word.

(*She puts out all the lights except a bracket at the fireplace.*)

That's enough light for you to smoke by, and it's enough for me to read by while I sup me glass of milk.

HUGH: Yes....

(*Standing in front of the fire and waving his hand towards the door through which the company has disappeared.*)

Well, there you are.

AUNT MOLL: How do you mean "There I are"?

HUGH: There's Knock for you. There's your comedy and tragedy — what was your ornamental phrase? — "trailing their skirts through the mud of Church Street". (*He laughs.*)

AUNT MOLL: There *you* are — if you only had the eyes to see it.

HUGH: I see them.

AUNT MOLL: You don't.

HUGH: I grant you they're all nice decent people.

AUNT MOLL: (*with contempt*) Nice decent people!

HUGH: Do you mean to say they're not all nice and decent?

AUNT MOLL: (*quietly and seriously*) I tell you, Hugh, there's a mort of tragedy and comedy sitting round that table in the next room — more tragedy than comedy I'm sorry to say.

HUGH: You're joking.

AUNT MOLL: I wish I was.

HUGH: What's tragic about any of them — except their awful provincialism?

AUNT MOLL: There are three plays for you there, maybe four, if you only had the guts to feel them and the eyes to see them.

HUGH: Plays? Ah, go on! I don't believe you for a minute.

AUNT MOLL: (*thoughtful, not dictating*) Of course you'd have to select, choose what you'd take and what you'd leave aside. Didn't someone say that genius was the art of selection? And you're no genius. You'd have to — sort of shape your material, just a little, a very little would be enough. Maybe you couldn't — maybe no dramatist could make that company inside into a play. Maybe it's only through the cinema you could catch it all, all the different stories, interlocking, moving away from each other, moving back to each other again, like figures in the lancers.

HUGH: Lancers?

AUNT MOLL: Maybe you're too young to have ever danced them. A figure dance, rowdy in a drawing-room, I've seen them danced in a kitchen in County Limerick, as dignified as an eighteenth-century minuet.

HUGH: Mother's party tonight seemed just a huddle of people, talking together anyhow and all getting in each other's way.

AUNT MOLL: I know. No construction. No stage management. But, God Almighty, boy, that's your job.

HUGH: My job?

AUNT MOLL: As a dramatist. To put some shape, some stage shape, on real life.

HUGH: Maybe. If there was only a subject there.

AUNT MOLL: I've told you. You have your choice of three or four.

HUGH: And I can't see even one.

AUNT MOLL: They tell me you're good at comedy, and I'm afraid there's not much comedy there —

HUGH: Oh come! Old Pettigrew and her sister.

AUNT MOLL: Hm, yes. But not as funny as they seem. There's your brother Jack and his wife — you'd better keep them in for the sake of normality, though it's a bit ironic that Jack, who was such a boyo, should be spancelled and tamed by that Mollie girl. Making him give up golf and take to gardening! Jack, who'd only recognise cabbage when it's boiled round a pig's head! Ha, ha! Oh, they're all right. They'll have a string of children, and Jack will die contentedly in his bed, aged eighty.

HUGH: You see; no play there.

AUNT MOLL: There's your father and mother —

HUGH: Normal again. The nicest people in the world, but utterly normal.

AUNT MOLL: Well, your father does take a drop too much now and again. I thought tonight he was distinctly elevated.

HUGH: Nonsense. And even if he was — the Captain's match. I have seen him tipsy but not enough to make a song and dance about it, and if you think I'm going to put my own father on the stage and show him drunk —

AUNT MOLL: Charles Dickens put his father in a book and didn't show him up so well. But no; I suppose we'll have to leave Joseph out, he doesn't get raging drunk, and, of course, poor Kate's a rock of morality — did she send me in me milk?

HUGH: No. Don't mind it for a minute. I'll get it. Go on. This is beginning to interest me.

AUNT MOLL: You ought to make yourself the villain of the play.

HUGH: I? What, under heaven, have I done?

AUNT MOLL: You, and Honor Bewley.

HUGH: Honor?

AUNT MOLL: Don't pretend to be so surprised. You broke her heart.

HUGH: I don't believe it.

AUNT MOLL: You did, when you went off to London seven years ago and left her behind.

HUGH: Nonsense. We were never engaged. There was nothing between us.

AUNT MOLL: There was everything between you except the one word "Honor, will you marry me?" Do you remember how gay she was long ago, and look at her now. That's what your seven years' desertion has done.

HUGH: I have nothing to do with her looks. She's had a hard time, nursing her paralysed father. That aged her, naturally.

AUNT MOLL: If she'd been married to you, she'd have thrown over her father, paralysed and all as he was. What is it Mr Shaw says? "Girls withering into ladies." Oh, but Honor Bewley's the withered lady.

HUGH: I don't believe you for a minute. She met me tonight without a flicker of embarrassment, she was icily calm.

AUNT MOLL: Don't you know why?... Ah, use your imagination, man. Don't you know what it's in her head to do?

HUGH: No ....

(*Something dawns on him.*)

I don't want to know. I mean — I mean —

AUNT MOLL: You're afraid.

HUGH: (*shaking it off*) Oh, let's fish round somewhere else. Let's be gay, macabre if you like. What about old Pettigrew and her monumental sister?

AUNT MOLL: Yes, make them as monumental as you like, but don't forget that there's something behind Sarah Pettigrew's gazebo of a dress.

HUGH: (*laughing*) A broken heart?

AUNT MOLL: No. An empty stomach.

HUGH: (*sobered*) Oh!

AUNT MOLL: I don't know for certain, Hugh, but I believe that those two women are hungry half the time. You know, apart from the big old house they have rent-free for the rest of their lives, they never had much money in their pockets; but they were the most generous creatures in the world — at least Sarah was; we don't know so much about the Lucy one. No beggar was ever turned from their door without a square meal and a shilling in his pocket. Well, now I hear there's neither bread nor a shilling for the decentest tinker walking the roads. I think they were living on the bit that came from the railways or some investments of the sort, but since they've failed — well, your father would know, he handles their investments, but of course I couldn't ask him. There's something to catch hold of there, Hugh.

HUGH: By Jove, yes. But it can't be true.

AUNT MOLL: People are hungry, Hugh, even in Knock, not only on the London Embankment. Didn't you notice the sort of grey look on their faces?

HUGH: No.

AUNT MOLL: That's what I'm telling you. You've no eyes, no imagination.

HUGH: I'll look closer next time. Well, who'd think that my oddities should turn out to be half-tragic figures? But when I write my play I'll keep them in for a kind of macabre relief. I'll have to get my nice fun, my romance, out of Jim Daly and Miss — I forget her name, but they seemed a bit gone on each other.

AUNT MOLL: Sallie Long. The rector's daughter.

HUGH: Oh yes. So she was.

AUNT MOLL: The rector's daughter and Jim Daly — in love with one another. Doesn't that suggest something to you?

HUGH: I don't think so.

AUNT MOLL: Don't you remember how great Jim's people always were with the Church? One uncle a Monsignor and the other a P.P. in Liverpool; two aunts nuns, and Jim himself, though he is a medical student, not wild at all, not likely to do anything rash, anything that would go against his family and his religion.

HUGH: You mean he'd like to marry her if she wasn't a Protestant?

AUNT MOLL: They're dying down about each other, and she won't go against *her* religion. We must give in, Hugh, that now and again Protestants are as hot on their faith as we are on ours. The thing is breaking their hearts.

HUGH: God!

AUNT MOLL: The whole town knows of it; I'm not making it up, 'tis the laugh of every public house. Old Daly is threatening all sorts. Poor Mrs Daly is just amiable, bewildered, the creature. What's to be the end of it, God alone knows.

HUGH: One or the other will give in.

AUNT MOLL: Neither will give in, they're both too proud.... I hear there's talk of her going to London.

HUGH: To forget him? I see. A good idea.

AUNT MOLL: (*darkly*) Maybe.

HUGH: Maybe? If not for that reason, why?

AUNT MOLL: I don't know, and I wouldn't tell you if I did.... Well, there's bits of a play for you, Hugh.

HUGH: Yes, but only bits. I'd have to bring you in to bind it all together.

AUNT MOLL: Let you leave me out of it.

HUGH: Indeed I won't. What are you, Aunt Moll? Comedy or tragedy?

AUNT MOLL: Just a cantankerous old woman.

HUGH: Yes, of course. But something else.

AUNT MOLL: Melodrama.

HUGH: I don't believe it.

AUNT MOLL: I've shot me man.

HUGH: Aunt Moll! A *crime passionnel*?

AUNT MOLL: Not at all. A Black-and-Tan.

HUGH: Good God! I think I'm going crazy.

AUNT MOLL: I shot him through the heart. Oh, none of your dirty shoot-him-in-the-back jobs for Aunty Moll.... There's a hat-box under me bed.

HUGH: What's in it?

AUNT MOLL: (*with a chuckle*) A relic. Human.

HUGH: Merciful heavens! And you used to teach me my catechism! (*He gets up; he is anywhere about the room; he is fearfully excited.*)

You're right, you're right, there's a play here somewhere. I don't quite know where, I don't quite know with whom, I'll have to fish round, try here and there, get them back, not really back, I only mean back in my mind — and in yours, Aunt Moll, for you must help me. But I don't want everyone together, just two or three at a time.... I think I'm beginning to see it now... those starving old women... and Sallie Long and London... how frightful... how perfectly ghastly.... But it's inevitable — or is it? Is it all in my own mind or must it⁻ — must it happen? Am I shaping events or are they shaping me? Is it all predestined?

(*He raises his voice and speaks with a harsh, unnatural note.*)

Will you all stand by, please. I'll summon you as I need you. We'll sit over this side, Aunt Moll. I must see them on the stage as I see them in my mind. I'll alter the lights and arrange the furniture as I go along.

AUNT MOLL: Use your imagination, Hugh.

HUGH: I'll try to.

(*He switches off all the lights and in the darkness pilots her to the extreme left of the stage. They sit on two chairs, facing diagonally from lower left corner to upper right. A faint light comes up. The back wall of the room has disappeared and has*

been replaced by a wall somewhere similar to it but with a
bench about four feet from the ground stretching across it, and
on the bench are sitting all the characters we have seen earlier
in the play with the exception of JACK *and* MOLLIE. *They sit*
quite motionless, like dummy figures, we see them dimly.)

HUGH: (*surveying them*) Yes, that will do.... I don't think we
need take it right from the beginning, Aunt Moll, I mean the
bit about my coming down here and telling mother I'm not
staying — oh but I say, I can't do myself, I've got to stage-
manage, construct. Besides I want to imagine a young man,
much more attractive than I am... a little tragic-looking...
yes, that's it.

(*As if evoked, a young man is standing by the fire.*)

And now, mother — you've gone out of the room by this
time, Aunt Moll, to get your bally milk.

AUNT MOLL: I've told you, I don't want to be in the play at all.

HUGH: What a hope! Just you wait!

(*During these two sentences* MRS RIORDAN *has come from the*
bench and taken her place beside the EVOKED HUGH. *The*
scenes which follow with the evoked characters should, if
possible, be a little different in production from the scenes
with the natural characters, the speeches a little slower and
more deliberate, the movements slightly stagey.)

EV. HUGH: No, I'm not staying.

MRS RIORDAN: Not staying?

EV. HUGH: Just till tomorrow morning.

MRS RIORDAN: But why? You've only just come. Is it a new
play? Is that why you've got to rush back to London?

EV. HUGH: No.

MRS RIORDAN: Then what is it? Oh, Hugh, I've looked forward
to this visit of yours for so long.

EV. HUGH: I know, but —

REAL HUGH: I'll break it there. Honor!

EV. HUGH: I know, but —

MRS RIORDAN: Hush. Someone's arrived. Don't make up your
mind yet, Hugh, we'll talk of it later.

REAL HUGH: And now for Honor.

(HONOR BEWLEY *has got off the bench and comes in through*
the door.)

MRS RIORDAN: Ah, how are you, my dear?

HONOR: (*shaking hands*) Am I the first?

MRS RIORDAN: Yes, but what matter? You can have a nice chat
with Hugh before all the others arrive.

HONOR: How do you do, Hugh?

EV. HUGH: (*meeting her awkwardly*) How are you, Honor?

HONOR: It's quite a long time since we've seen you.

EV. HUGH: Four years.

MRS RIORDAN: Will you excuse me, Honor dear, if I just slip into the dining-room and have a look at the supper-table? Maggie's as good as gold, but forgetful.
(*She goes out.*)

HONOR: (*smiling*) Your mother was always diplomatic.

EV. HUGH: I was so sorry to hear of your bereavement. I meant to have written — but you know how it is.

HONOR: Of course. You were so busy with your writing. I quite understood.

EV. HUGH: You're looking —
(*He pauses for a word.*)

HONOR: Older? Tired?

EV. HUGH: Well — grave. Very grave.

HONOR: I'll try not to be at your party. I'm sure I am looking old and tired, but father's was such a long illness and I nursed him myself. He suffered so much, his death was what is called a "blessed release".

EV. HUGH: Mother told me that he left you quite well off and you still have the nice house. You'll live on there, of course?

HONOR: It's being auctioned next week.

EV. HUGH: Honor! Why?

HONOR: Oh, I have other plans.

EV. HUGH: (*laughing*) I believe you're going to get married.

HONOR: (*pained*) Hugh!

EV. HUGH: I shouldn't have said that. I'm sorry.

HONOR: It doesn't matter.... Listen, Hugh, after the next few days I shall never see you again.

EV. HUGH: Honor!

HONOR: Never again. So for your sake — for both our sakes — I want to say something to you quite frankly. You remember I had barely met you till I was over seventeen. I was away at school or you were away at school. I was a very religious girl; I wanted to be a nun; I thought I had a vocation, I still think I had a vocation, and father didn't object and then — and then —

EV. HUGH: And then I came along.

HONOR: Exactly. You came along. It was fun for you those long summer holidays and the Christmas after.

EV. HUGH: I loved you very much, Honor, I did indeed.

HONOR: I know you thought you did; but when there was a

275

question of your going to London and being very poor and having to make your own way —

EV. HUGH: I couldn't bear the idea of being spancelled and strangled by an engagement of marriage. I couldn't, Honor, I couldn't. That evening, walking home from the dance at the Bank — do you remember? — (*she nods*), I was going to London the next day, it was on the tip of my tongue to ask you to marry me, and I just managed not to; and I came home and threw myself on my bed and said, "I'm free, I'm free, thank God, I'm still free".

HONOR: I was free too, but I didn't want to be free. And you hardly ever wrote, so I knew it was all over. And then I set myself to forget you, and it took me a few years, but I succeeded at last; and now you are less to me than any stranger I might pass in the street. I suppose you "broke my heart" as they used to say, but it's mended again; and now that father's dead I'm free to do what I should have done after I left school.

EV. HUGH: You mean — become a nun?

HONOR: Yes.

EV. HUGH: You make me feel an awful brute.

HONOR: You needn't feel that. I think you should never forget the rather mean way you treated me; but maybe it was for the best, for if I had been a nun I couldn't have looked after poor father. Anyway, all's over now, Hugh, and let's shake hands quickly as old friends before the others come in.
(*She holds out her hand.*)

EV. HUGH: Honor, perhaps even still —

HONOR: Nonsense. You're quite out of my heart. God bless you, Hugh; may you be as happy as I shall be.
(*She shakes his hand warmly.*
MR RIORDAN *comes in; he has been drinking, and it makes him excited and brusque.*)

RIORDAN: Hallo. What are you two colloguing about? Sorry, Honor. I should have shaken hands with you, but I'm a bit put out this evening. What do you think of this fine lad of mine?

HONOR: I think he's looking very well, Mr Riordan.

RIORDAN: Yes, why shouldn't he? Living on the fat of the land in London. Wish I had the chance of getting away for a bit.

HONOR: You have been looking pulled down for the last couple of months.

RIORDAN: Nonsense. Never better, never better. Where's your mother, Hugh? I must see Kate. Business. I've to telephone to Dublin at once.

HONOR: I'll get her, Mr Riordan, she's in the dining-room, I think.

EV. HUGH: No, let me go.

HONOR: Don't bother.

RIORDAN: Yes, both of you go if you don't mind. It's a little bit of private business — nothing important you know, but private.

(EV. HUGH *opens the door for* HONOR *and she goes out.*

EV. HUGH *gives his father a searching look.*)

RIORDAN: (*resenting it*) You think I've been drinking? Well, I have, and so would you if you were in my shoes.

EV. HUGH: I'm sorry. Can I do anything — help in any way?

RIORDAN: No, you can't. But thanks all the same.

(EV. HUGH *goes out.*)

AUNT MOLL: I don't like this, Hugh. Joseph isn't a bad boy.

HUGH: Hush, Aunt Moll. Remember it's half play-acting.

(MRS RIORDAN *comes in.*)

MRS RIORDAN: You wanted me, Joseph?

RIORDAN: Yes. You know those Blenkinsop shares you have?

MRS RIORDAN: Blenkinsop?

RIORDAN: Yes; Blenkinsop, Blenkinsop. I want you to lend them to me; I must raise some money on them at once.

MRS RIORDAN: Oh.

RIORDAN: I'll be able to give them back to you in a couple of months.

(MRS RIORDAN *says nothing.*)

You trust me, don't you? You don't think I'm going to make away with them?

MRS RIORDAN: Of course not. But — but I haven't got them.

RIORDAN: Not got them?

MRS RIORDAN: I sold them, three months ago.

RIORDAN: Behind my back, without telling me a word?

MRS RIORDAN: Yes, Joseph.

RIORDAN: In the name of Heaven, why? What have you been doing?

MRS RIORDAN: Nothing wrong, Joseph, but I knew you'd be angry. It was for Hugh.

RIORDAN: Hugh? What did he want money for? Hadn't he his allowance? Debts?

MRS RIORDAN: No, it was money for his play. He could only get it on by putting some money into it himself and, of course, he hadn't a penny beyond his little allowance.

(MR RIORDAN *sits down, collapsed.*)

You're not angry with me, Joseph?

RIORDAN: No, I'm not angry, I'm beyond that.

MRS RIORDAN: You're frightening me. What's happened?

RIORDAN: I've been a blasted fool, Kate. I've been worse. A criminal. I've been gambling with other people's money.

MRS RIORDAN: Joseph!

RIORDAN: Miss Pettigrew's and her sister's, of all unfortunate people. I thought I could double their money for them — no, I didn't really do it for their sakes; if I'd doubled it I'd have kept the makings for myself — and now, unless I can find three hundred pounds by tomorrow morning it's all gone.

MRS RIORDAN: Ah, the poor women!

RIORDAN: They won't starve, I won't let them starve anyway. Oh, my God, what a fool I've been, what a blasted fool.

MRS RIORDAN: I've thirty or more pounds in the bank, Joseph.

RIORDAN: Yes, I'll use that to go on with, and then I'll think of some way — there must be some way.

(JIM *and* SALLIE *come in, there are mutual greetings.*)

RIORDAN: (*irritably*) Are we all here? Can't we have supper now, Kate. I'm starving.

MRS RIORDAN: I'm expecting a couple more, dear.

RIORDAN: Who?

MRS RIORDAN: Miss — Miss Pettigrew and Mrs de Lacy.

RIORDAN: Oh, my God!

JIM: You say that as if you didn't like them, as if you weren't their best friend — which they always swear you are.

SALLIE: Friend? Why, Jim — you've been away in Dublin, but if you could see the way Mr Riordan flirts with Miss Pettigrew at the badminton, it's — it's quite shameless. I wonder you allow it, Mrs Riordan.

MRS RIORDAN: (*trying to smile*) I know, dear. Shocking, isn't it? But — you're not looking quite yourself. Are you feeling quite well?

SALLIE: (*quickly, brazening it out*) Never felt fitter, Mrs Riordan. Running round a little too much perhaps.

MRS RIORDAN: You should take care of yourself.

(*Taking in* JIM *with her eyes.*)

Ah yes, of course.

RIORDAN: (*slapping* JIM *on the back*) Young people will be young people.

JIM: (*uncomfortable*) Yes, yes. Playing golf today, Mr Riordan?

RIORDAN: No, Jim. Too busy, too busy. I forgot, aren't Jack and Mollie coming?

MRS RIORDAN: Not till after supper, Joseph.

(*The door opens and* HUGH *admits* MISS PETTIGREW *and her sister.*)

MISS PETTIGREW: We met Mr Hugh in the hall — how do you do, Mrs Riordan? My sister says he's grown. Sallie, my dear, (*she kisses her*) and Jim, of course, never very far away, ha, ha! And there's Mr Riordan hiding from me, positively hiding from me. I see you, you naughty man; come here and shake hands with me.

(*He comes forward unwillingly.*)

Hold up your head! I believe Kate has been giving you a good dressing-down, and I'm sure you deserved it. Have you, Kate?

(MRS DE LACY *meanwhile is making proper salutations.*)

MRS RIORDAN: No, oh no.

MISS PETTIGREW: Of course you couldn't. None of us could have the heart to do anything or say anything against dear Mr Riordan, our best friend, our oldest friend.

(HONOR *opens the dining-room door.*)

HONOR: Supper's ready now, Mrs Riordan.

MRS RIORDAN: Thank you, dear. Come along everyone.

(*And, talking easily and moving easily, they all go into the dining-room and the door is shut.*)

AUNT MOLL: And that, I suppose, properly worked up, is your first act?

HUGH: I'm not sure. I'd like to run the play straight through in a series of little scenes.

AUNT MOLL: Taking how long?

HUGH: Maybe an hour, maybe an hour and a half.

AUNT MOLL: Nonsense. No audience would stand it. Not an audience of men anyway. Never can sit for more than half an hour without wanting a smoke or a drink or — or something. No self-control.

HUGH: They stick it at the pictures. I'll try them anyway. The fact is, Aunt Moll, you've no self-control; you are dying for your milk.

AUNT MOLL: Of course I am. It's beyond me hour.

HUGH: (*going towards the dining-room door*) I'll get it for you.

AUNT MOLL: (*calling after him*) And me Marie biscuits.

HUGH: (*disappearing*) You'll get them.

AUNT MOLL: The creature. His mother all over. Feckless. I'll warrant he'll forget the biscuits — or the milk, no system, no imagination. Ah well, I've me "Manchester Guardian".

(*She picks up the paper but before she has time to start to read it* HUGH *is back with a glass of milk, two Marie biscuits, and a glass of claret.*)

HUGH: Here's your milk, Aunt Moll, *and* your biscuits.

AUNT MOLL: Thank you. (*She has a good gulp of milk.*)

HUGH: (*after a sip of claret*) I know I should have used them more, those two old women for queerities' sake. I could do them as easily as I — as I — but they're all there, in my mind. I can plug them in later on if it's necessary. Just now, just for a first draft I wanted to bring them in bare and neat — like a very dry sherry. But don't fret, Aunt Moll, I'll enrich it all later. What I want you to do now is run upstairs and get into a mackintosh and a very plain hat.

AUNT MOLL: I certainly will do nothing of the kind. At this hour of night!

HUGH: Oh yes, you will. Don't you understand, I'm master here this evening. Whatever I say, goes. I clap my hands, presto! — and you disappear.

AUNT MOLL: (*going*) Well, I never! (*She goes out.*
There is a sound of ping-pong balls from the dining room, sound of people scoring and laughter. The door opens and SALLIE LONG *comes in. She moves to the fire and stands there rather wearily. A few seconds later* JIM DALY *comes after her.*)

JIM: You slipped away. Why did you? We were all so jolly.

SALLIE: Yes, you were.

JIM: Don't you like table-tennis — ping-pong or whatever they call it?

SALLIE: I used to.

JIM: Why wouldn't you play this evening?

SALLIE: Aren't you almost a doctor?

JIM: Yes.... I forgot, for a minute.

SALLIE: Go back to the others. They'll miss you.

JIM: They won't. I've been knocked out.

SALLIE: Still, they'll miss you.

JIM: Look here, Sallie, things can't go on like this.

SALLIE: Why not?

JIM: I'll marry you tomorrow, like a shot.

SALLIE: Yes. On the old conditions. Oh Jim, my dear, don't let's go over it all again. We've argued and argued. There's no possible solution.

JIM: You can't bring yourself to do it?

SALLIE: Turn Catholic? No. Isn't it queer that I could let myself do with you — what I did, and yet I can't go back on my faith? I could never bring myself to say that I believe in things I don't believe in, things that I hate in my heart. You can't give up your faith either. I respect you for it, respect me.

JIM: I do. You'll always be the only woman —

SALLIE: Stop. Don't make rash promises, and don't look so awfully solemn. After all, isn't it a very old story — the medical student and the clergyman's daughter? Aren't there vulgar jokes about it — or comic songs?

JIM: Oh, shut up.

SALLIE: When Jack and Mollie came in tonight there were mildly facetious jokes made about her "condition" — isn't that what it's called? Everyone was as pleased as punch. Suppose that I went into that room this minute and told them of *my* condition, what would they say?

JIM: You wouldn't.

SALLIE: Of course not. But suppose I did and said you were the father?

JIM: But what's going to happen?

SALLIE: I'm going to London next week.

JIM: To London?

SALLIE: Well, Jim, father's awfully broad-minded, but my having my bastard at the Rectory would be a little bit thick.

JIM: Who are you going to in London?

SALLIE: School friend.

JIM: I don't believe you.

SALLIE: Well, it's an easy thing to say.

JIM: I want your address.

SALLIE: Why? Don't you see it's all over Jim?
(*He starts to protest.*)
Oh, very well, you shall have it, but I don't promise to write.

JIM: I'll write often.

SALLIE: (*sure that he won't*) I'm sure you will. When do you go back to Dublin?

JIM: Tomorrow morning.

SALLIE: Oh.... Then tonight is goodbye.

JIM: No, of course not.

SALLIE: Yes, it is. (*Quite lightly.*) Goodbye, Jim.

JIM: You're horribly cruel.

SALLIE: I mean to be.

JIM: You're putting me in the wrong all the time.

SALLIE: I'm not, I'm not. Oh, forgive me, my dear and — there's one thing — thank your mother from me, somehow I can't, and tell her how sweet and nice she's been. I think she'd have liked me for a daughter-in-law — if things had only been different.

JIM: I'll tell her. Father's been a beast.

SALLIE: Ah no. Behaved just the way you'll behave to your

children — your legitimate children. We'd better go back to the others, they'll be wondering.

JIM: Yes, come along.

(*As they are going* SALLIE *stops. She holds out her arms to him.*)

SALLIE: Jim, goodbye.

JIM: (*kissing her passionately*) Oh, my dear, my dear.

SALLIE: My poor Jim.

(*They go into the next room.* HUGH *walks about the room slightly rearranging the furniture and talking as he does so.*)

HUGH: A big dining-room in an old Georgian house; it's a sitting-room too, for of course they only use the drawing-room when they give a party and that they haven't done for years — Mrs de Lacy's mourning makes such a convenient excuse. A few worthless old portraits on the walls, some good mahogany furniture, gimcrack candlesticks on the fine Adams mantelpiece, two pictures of comic cats by Louis Wain. The light is cold and dim.

(*He does something to the light switches.*)

Yes, like that.

(MISS PETTIGREW (SARAH) *and* MRS DE LACY (LUCY) *come in, taking off their wraps, showing themselves in the dresses we saw them in at the party. They sit beside the fire.*)

MISS PETTIGREW: Look, Lucy, fancy! The fire is still in.

MRS DE LACY: So it is.

MISS PETTIGREW: Those beech logs are wonderful, they last so long. Why it's nearly three hours since we left for the Riordans. Shall I put another log on?

MRS DE LACY: Better go to bed. There are only two logs left in the basket, you'll have to cut some more tomorrow.

MISS PETTIGREW: Yes, indeed I will.

MRS DE LACY: I wish I could help you, but — my heart.

MISS PETTIGREW: Of course, Lucy. And I don't mind cutting logs a bit, it's warming work. I always say that about logs, they warm you while you're making them and they warm you when they're burning.

MRS DE LACY: I wish to goodness you wouldn't be for ever looking on the bright side of things, Sarah, it's — it's most irritating.

MISS PETTIGREW: Is it, Lucy? I'm sorry but I can't help feeling gay tonight after that lovely party.

(*She starts to hum* "So, we'll go no more a-roving".)

MRS DE LACY: Do be quiet. You were ridiculous tonight. You were as gay as — as a three-year-old.

MISS PETTIGREW: Was I, Lucy? Did I chatter too much?

MRS DE LACY: You did.

MISS PETTIGREW: Isn't that dreadful of me? But the lights, and all the young people, and the lovely food, and that mulled claret — they went to my head I suppose.
(*She gets up and starts to waltz, singing.*)
"So, we'll go no more a-roving
So late into the night."

MRS DE LACY: Sit down and behave yourself.

MISS PETTIGREW: (*still dancing*) No, join me, partner me. You always used to be gentleman when we practised dancing long ago together. Come on, Lucy.

MRS DE LACY: Ridiculous. At our age.

MISS PETTIGREW: (*waltzing to her*) Come on.
(*She pulls her up. Far away a ghostly piano and violin are heard playing the waltz from "The Merry Widow".*)
That was the waltz they played — do you remember? — at the Hunt Ball the night Bob proposed to you.

MRS DE LACY: I remember.

MISS PETTIGREW: Mr Clarke-Barry's band, wasn't it? We had met Mr de Lacy at the Dublin Exhibition. That was nineteen hundred and seven, wasn't it, Lucy?

MRS DE LACY: Yes. The Morgans introduced us.

MISS PETTIGREW: How happy you were that evening after the ball. You came into my room; we brushed each other's hair, and you told me about Bob.

MRS DE LACY: I remember.

MISS PETTIGREW: We were both so happy. Bob was so handsome.

MRS DE LACY: But no good as a husband. You were luckier, Sarah, after all.

MISS PETTIGREW: Because I never loved anyone? Or at least no one ever loved me. Was I, Lucy?

MRS DE LACY: Of course you were.

MISS PETTIGREW: I don't know. When I saw those young people tonight — Jack and Mollie and Mr Daly and Miss Long — I felt I could almost cry.

MRS DE LACY: Nonsense. Jack and Mollie are the most ordinary people. Bob and I — I admit that Bob was hopeless as a business man and as a husband — but we were never ordinary.

MISS PETTIGREW: Maybe Mollie doesn't think Jack ordinary.

MRS DE LACY: Rubbish. I won't dance any more. It's ridiculous, at our age.
(*They stop dancing.*)

MISS PETTIGREW: I danced three times tonight, with Mr Riordan and Mr Daly and Jack.

MRS DE LACY: I saw you. Disgraceful.

MISS PETTIGREW: Was it? I'm sorry. But it was all so lovely. If only Hugh hadn't behaved so queerly. What was the matter with him, do you think?

MRS DE LACY: Oh, just nerves and foolishness, I suppose. I'm sure he leads a most dissipated life in London; I'm told all young men there do.

MISS PETTIGREW: Kate always says he's the steadiest of boys.

MRS DE LACY: Hm!... Read the papers. Murders. Suicides. Night clubs.... By the way, what was he saying about your bag?

MISS PETTIGREW: My bag? Oh nothing. Just nonsense.

MRS DE LACY: It sounded nonsense to me but you got so flustered I thought for a minute there must be something in it.

MISS PETTIGREW: In it? In the bag?

MRS DE LACY: In what he was saying.

MISS PETTIGREW: Well — in a way — there was.

MRS DE LACY: There was? What do you mean?

MISS PETTIGREW: You'll be cross with me, Lucy, I know, but I couldn't resist it, and no one saw me, I'll swear to that, and Hugh wasn't in the room at the time so I don't know how he suspected, and anyhow I didn't let him open my bag, and we haven't tasted butter for a week —

MRS DE LACY: What on earth are you talking about?

MISS PETTIGREW: Those little rolls with the sausages inside them — weren't they lovely?

MRS DE LACY: They were very nice. I only had one; I'd have liked another but the plate never came round again.

MISS PETTIGREW: It came round to me. And I thought — a couple of them for our breakfast —

MRS DE LACY: Sarah!

MISS PETTIGREW: Yes. I slipped them into my bag, two of them.

MRS DE LACY: You stole them?

MISS PETTIGREW: It wasn't exactly stealing, Lucy. Kate Riordan would strip her table for us and well you know it. But I couldn't ask her for food.

MRS DE LACY: I should think not.

MISS PETTIGREW: (taking the rolls out of her bag) Look, there they are. They smell so nice.... You're furious with me, Lucy?

MRS DE LACY: (after a pause) I should be, but I'm not. My God, that shows how low we've sunk.

MISS PETTIGREW: Things will be better in a little while when the hens begin to lay again.

MRS DE LACY: To be depending on half a dozen hens! The Pettigrews to be waiting on six white Wyandottes. Thank God Papa never lived to see this day.

MISS PETTIGREW: They're very red in the comb, they'll be laying any day now. And we're never cold, Lucy, with all the old trees on the place. And I don't mind cutting up the logs, not a bit. There's others worse off than we are. (*Timidly.*) Would you eat the roll now?

MRS DE LACY: It would choke me.

MISS PETTIGREW: Indeed I don't feel hungry either. I'll heat them for the breakfast. That mulled claret — it warmed the cockles of the heart, didn't it, Lucy? I thought Mr Riordan took a little too much whiskey before the evening was over. Did you think so, Lucy? Indeed one shouldn't say a word against him, he's such a kind man and has been the best of friends to us.

MRS DE LACY: That reminds me — he gave me a letter when we were leaving.

MISS PETTIGREW: What was in it?

MRS DE LACY: I hadn't a chance to read it.

MISS PETTIGREW: Maybe the shares are paying again.

MRS DE LACY: Maybe they are. He said it might be years before we'd get a dividend, but that in the long run they were as safe as could be.

(*She takes a letter from her bag.*)

MISS PETTIGREW: Hurry and see what he says.

MRS DE LACY: (*opening the letter*) The light's dim. (*Reading.*) "Dear Mrs de Lacy — As an old friend of yours and of your sister's . . . not offended . . . sake of old times" . . . well, well . . . .

MISS PETTIGREW: What is it?

MRS DE LACY: He's sent a cheque, he's offering us money.

MISS PETTIGREW: Money?

MRS DE LACY: Twenty pounds, to tide us over the winter, he says.

MISS PETTIGREW: Twenty pounds! Oh, isn't he the generous man?

MRS DE LACY: Indeed he is.

MISS PETTIGREW: We could get a few clothes, and maybe a little goat, and we'd have milk for our tea and meal for the hens and — and —

MRS DE LACY: We'd have nothing of the sort.

MISS PETTIGREW: Why not? What would you spend it on?

MRS DE LACY: Good friend as Joseph Riordan is I'd die sooner than take anything from him. He's done his best for us, he's looked after our stocks and shares and 'tisn't his fault that all has gone wrong with us. If I took this money from him I could never walk into his house again and hold my head up.

MISS PETTIGREW: But you weren't cross with me for taking the rolls.

MRS DE LACY: I should have been. Never must you do such a thing again. Promise me, Sarah.

MISS PETTIGREW: (*starting to cry*) I can't promise. I can't trust myself not to. You're strong, Lucy, I'm weak, I'm hungry. I want nice clothes, I want nice food. Don't I know that I look a fright going around in old Aunt Julia's clothes of thirty years ago. I make a joke about it and say I'm all in the fashion, but of course I'm not. I'm — I'm comic.

MRS DE LACY: You're not. You're a lady whatever clothes you wear.

MISS PETTIGREW: I'm tired of being a lady, tired of this poverty, tired of trying to keep up an appearance and knowing that everyone sees through it, and that the men lounging outside the public houses and seeing me pass talk of me as "poor ould Miss Pettigrew".

MRS DE LACY: They don't. How do you know they do?

MISS PETTIGREW: I don't know for certain, but I just know.

MRS DE LACY: If we're poor it's through no fault of our own.

MISS PETTIGREW: That makes no difference. Maybe they'd think more of us if we had lost it card-playing or horse-racing. Not that I care what they think. But, twenty pounds! Oh, however will you thank Joseph Riordan?

MRS DE LACY: I'll write to him very nicely and tell him we're in no need.

MISS PETTIGREW: You'll send back the cheque?

MRS DE LACY: Of course.

MISS PETTIGREW: You'll tell him we're in no need? That'll be a lie he won't easily believe.

MRS DE LACY: He's gentleman enough to take it as it's meant to be taken, as a polite refusal of his help. After all, it isn't his fault that our shares have come to nothing.

MISS PETTIGREW: No.... But to send back all that money.... Lucy!

MRS DE LACY: I won't send it back. I'll burn the cheque — now.

MISS PETTIGREW: No, no, please, Lucy, wait till the morning.

MRS DE LACY: There's enough fire left to burn it.

MISS PETTIGREW: Wait till the morning. Maybe you'll think different in the morning.

MRS DE LACY: That's what I'm afraid of, Sarah, I might think different in the morning. Isn't it queer the difference good food and a drop of wine make? I'm feeling very high and moral now, I mightn't feel so moral in the morning.
(*She burns the cheque.*)

MISS PETTIGREW: (*in a little voice*) I'll burn the rolls if you like, Lucy.

MRS DE LACY: No, no, child, keep them. Have the two of them for your breakfast.

MISS PETTIGREW: I couldn't eat them; they'd stick in my throat.

MRS DE LACY: They'll do nothing of the sort. I'll share with you if that will help you. Maybe it will do my pride good to eat stolen food.
(MISS PETTIGREW *begins to cry.*)
There, there, I didn't mean to start you crying.... I declare I believe I'm crying myself.
(*She puts her arms round her sister and the scene fades.*)

HUGH: (*moving about in the darkness as if he were arranging furniture, which he probably isn't.*) A white bed here, an image of the Blessed Virgin, a little lamp, and Honor in her nightdress kneeling before it; she has said her prayers, she is going to bed.
(*A light comes up and we see* HONOR *kneeling in her white nightdress.*)

HONOR: I thought I had utterly forgotten; I thought I had torn him entirely out of my heart. But I was deceiving myself and I was trying to deceive you, Holy Mother. This flower, this daisy he gave me long ago, I have kept it. Now I tear it to pieces. See! It's all gone, it's all forgotten. I'm empty now, empty of every human affection.
(*She takes her Thomas à Kempis from the bed and reads.*)
"Lord, how oft shall I resign myself and wherein shall I forsake myself?... I have said to thee full oft and yet I say again; forsake thyself, resign thyself and thou shalt enjoy great peace. To this enforce thyself, this pray thou, this desire thou, that thou may be despoiled of all manner of self, and thou, bare, follow Jesus only and die to thyself and live everlastingly in me. Then shall end all vain fantasies, wicked conturbations and superfluous cares; then also shall go away inordinate dread and inordinate love shall die."
(*The scene darkens and closes.*)

HUGH: And now, as slap contrast, we move from a girl's bedroom in Ireland to a back sitting-room in London, probably in one of those awful terraces near Paddington Station. It's late afternoon and there's a touch of fog outside and it's neither cold nor hot. There's a ghastly red wallpaper on the walls and imitation eighteenth-century prints — for we'd like to pretend we're Harley Street, but of course we're miles too far west. And a maid with a dirty apron has shown us in and here we are, poor old Aunt Moll and Sallie Long.

(*And there they are, in mackintoshes and hats, sitting opposite each other at the centre table.*)

AUNT MOLL: I don't like this place.

SALLIE: It's all right.

AUNT MOLL: What is he like, this doctor of yours?

SALLIE: All right.

AUNT MOLL: I don't believe you.

SALLIE: Well, of course, he couldn't be quite all right to be what he is and to do what he's prepared to do.

AUNT MOLL: Hm.

(SALLIE *shivers and catches her breath in a sob.*)

Sallie, come away, come out of this place, it's evil.

SALLIE: No. I'm going through with it.

AUNT MOLL: Have courage. Think of Bernard Shaw.

SALLIE: It's pretty easy for him. He never had to bear an illegitimate baby; he need only talk light-heartedly about them.

AUNT MOLL: Child, I'll do anything I can to help you.

SALLIE: Dear Aunt Moll, you've done so much coming with me to London like this — don't leave me now. Call me a little coward if you like. I am, but I couldn't face mother; she's fond of me, she'd forgive me like a shot, but she'd be so sorry, so terribly sorry: and father — he wouldn't be cross, but he'd be so hurt and sorry. Oh, I couldn't bear people being sorry for me!

AUNT MOLL: I know. But don't let them be sorry. Be proud, be gay.

SALLIE: You're talking out of your reading, Aunt Moll, not out of common sense. There's nothing proud or gay in having an unwanted fatherless baby. And I'm not going to do it, I'm not going to do it. (*Getting more and more hysterical.*) Go on, walk out of here, don't get yourself mixed up in anything dirty and questionable. I thought you were my friend, the only real friend I had in Knock, but you're as conventional as the rest. Go back by the train tonight, eight forty-five from Euston, isn't it? Tell in Knock tomorrow afternoon where you saw me last, in a questionable doctor's waiting-room near Paddington.

Tell them all I was going to do, have done to me, tell Jim's parents —

AUNT MOLL: You're talking nonsense. Pull yourself together. You know I'm your friend.

SALLIE: I'm sorry, Aunt Moll, I'm sorry.

(DOCTOR SMITH *comes in, a greasy, plausible man.*)

DOCTOR SMITH: (*to* SALLIE) Good afternoon, Mrs Smith.

SALLIE: Good afternoon, Doctor Smith. This is my aunt, Miss — Miss —

AUNT MOLL: Smith.

DOCTOR SMITH: Good afternoon, Miss Smith. We talked the matter over very fully the last time you were here, Mrs Smith.

SALLIE: Yes, we did. I have the money here. (*She opens her bag.*)

DOCTOR SMITH: In notes?

SALLIE: In notes. (*She counts them out.*)

DOCTOR SMITH: I'll ring for Nurse Smith. (*He does so.*)

AUNT MOLL: Is everyone here called Smith?

DOCTOR SMITH: It is a convenient name, Miss — er — Smith. (*Taking the notes.*) Thank you.

SALLIE: You haven't counted them.

DOCTOR SMITH: I am sure that will not be necessary. I know a lady when I meet one.

AUNT MOLL: How long will it — I mean, how long, I mean —

DOCTOR SMITH: Oh, a short time, a very short time.

AUNT MOLL: I mean, how soon will my niece be out and about?

DOCTOR SMITH: Oh, a short time, a very short time. Ah, here is Nurse Smith.

(NURSE SMITH, *not too smart a nurse, appears.*)

Miss Smith, will you take Mrs Smith downstairs. I shall follow you in a few minutes.

(NURSE SMITH *makes* SALLIE *get up and come with her. As she passes to go out* AUNT MOLL *goes to her.*)

AUNT MOLL: My darling child.

SALLIE: If anything happens, tell Jim that — no, better tell him nothing. (*She goes out.*)

DOCTOR SMITH: Nothing bad can possibly happen, Miss Smith. As I said, in a short time, a very short time —

(*The scene suddenly goes black. The platform at the back on which the bench was is illuminated as a surpliced clergyman appears.*)

CLERGYMAN: I am the resurrection and the life, saith the Lord, and whoso liveth and believeth in Me shall never die. For the trumpet shall sound and the dead shall be raised incorruptible

and we shall be changed.... For as much as it hath pleased
Almighty God to take unto himself the soul of our dear sister
here departed, we therefore commit her body to the ground;
earth to earth, ashes to ashes, dust to dust.
(*His voice fades away and scene darkens.*
A light comes up. JIM DALY *is sitting by the fire writing on a*
pad on his knee.)

JIM: Darling Mums — I have got my final with flying colours and
apparently a medal thrown in, gold they tell me, but I expect
brass or maybe leather. Anyhow I've made up my mind to take
a special course, so I won't be able to get home before the
summer. Any news of Sallie? She hasn't answered my last two
letters. The weather here is pretty good. I'm going to a Rugger
dance at the Metropole tonight and on Thursday I'm going —
(*The scene fades. We see* HUGH *and* AUNT MOLL; *she is without*
mackintosh and hat, she seems to be crying.)

HUGH: What *is* the matter, Aunt Moll?

AUNT MOLL: I'm foolish, I suppose, but it seemed so real.

HUGH: Nonsense. It's all in my mind. A figment of the imagination, as they say.

AUNT MOLL: Is it? Are you sure?

HUGH: Certain. I'm not a storyteller for nothing. Ssh! I hear them
getting up inside; they'll be in in a minute. I'll prove to you it's
all fancy. I'll ask Miss Pettigrew to show me what's in her bag,
she'll let me search it; there'll be no sausage rolls there and that
will prove to you how imaginary the whole thing is.

AUNT MOLL: Please God.
(*The door from the dining room opens, everyone comes in as*
they went in at the beginning of the play.)

JIM: Whew! I've eaten too much, Mrs Riordan.

JACK: Same here. You certainly gave us a meal tonight, mother.

MISS PETTIGREW: Quite a collation, Mrs Riordan. Wasn't it,
Lucy?

MRS DE LACY: Sumptuous.

MRS RIORDAN: Well, indeed, I'm glad you liked it, but I think
you hardly took a pick.

SALLIE: Indeed no.

RIORDAN: I think we've all done remarkably well, mother, except
Hugh. And you were the belle of the ball, Hugh, and you only
looked in for a minute to get a glass of milk for Aunt Moll.

HUGH: Oh, I stole a glass of claret for myself, Daddy.

RIORDAN: Claret? Sure that's no drink for a man.

MISS PETTIGREW: (*coyly*) We missed you, Mr Hugh.

HUGH: I'm sorry. I was talking to Aunt Moll.

MRS RIORDAN: Oh, did you get your milk, Aunt Moll? I forgot about it.

AUNT MOLL: Oh yes, Aunt Moll got her milk. She took care she got her milk; she saw to it herself.

HUGH: You mean I got it for you.

RIORDAN: I think we might have a game or a song or something. How soon will the table be cleared, Kate? Can't we play ping-pong?

MRS RIORDAN: You must give Maggie ten minutes.

JIM: After that supper? Have a heart, Mr Riordan.

MRS RIORDAN: I thought later on we might clear the floor and have a bit of a dance.

JIM: Fine.

MOLLIE: I'm not allowed to dance.

MRS RIORDAN: Of course not, dear.

RIORDAN: Then let's have a song. I'm in the humour for a bit of music. After all, I nearly won the Captain's prize.

MRS RIORDAN: Yes, I think a little music would be nice. Would you like some music, Mrs de Lacy?

MRS DE LACY: As long as it's not jazz.

MISS PETTIGREW: Oh, I love jazz. Of course I can't dance it. (*She laughs sillily.*)

MRS RIORDAN: Honor, will you — ?

HONOR: A terrible cold. Really, truly, Mrs Riordan, not just an excuse.

MRS RIORDAN: Isn't that too bad. Miss Long?

SALLIE: I only sing when mother wants the room cleared.

JIM: Oh, nonsense, Sallie.

SALLIE: No, quite imposs. (*Turning to* JACK.) But, Mr Jack?

JACK: Nothing doing.

MISS PETTIGREW: But you sing most beautifully.

JACK: Never had a lesson in my life.

MISS PETTIGREW: Like the nightingales — not that I've ever heard one; there are none in Ireland I believe, quite extraordinary.

JIM: Come on, Jack. Give us a rouser.

RIORDAN: Yes, start it rolling, Jack, something lively. Hugh, put a freshener in that, will you? (*He hands him his glass.* HUGH *goes into the dining room with it.*)

MRS RIORDAN: Yes, do, dear. Mollie will play your accompaniment, won't she?

JACK: I should rather think she will. That's the reason why I married her.

MOLLIE: The only reason?

JACK: No, not the only reason. Come on, let's get it over.

AUNT MOLL: The song I asked you for, Jack.

JACK: "So, we'll go no more a-roving"? All right.

MISS PETTIGREW: Now I think this is going to be delightful. We hear so little music in Knock nowadays. I remember long ago what a lot of music there used to be at little parties like this. Do you remember, Lucy, how you and I used to sing that duet "Oh, that we two were maying"? And you were magnificent, Lucy, in "When sparrows build".

MRS DE LACY: Hush.

MISS PETTIGREW: These gramophones and wireless have killed all real music, that's what I always say. Give me the good amateur every time, every time, every —

HONOR: A cushion behind you, Miss Pettigrew?

MISS PETTIGREW: Thank you, dear. Ah, they're beginning. How well Mollie plays.

MRS DE LACY: Ssh!

MISS PETTIGREW: All right, my dear. I hope I know good music when I hear it.

(MOLLIE *plays quite well.* JACK *sings well in an untrained voice.*)

JACK: (*singing*)   "So, we'll go no more a-roving
          So late into the night,
      Though the heart be still as loving,
          And the moon be still as bright.

          For the sword outwears its sheath,
          And the soul wears out the breast,
      And the heart must pause to breathe,
          And even love have rest.

          Though the night was made for loving,
          And the day returns too soon,
      Yet we'll go no more a-roving
          By the light of the moon."

(*The song captures the room.*

MR *and* MRS RIORDAN *sit back vaguely pleased.* MR RIORDAN'*s whiskey has been brought to him somewhere in the song by* HUGH, *who remains in the background.*

MISS PETTIGREW *and her sister become sentimental but not comically so.*

JIM *is very quiet.*

HONOR *is holding herself in stonily.*

SALLIE *is on the verge of a breakdown.*
No one could guess what AUNT MOLL *thinks, she is very quiet.*
HUGH *watches it all, takes it all in in growing excitement.*
The song stops, there is an instant of silence.)

MRS RIORDAN: Thank you, dear. How well you play, Mollie.
(*A little conventional murmur of thanks runs round the room.*
SALLIE *gets up and crosses to the fire, swaying a little on her feet.*)

SALLIE: I can't — Jim —

HONOR: (*at her side at once*) My dear, you're a little faint, aren't you? May we go into the hall, just for a minute, Mrs Riordan?

MRS RIORDAN: Of course. But —
(*Almost before she can answer* HONOR *has got* SALLIE *out of the room.*)

RIORDAN: What's happened? Is she ill?

AUNT MOLL: Not at all, Joseph. Don't be ridiculous.

MRS RIORDAN: Just a touch of faintness.

MOLLIE: It *is* hot in here.

MISS PETTIGREW: Such a good supper.

HUGH: (*who has got* JIM *aside; he talks to him with intensity, but in a low voice so that the others don't hear him.*) She *is* ill and you know why. You know. Why don't you go to her? Why don't you?

JIM: I? I? —

HUGH: (*almost shaking him*) Yes, you. You!

MISS PETTIGREW: It's such a pleasant party, Mrs Riordan, one of the nicest I've been to this winter, but of course Mr Hugh's being here makes all the difference.

HUGH: (*turning from* JIM, *and now he affects a gaiety*) Yes, and now I'm going to have a joke on you all, at least I'm going to try a mild little joke on you, Miss Pettigrew. I want to search your bag.

MISS PETTIGREW: My bag?

HUGH: Yes. What have you got in your bag?

MISS PETTIGREW: (*with a nervous, affected laugh*) Do you think I've taken some of your mother's silver forks?

HUGH: Of course not. But may I search it?

MISS PETTIGREW: Certainly not.

MRS RIORDAN: What a crazy notion.

RIORDAN: What's the idea, Hugh? Is it a game?

HUGH: (*holding himself in, trying to speak lightly*) No, not exactly a game, Daddy, but all the future, all truth, all reality depends on the answer to my question. Aunt Moll, *you* know what I mean?

AUNT MOLL: I do.

(HONOR *and* SALLIE *come in.*)

HONOR: We're feeling quite all right, Mrs Riordan. It was just your very good supper and your very hot fire.

MRS RIORDAN: I think it's high time for a nice round game or some more music. Would you like that, Mrs de Lacy?

MRS DE LACY: Yes, indeed. Anything you choose.

HUGH: (*wildly*) No, no. There are more important things going on in this room than a little music or a good round game. Miss Pettigrew, what's in your bag?

MRS RIORDAN: Hugh, dear —

AUNT MOLL: As Mr Shaw says, "Press your question, press your question."

HUGH: I won't, I can't, I couldn't bear to find it was true. Oh, have it your own way. (*He goes out quickly.*)

MRS RIORDAN: I'm sorry, he's so overtired. No sleep coming over and he has to go back tomorrow.

MISS PETTIGREW: Tomorrow? So soon?

MRS RIORDAN: Yes, some new play coming on, I think. Jack dear, turn on the wireless, there's sure to be a dance band somewhere, and let's have a game of Slippery Sam. You might as well bring in the claret cup and the sandwiches from the sideboard — and the decanter and siphon. Aunt Moll, are you going to play?

(*But* AUNT MOLL *can't answer, she has her head in her hands.*) What's the matter? Aren't you well?

AUNT MOLL: (*getting up and going to the door*) I'm a stupid old woman. Let me be, Kate. I'm going to Hugh. (*She goes out.*)

RIORDAN: Poor old Aunt Moll, she's beginning to break up. Give me the cards, Kate. I'll deal.

(*They pull their chairs round the table, talking and laughing, but before the game starts the curtain has fallen.*)

THE END

A SELECTED CHECKLIST

compiled by Frances-Jane French

Plays

The Cross-Roads, (Maunsel & Co.), Dublin, 1909.

Two Plays: Harvest and *The Clancy Name*, (Maunsel & Co.), Dublin and London, 1911.

Patriots, (Maunsel & Co.), Dublin and London, 1912.

The Dreamers, (Maunsel & Co.), Dublin and London, 1915.

The Lost Leader, (Eigras Press), Dublin, 1918.

The Whiteheaded Boy, (Talbot Press), Dublin, [1920].

The Round Table, (G.P. Putnam's Sons), London and New York, 1924, revised 1928.

Crabbed Youth and Age, (G.P. Putnam's Sons), London and New York, 1924.

The White Blackbird. Portrait [two plays], (Talbot Press), Dublin and Cork, 1926.

Give a Dog . . . . , (Macmillan & Co.), London, 1928.

The Big House: four scenes in its life, (Macmillan & Co.), London, 1928.

Ever the Twain, (Macmillan & Co.), London, 1930.

The Far-off Hills, (Chatto & Windus), London, 1931.

Is Life Worth Living? [*Drama at Inish*] , (Macmillan & Co.), London, 1933.

More Plays (*All's Over Then?*; *Church Street*), (Macmillan & Co.), London, 1933.

Killycreggs in Twilight and Other Plays, (*Is Life Worth Living?*; *Bird's Nest*), (Macmillan & Co.), London, 1939.

"Let Well Alone" in *The Bell* (Dublin), January 1941, 54-67.

The Lucky Finger, (Samuel French), New York, 1949.

Two One Act Comedies: Never the Time and the Place, and Crabbed Youth and Age, (H.R. Carter's Publications), Belfast, 1953.

Prose

A Young Man from the South, (Maunsel & Co.), Dublin, 1917.
[Autobiographical novel]

Dark Days, (Talbot Press), Dublin, and (T. Fisher Unwin), London, 1918. [Political Sketches of Life in Ireland]

Eight Short Stories, (Talbot Press), Dublin [1920].

Three Homes [in Co. Cork] *Lennox Robinson, Tom Robinson & Nora Dorman*, (Michael Joseph), London, 1938. [Autobiographical]

Curtain Up: An Autobiography, (Michael Joseph), London, 1942.

Towards an Appreciation of the Theatre, (Metropolitan Publishing Co.), Dublin, 1945.

Pictures in a Theatre: [The Abbey Theatre] *A Conversation Piece*, (Abbey Theatre), Dublin, [1947].

Ireland's Abbey Theatre: A History, 1899-1951, (Sidgwick & Jackson), London, [1951], and (Samuel French), New York.

I Sometimes Think, (Talbot Press), Dublin, 1956. [Essays]

Works Edited by Lennox Robinson

Further Letters of John Butler Yeats; Selected by Lennox Robinson, (Cuala Press), Dundrum, 1920.

A Golden Treasury of Irish Verse, (Macmillan & Co.), London and New York, 1925.

The Irish Theatre: Lectures delivered during the Abbey Theatre Festival held in Dublin in August 1938, (Macmillan & Co.), London, 1939. [Contains contributions by A.E. Malone, Frank O'Connor, F.R. Higgins, T.C. Murray, Walter Starkie, Ernest Blythe, Micheál MacLiammóir, Lennox Robinson]

Lady Gregory's Journals, 1916-1930, (Putnam & Co.), London, 1946, and (Macmillan Co.) New York, 1947.

Contributions to Books

"The Man and the Dramatist", in *Scattering Branches*, edited by Stephen Gwynn, (Macmillan & Co.), London, 1940. [Tributes to the memory of W.B. Yeats]

Contributions to Periodicals

"Lady Gregory" in *Ireland Today* (Dublin), July 1936, I, 20, 49-50. [An Appreciation]

Biography

Lennox Robinson, by Michael J. O'Neill, (Twayne Publishers Inc.), New York, 1964.

General

The Journal of Irish Literature, Vol IX, No. I (January 1980); *A Lennox Robinson Number*.